PRAISE FOR BLUE COLLAR JESUS

"As a lineman for the power company I would start each day with a safety tailgate meeting. Now that I am retired Jay's devotions are my safety tailgate to start each day."
~ DAVE SHEELY, *retired NIPSCO lineman*

"Jay's writings inspired my recovery group to dig deep into their hearts and seek lasting sobriety."
~ DONNA RIEDEL, *nurse*

"Blue Collar Jesus enables me daily to relate to Scripture and apply it to my own personal growth."
~ KATHY KESLING, *food service manager*

"These daily Spirit-filled devotions pulled from Scripture verses enlighten and inspire. The lessons shape an awareness of God's will, which help us take our next steps with Christ."
~ TODD KELLER, *purchasing agent*

"I use these writings for family devotions each day with my three kids. They have inspired great conversation at the dinner table."
~ TONYA PARRETT, *mom*

"Jay is one of those remarkable writers who can make complex lessons in Scripture totally relatable to anyone. We begin each day reading his thoughtful take on just one verse or a single line of Scripture. It always encourages consideration of our own 'next step' in our walk with Jesus, and makes that clearer and more doable. We have enjoyed Jay's devotions for years and now it is exciting to see it available to a wider audience."
~ PHIL AND KATHIE HEMPEL, *bee keepers*

"I enjoy Blue Collar Jesus every morning with my first cup of coffee. I find it authentic and transparent and very readable."
~ GINNY BEUKER, *widow in her 80s and still going strong*

Blue-Collar JESUS

Pastor Jay Loucks

Blue-Collar JESUS

A daily devotional for the *blawed* but *hopebul*
as we take our next step with Christ

Lectionary Year A

Pastor Jay Loucks

Hermits Hope Publications
LaPorte, Indiana

Blue-Collar Jesus:
A daily devotional for the flawed but hopeful as we take our next step with Christ

Copyright© 2019 by Jay Loucks

ISBN-13: 9781686366857
Library of Congress Control Number: 2019910427

Hermits Hope Publications
6006 North Fail Road
La Porte, Indiana 46350
www.lambschapelumc.org
jaylouckslambschapel@gmail.com
(219) 380-7477

Unless otherwise indicated, all scripture taken from the HOLY BIBLE, NEW INTERNATIONAL VERSION®. Copyright© 1973, 1978, 1984 by International Bible Society. Used by permission of Zondervan Publishing House. All rights reserved.

All rights reserved. No part of this book may be reproduced without written permission from the publisher, except by a reviewer who may quote brief passages in a review; nor may any part of this book be reproduced, stored in a retrieval system or transmitted in any form or other without written permission from the publisher.

This book is manufactured in the United States of America.

Editor: Janet Schwind
Cover & Interior Design: Suzanne Parada

INTRODUCTION

When Jesus began his public ministry, he became wildly popular with folks. The Bible says they were amazed at his teaching. And everything seemed to be sailing along just fine—that is, until he claimed he had been sent from his Father in heaven. That was just too much for them to accept. And the apparent reason is revealed in their response when they said, "Wait a minute. We know this guy. He is Joseph's boy, the carpenter from Nazareth."

Some of them probably even ate off tables Jesus had built for them. I'm convinced it's no small matter that when God decided to send his son into the world to reveal himself to the people, he chose not to send him as a ruling king or even as an academic. No, he sent him as a humble blue-collar worker. And when Jesus launched his teaching ministry, he did it in such a way that it was easy for his audience to relate. He spoke of sheep and vineyards and fruit trees so no one would be left behind. It was a blue-collar message for blue-collar folks. But thirty years ago, when I embarked on this process of trying to discover who God was and what he wanted from me, I quickly discovered that almost all the material available for me was written by academics who were disconnected from my experience of being raised on a farm and working as a construction worker.

I have written this book with people like us in mind. As a proud member of Alcoholics Anonymous, I can assure you I've had enough struggles along the way to relate to your struggles as well. It has taken those thirty years of study and prayer to get to a place where I believe I have something valuable to share. In 2015 I began to write a daily reflection based on the readings from the Revised Common Lectionary. I chose the lectionary because I have preached from it for the past 18 years and because it is a journey that takes us through the teachings of the Bible in a three-year process.

It was a struggle for me at first because I'm not naturally given to the discipline of journaling. But I was taught if I was patient and simply read the Scriptures laid out for me each day, there would always be something in the reading that jumped out at me. I had my doubts at first, but I discovered there always seemed to be a verse or two that caught my eye. And every day when it did, I simply wrote down the verse and then waited to see what the Lord would reveal to me.

Some days I'd write about a personal struggle and other days I'd speak to something new I was learning. But every day my perspective revealed my blue-collar roots. The encouraging part for me was that these thoughts would stick with me for the rest of the day and I would have Jesus on my mind as I went to work.

I am 100 percent convinced that what the Lord has done for me, he will do for you as well. Slow and steady, one day at a time, you'll discover your life is being reshaped by the carpenter from Nazareth.

Over time many other folks became interested in my writings and so I began to share them. Each morning they would get up and find on their computer the Scripture for the day as well as my thoughts on it. It has become so popular that I decided to offer it in this book for everyone.

Psalm 19 promises us that reading God's word will make us happy and wise. That's a promise given directly to you by a God who cannot lie.

And finally, just a friendly warning: the worst day to start spending time alone with Jesus is tomorrow. Take this book today and let it be your companion on a journey of faith. As you do, you'll discover our focus is always on the principle of taking our next step with Jesus. It will be a journey that will do more for you than you could ever hope or imagine.

Thursday | NOVEMBER 28

When you ask, you do not receive, because you ask with wrong motives, that you may spend what you get on your pleasures. | James 4:3

Morning, Lord

James is telling us not to ask for our own selfish pleasure. How many of our prayers, in the past, have been crafted to bring us more pleasure? We're a people who live a privileged life, more so than any generation in history. Yet we pray as though we somehow need more.

Most of us simply don't need any more stuff. If we don't need any more stuff, then what is it that we do need? According to James, we need the godly wisdom to love and serve Jesus Christ. Our prayers should reflect that desire.

James said God never grows weary in our asking for wisdom. I read that a good way for me to pray in the morning goes like this: "Hi, Lord, it's Jay. What are you up to today? Can I be a part of it?"

Next, if we're willing to pray that prayer, then we need to be about the business of noticing just what God is up to throughout each day. If we keep on pursuing him and his incredible wisdom, he will include us in his day's activities. It might be something really big that rocks our world, or it might be a simple opportunity to offer a word of encouragement to someone who's hurting.

Nothing is too big, and nothing is too small; he's intimately involved with both. We simply need to ask. Shalom!

TODAY'S READINGS
Psalm 122 | Daniel 9:15-19 | James 4:1-10

Friday | NOVEMBER 29

> By faith we understand that the universe was formed at God's command, so that what is seen was not made out of what was visible. | Hebrews 11:3

First Cause

The teens in our church are studying creation. When one of them asked me what I believed about the creation account in Genesis, I told him I believe Genesis answers the "Why?" of creation. I think trying to make it answer the "How?" question becomes a slippery slope.

Our kids want to be informed for when they get in conversations at school with their teachers and classmates. I encourage them that there's a very logical argument for the creation account. I'm convinced it required intelligent design to create our universe. I simply do not have enough faith to believe "nothing" was capable of creating all this. So, I do believe the God we worship in church each Sunday created the heavens and the earth and everything in them. I'm also convinced he did it "ex nihilo" or "out of nothing." Think about that—only God can create something out of nothing.

Now, how he created everything, and what the timeline was, I'm not sure about that. What I am totally convinced of is that however the world was created, God did it. I don't necessarily have to stand opposed to the scientific community; I'm not a scientist. I'm just passionate about giving God all the credit for his glorious creation. For example, if some day it can be proven there was an actual "Big Bang," I don't need to be afraid of that.

As long as it was God who was doing the banging, I'm fine with it. What's important to me is that no matter how we explain the beginning of the universe, we embrace the truth that God did it. Shalom!

TODAY'S READINGS
Psalm 122 | Genesis 6:1-10 | Hebrews 11:1-7

Saturday | NOVEMBER 30

Noah did everything just as God commanded him. | Genesis 6:22

Keep Building

Noah is a good example for us. It's not like God asked him to simply build another boat. He didn't even know what a boat looked like. Then he spent all those years building a boat—not to mention the task of gathering up the animals. And all the while he was preaching a message of repentance.

Not one single person accepted his message. And that went on for decade after decade. He just kept building the ark and preaching the word, faithfully submitting to God's call on his life. All the while, as far as I can tell, nothing happened to give him any encouragement. No one responded favorably. As a matter of fact, Noah was a laughingstock. But, he faithfully pursued God's plan for his life.

There's a message in this for us. God has given each of us a life to live for our good and his glory. It may not end up making sense to anyone else. However, we are to embrace the task at hand and get up each day and faithfully pursue his plan for our lives. And we do that regardless of the response we get from others.

My task is to pastor my church. There have been times when I have been greatly encouraged, and yet, there have been seasons when I wondered why I wasn't getting a better response. But Noah's example for me is to faithfully preach the word and let God take care of the rest. Shalom!

TODAY'S READINGS
Psalm 122 | Genesis 6:11-22 | Matthew 24:1-22

Sunday | DECEMBER 1

> Rather, clothe yourselves with the Lord Jesus Christ, and do not think about how to gratify the desires of the flesh. | Romans 13:14

Clothing Ourselves

This is a beautiful word picture. We are to put on Christ. I take that to mean if we clothe ourselves with the Lord Jesus Christ, we will act and think the way he acted and thought. The motivation for everything in his life was to do the Father's will. He said he couldn't do anything without the Father's will to guide him.

So, if we're going to clothe ourselves with him, then we too need to make the Father's will our number one priority. To do that, we must spend time searching his heart for his will for our lives. And then we must always be willing to do the next most responsible thing.

Once again, I see two parts to this discipline. First, we must search the Father's heart, and then second, we must be willing to always do the next most responsible thing he reveals to us. That's why our daily time alone with God is so essential. We must find solitude and silence for a time each day so we can discern his will for us.

As we humbly submit our will to his, we are clothing ourselves in the Lord Jesus Christ. There is nothing more satisfying than knowing we're in the center of God's will. I'm convinced that having this focus will prevent us from thinking about how to gratify the desires of our flesh. Shalom!

TODAY'S READINGS

Psalm 122 | Isaiah 2:1-5 | Matthew 24:36-44 | Romans 13:11-14

Monday | DECEMBER 2

Our help is in the name of the Lord, the Maker of heaven and earth. | Psalm 124:8

Help, Lord

Psalm 124 calls to mind a time when God's people's fate hung in the balance. They were facing certain destruction. And they certainly would have been destroyed if not for a miracle of epic proportion, against enormous odds. God came to their rescue.

While it appeared as though their demise was certain, God had other plans. They not only survived, but they destroyed their would-be assassins. This is a beautiful psalm for us to pray when the odds are stacked against us.

I pray this psalm with the monks of St. Meinrad every day during our noon prayer. It's a daily reminder that God, the creator of heaven and earth, stands ready to support and protect his people. The One whose hand flung the stars in place is ready and willing to fight our enemy on our behalf. And we're reminded that not only did he create everything, but it was easy for him to do it.

Our God is amazing and all-powerful. So, when he decides to fight for us, there's no enemy too strong for him. When he places our enemy in his sight, victory is certain. So, we cry out with the apostle Paul, "If God is for us then who can be against us? If God is on our side, how can we be denied? No, in all these things we are more than conquerors through Jesus Christ our Lord. And nothing can separate us from the love of God." Hooray for us! Yay God! Shalom!

TODAY'S READINGS
Psalm 124 | Genesis 8:1-19 | Romans 6:1-11

Tuesday | DECEMBER 3

> ...the world was not worthy of them. They wandered in deserts and mountains, living in caves and in holes in the ground. These were all commended for their faith, yet none of them received what had been promised, since God had planned something better for us so that only together with us would they be made perfect. | Hebrews 11:38-40

Something Better

What would it look like to live a life the world is not worthy of? Much of my life has been spent in a desperate and often futile attempt of trying too hard to fit in and to be honored by my peers, or worse. The idea of living a life so focused on being connected to the will of God and becoming unworthy to the rest of the world is almost a foreign concept to me. I feel like I have a tight grip on Jesus with one hand but still refusing to let go of the world with the other.

One of the things I've been thinking about lately is to keep taking my next step and grow deeper and deeper into an all-absorbing relationship with Jesus. I want my spirit to be so enmeshed with his that in my transition from this life to the next, I won't know the difference between here and heaven. I'll try making one change today that'll get me closer to the person God is calling me to be. How about you? What one change, however small, will you make today? Shalom!

TODAY'S READINGS
Psalm 124 | Genesis 9:1-17 | Hebrews 11:32-40

Wednesday | DECEMBER 4

I rejoiced with those who said to me, "Let us go to the house of the Lord." | Psalm 122:1

Temple Worship

I assume the psalmist is talking about the temple of the Lord here. It was a glorious, joy-filled experience for God's people to travel to the temple and to offer sacrifice and receive forgiveness. We do not journey to Jerusalem any longer, because we have the privilege of worshipping God right here in our own communities. We no longer sacrifice animals, but we do bring the sacrifice of praise.

As we're led in worship each week, we're experiencing the same God that the psalmist longed to encounter. I love to worship with the people of God. I get so excited to worship the Lord in song, preach and offer communion that by the time I get to the blessing, I'm downright giddy. I always ask our children to come on stage and help me with the benediction. We stand on the stage together with our arms reaching to heaven and I declare, "You have heard the gospel preached. You have repented of your sin. You have received the body and blood of Jesus Christ, so it's going to be a great week. You can go in peace. In the name of the Father and the Son and the Holy Spirit."

I could float off the stage, surrounded by those precious children helping me bless God's people. Our public worship together is the most important hour of my week. I'm so thankful God has blessed me with the honor of being a shepherd to his people. So, let's continue to receive God's blessing in our houses of worship, as they continue to be the places where folks can experience the presence of the Lord. Shalom!

TODAY'S READINGS
Psalm 124 | Isaiah 54:1-10 | Matthew 24:23-35

Thursday | DECEMBER 5

> Therefore it is necessary to choose one of the men who have been with us the whole time the Lord Jesus was living among us, beginning from John's baptism to the time when Jesus was taken up from us. For one of these must become a witness with us of his resurrection. | Acts 1:21-22

He's Alive!

All of human history pivots on the resurrection of this carpenter from Nazareth. If Jesus isn't raised from the dead, then we are to be pitied over all people. The message the apostles proclaimed was that the Jews conspired with the Romans to execute Jesus. And he died, but he didn't stay dead. The apostles then went to their deaths declaring Jesus was raised from the dead. They were eyewitnesses to his life and death and resurrection and even watched him ascending toward heaven. And they consistently proclaimed that stunning news—even under penalty of death.

Church tradition holds that each of these men, except John, were put to death simply because they refused to stop telling folks that the Jews had Jesus executed but that he didn't stay dead. When forced to either take back this outrageous claim or suffer a horrible death, every one of them proclaimed God raised Jesus from the dead. And folks, this is our legacy as well.

Two thousand years later we still believe God raised him from the dead. And it's our mission in life to share the good news of his resurrection with anyone who will listen. How might you share the good news today? Shalom!

TODAY'S READINGS
Psalm 72:1-7, 18-19 | Isaiah 4:2-6 | Acts 1:12-17, 21-26

Friday | DECEMBER 6

Whether you turn to the right or to the left, your ears will hear a voice behind you, saying, "This is the way; walk in it." | Isaiah 30:21

This Way

We can have the same kind of relationship with God today that his people shared with him in those days. If we are willing to meet him on his terms, he will always show us the way. As we submit our will to his, and as we give ourselves over to his control, we will develop a keen sense of God's direction for our lives. We will intuitively know which path to choose. That's why it's so important we spend time with him every day in silent solitude. Nothing will take the place of time alone with him.

Jesus is our example. Often, we see him, in the gospels, with choices to make, going off by himself to pray. Each time he does, God basically says to him, "This is the way, walk in it." And God's way for him wasn't always the direction Jesus was hoping for.

As he prayed in the garden before his arrest, Jesus asked the Father for a way out of his suffering. But God said through his silence, "This is the way, walk in it." This tells me that we won't always get the answer we're looking for. But we can know if we silently give ourselves to God, he is always about the business of directing us for his glory and our ultimate good. Listen for the ways he might be speaking to you today in your inner man, guiding you in the way you should go. Shalom!

TODAY'S READINGS
Psalm 72:1-7, 18-19 | Isaiah 30:19-26 | Acts 13:16-25

Saturday | DECEMBER 7

> John replied in the words of Isaiah the prophet, "I am the voice of one calling in the wilderness, 'Make straight the way for the Lord.'" | John 1:23

Spiritual Excavation

John the Baptist is an interesting study for Advent. Advent is designed to prepare us for the coming of the Christ child, as well as the return of Jesus in all of his glory. It's four weeks out of the year when we focus on the coming of Christ.

When John declared, "Make straight the way for the Lord," it would have brought to the folks' minds the preparation that preceded the coming of Caesar. Whenever the Roman emperor would travel, there would be a construction crew that would go out ahead of his entourage and build a road fit for a king. They would clear away trees and fill in the valleys and level off the hills. I always imagine a bulldozer smoothing out the road in preparation for the king's arrival.

So, during Advent each year, we are to clear away the clutter in our lives, remove any spiritual obstacles that will impede our progress and get ready for the coming of the Lord. Advent ushers in the Christmas season by reminding the followers of Jesus Christ that not only did he come to us as the Bethlehem baby, but he is coming back to us again—as the Lord of glory. Let's think of how we will prepare ourselves for this holy season. Shalom!

TODAY'S READINGS
Psalm 72:1-7, 18-19 | Isaiah 40:1-11 | John 1:19-28

Sunday | DECEMBER 8

Produce fruit in keeping with repentance. | Matthew 3:8

Fruit Inspector

John the Baptist was the kind of guy who thought, "Don't tell me; show me." He saw how the religious leaders treated the poor and the outcast, saying one thing but not following up with their actions. He knew they hadn't heard and embraced his message of salvation for everyone. The men who Matthew is referring to here were religious elitists. They believed the Kingdom of God was reserved only for those who obeyed all the religious rules they had created.

But John knew these men only made a show of obeying the rules; in their hearts, where it really mattered, their lives were far from where God wanted them to be. For John was preparing the folks for the Kingdom of God, which is reserved for those who humbly realize that apart from God's grace and kindness, they'd never be able to perform well enough to please him.

So, for us, 2,000 years later, our path to citizenship in the Kingdom of God is still exactly the same. It begins with pure humility, as we stop trying to convince ourselves and everyone else we are good enough on our own. Instead, we surrender our will to the One who has humbly demonstrated his love for us in that while we were still his enemy, he died for us. And it is in our daily act of humble understanding that we may participate in the Kingdom of God, producing fruit in keeping with repentance. How will we help someone who's hurting take their next step today? Shalom!

TODAY'S READINGS
Psalm 72:1-7, 18-19 | Isaiah 11:1-10 | Romans 15:4-13 | Matthew 3:1-12

Monday | DECEMBER 9

...and to make it your ambition to lead a quiet life: You should mind your own business and work with your hands, just as we told you... | 1 Thessalonians 4:11

Tend To...

This is a great verse to encourage all of us who are trying to take our next step toward Christ. It is a reminder that every day we get up and go to work for the glory of God. When we mind our own business and tend to our daily tasks, no matter how complicated or mundane, we are witnessing to our faith. People are watching us. They may only know that we attend church each Sunday. But our actions can speak louder than our words.

So, take heart, Christian, your daily grind is a great witness for the glory of God. People need to look at us and see that we are always mindful of the details at work, like being on time and operating with kindness and integrity even in the smallest of things, and to generally be a joy to work with, abstaining from office gossip and complaining.

The Bible says we are to do our work as though we're answering to God as our supervisor. Which means that each day we mind our own business and work hard, our routine is our act of worship! What are some ways in which you can live out your faith in the workplace? Shalom!

TODAY'S READINGS
Psalm 21 | Isaiah 24:1-16 | 1 Thessalonians 4:1-12

Tuesday | DECEMBER 10

Be exalted in your strength, Lord; we will sing and praise your might." | Psalm 21:13

Be Exalted

Did you know that the Psalms are actually to be sung? Of course, we have lost the music that goes with them. When I have the opportunity to pray with the monks at Saint Meinrad, I am always moved by the way they sing the Psalms. I am convinced that in these inspired songs, we have been given hymns that will bring us strength in spite of our fears and inspire us to remain faithful to the God who saves us. In truth, God has ordained us to find strength through his praises.

I try to be a bit intentional about praying through these precious songs every month. I find it amazing how they grab me in the midst of whatever struggle I find myself in and pick me up out of the mud and gunk of life. It reminds me that praise is a choice that does not depend on my feelings.

I have to choose each day to pray these glorious hymns to God. And I believe there is no music more pleasing to his ears. What can you praise God for today, even if you don't feel like praising? Shalom!

TODAY'S READINGS
Psalm 21 | Isaiah 41:14-20 | Romans 15:14-21

Wednesday | DECEMBER 11

On that day the Lord made a covenant with Abram... | Genesis 15:18a

Covenant Cutter

This covenant God made with Abram was unconditional. In a normal conditional covenant between two parties, each party is expected to provide a good or a service or payment. If either party fails to perform their part of the covenant, it is deemed null and void. It was customary for two men to lay out animal halves and pass through them.

This would signify that if they did not perform up to the agreement then they would receive the same fate as the sacrificed animals. I'm sure that you've heard the phrase, "cut a deal."

But notice how Abram is sleeping when this deal was sealed. It was God and God alone who was required to perform. That's why scholars call this an unconditional covenant. God is going to make Abram's family numerous like the stars in the sky. And God will give Abram possession of all the land. Neither of these promises is conditional upon Abram's performance. God is going to follow through with what he promised.

So, what does this ancient covenant between God and Abram have to do with us today? Well, I was thinking that we serve a God who cannot lie. So, when he says things like he's coming back to get us, we can bank on it. When the timing is perfect, he will transcend time and space and rapture his church. It's an unconditional covenant cut by a God who cannot lie. Think about this covenant today and how it might impact your life. Shalom!

TODAY'S READINGS
Psalm 21 | Genesis 15:1-18 | Matthew 12:33-37

Thursday | DECEMBER 12

At this they wept aloud again. Then Orpah kissed her mother-in-law goodbye, but Ruth clung to her. | Ruth 1:14

Defining Moments

This was a defining moment in Ruth's life. She could follow her sister-in-law Orpah back to their families and their false gods. Or she could cling to Naomi and her God—the God of the Hebrews. Ruth would have no way of knowing it, but the fate of a nation hung in the balance at that tearful roadside meeting.

She is putting all her faith in Naomi. Ruth will look to Naomi for spiritual guidance. She will obey everything Naomi asks her to do. Naomi knows well the Hebrew practice of the kinsman redeemer. And she is faithful to guide Ruth through the process. As the story plays out, Ruth takes on the leading role, but Naomi's influence in all Ruth does is constant. She will guide Ruth to approach Boaz as her kinsman redeemer and Boaz will take Ruth as his wife.

Together they will begin a heritage that will not only include kings David and Solomon, but Jesus Christ himself will come from Ruth's family tree. When you stop and think about it, the history of the nation of Israel pivoted on this impromptu roadside meeting.

So, the lesson for us today is to choose wisely whom we will cling to. Each of us is influenced greatly by those we follow. Who is your Naomi today and why? Shalom!

TODAY'S READINGS
Psalm 146:5-10 | Ruth 1:6-18 | 2 Peter 3:1-10

Friday | DECEMBER 13

Since everything will be destroyed in this way, what kind of people ought you to be? You ought to live holy and godly lives. | 2 Peter 3:11

Forever Stuff

It is right and good to hold loosely those things that will be destroyed on the Lord's return. Think about it. Someday all our possessions will be gone. This truth should have a great bearing on how we use our resources. In the end only the things that have brought glory to God will survive. So, what should we concentrate on?

Well, Peter concludes this passage by exhorting us to grow in the grace and knowledge of our Lord and Savior, Jesus Christ. In the end, when Christ returns, only what was done for Christ will matter. That's why it is so crucial we spend our time knowing and serving the people he died for.

We dedicate ourselves to spending time alone with him. Day after day, we surrender our will to his. And we use ourselves up by finding hurting people and helping them take their next step toward our Lord and Savior, Jesus Christ. The time we spend alone with him, serving others, and in our corporate worship on Sunday pays eternal dividends.

When Christ returns, we won't be bragging about our collection of stuff or our retirement account. So, let's take a moment and look at our schedule for today. How are we spending our time on tasks of eternal value? Shalom!

TODAY'S READINGS
Psalm 146:5-10 | Ruth 4:13-17 | 2 Peter 3:11-18

Saturday | DECEMBER 14

John answered, "Anyone who has two shirts should share with the one who has none, and anyone who has food should do the same." | Luke 3:11

Do/Don't

Even before Jesus began to proclaim the message of the Kingdom of God, John was already telling the folks to find hurting people and help them. Did you notice when asked what to do, John didn't launch into a sermon on "thou shalt nots"?

No, he commanded them to be proactive about finding hurting people and helping them. Dare we say this is the first command in the New Covenant for the people of God? And when asked by those in power what they should do, John basically said, "Stop taking advantage of the vulnerable." For John the Baptist, it wasn't enough for them to abstain from sinful activity. He wasn't simply calling people out of the darkness—he was calling them into the light.

For far too many Christians these days, the message of the gospel has been watered down to a list of "don'ts." Thou shalt not do this and thou shalt not do that. By that standard anyone with a certain amount of self-discipline would be able to modify their behavior enough that they would pass muster.

I think it's interesting that John drew his listeners' attention to the melon-shaped rocks that lined the desert floor. If you think about it, even a rock can abstain from sin. Rocks don't lie or steal or cheat. But no one would describe a rock as a child of God. That's because it is not enough to simply abstain from evil. What can you do today to help someone who's hurting? Shalom!

TODAY'S READINGS
Psalm 146:5-10 | 1 Samuel 2:1-8 | Luke 3:1-18

Sunday | DECEMBER 15

You too, be patient and stand firm, because the Lord's coming is near. | James 5:8

Today

This is a perfect verse for us to consider during Advent. It's the season when we prepare for the coming of the Christ child at Christmas and also look forward with hope to his second coming. James seemed to think the Lord would return soon. He did not.

So, what are we to make of the call to be patient and stand firm for the coming of the Lord? I think what James and the other writers of the New Testament would have us embrace as truth is that we should live out every day of our lives as though this may be the day. And so the question we need to ask ourselves is, "What would I do differently if I knew Jesus would return today?"

For one thing, I would not be concerned with long-term financial planning. I would be content with enough to get me through the day. Another concern of mine, if I really believed that Jesus would return today, is that I'd be certain I wasn't quarreling with anyone. I don't want Jesus to come back and find me bickering.

The other thing I thought of was, if Jesus is coming back today, then I want to be found faithful in helping hurting people take their next step toward Jesus Christ. What would you do differently if you knew Jesus was coming back today? Shalom!

TODAY'S READINGS
Psalm 146:5-10 | Isaiah 35:1-10 | James 5:7-10 | Matthew 11:2-11

Monday | DECEMBER 16

Why, my soul, are you downcast? Why so disturbed within me? Put your hope in God, for I will yet praise him, my Savior and my God. | Psalm 42:11

Why Sad?

One way to cure depression is praise. When we read the Psalms or sing praises to God, we are reminded of his faithfulness and his capacity to bring us joy, regardless of our circumstances. We serve a God who is ready and able to bring us peace.

He stands sovereign over every detail in our lives. And he desires only good for us. So, even though we may suffer temporarily, our hope can spring eternal. But we have to make the effort to get out of our own head, where all that negativity is so prevalent. Singing and reading psalms, hymns, and spiritual songs takes our focus off our problems and focuses us, instead, on our solution: God Almighty.

What about the days when we don't FEEL like praising God? I embrace the philosophy that "you fake it 'til you make it." In other words, we won't think our way into right acting, but we can act our way into right thinking. On days when we don't feel like singing and praising God, we know those are the days we need to offer praise the most. That's why there is always a psalm in our daily readings.

Read Psalm 42 again and notice how the psalmist goes from utter despair to joyous praise. Try writing a psalm of praise yourself today. Shalom!

TODAY'S READINGS
Psalm 42 | Isaiah 29:17-24 | Acts 5:12-16

Tuesday | DECEMBER 17

Why are you in despair, O my soul? And why have you become disturbed within me? Hope in God, for I shall again praise Him, for the help of His presence. | Psalm 42:5

My Soul

From the time I was 18 years old, I have suffered from depression and anxiety. I have been on innumerable medications and sat in countless hours of therapy. Both approaches were helpful at times, but what I've discovered over the last few years is that my mental and emotional stability is directly related to my willingness to turn from my despair as I enter into the presence of God and renew my hope in his amazing love.

As I disciplined myself to make this change in my daily life, slowly but surely, my depression and anxiety have been overcome by hope. It took about three years to arrive at a point in my life where I no longer needed medication of any kind.

I am a slow learner, but God is a great teacher. So, today I will hope in his amazing and steadfast love, and I will receive his blessing as I choose to turn to him. I pray you will as well. What part of your life will you turn to God for and receive his amazing hope and love? Shalom!

TODAY'S READINGS

Psalm 42 | Ezekiel 47:1-12 | Jude 1:17-25

Wednesday | DECEMBER 18

"What do you want with us, Son of God?" they shouted. "Have you come here to torture us before the appointed time?" | Matthew 8:29

What Now

We can learn something about demonology from this text. First of all, we see the demons inhabiting people. When they begged for Jesus to cast them into the pigs, it indicates they needed a living host to survive. Second, it's obvious they understood who Jesus was, better than the crowd did. They called him "Son of God." And it's obvious from the context, they knew they were subservient to him. They recognized Jesus had the authority to torture them. And finally, they created chaos; whether they possessed the men or the pigs, they were bent on destruction.

So, some obvious takeaways for us are: Jesus believed demons existed. He understood they were extremely evil and that he had absolute power over them. This leaves us with the fact that demon possession was real in Jesus' day.

I can't think of any scriptural reference to indicate they no longer exist. We can conclude that demon possession is real today—that they are bent on destruction, probably through chaos. But Jesus Christ still stands sovereign over them and their activities.

Have I missed anything? Let's thank God that Jesus has the capacity and the compassion to protect us from our enemy, and that in the end, we win. Shalom!

TODAY'S READINGS
Psalm 42 | Zechariah 8:1-17 | Matthew 8:14-17, 28-34

Thursday | DECEMBER 19

> So the law was our guardian until Christ came that we might be justified by faith. | Galatians 3:24

Guardian Jesus

In the first century, a little boy would have a guardian, who would do things like escort him to and from school. When the boy reached a certain age, it was no longer necessary for him to be under an escort.

This is the word picture the apostle Paul paints for us here regarding the law. I can just picture the guardian walking with the little boy, saying things like, "Don't step in that puddle" and "Stop swinging that stick around."

Paul says it's the function the law performed. It pointed out when we were outside of the Lord's will. But he says, "Now that faith has come, we are no longer under the supervision of the law." We have a higher calling. It is more than being in a position where the law no longer has authority over us.

We are compelled now, each day, by the power of the Holy Spirit to take our next step with Christ. Because of Christ's presence in our lives now, each of us is being directed daily by his wonderful guidance. He is our loving guardian, showing us our next step.

God might be dealing with me in an area you have already brought under the lordship of Jesus Christ. The point is, each of us has a next step to take today on our faith journey. It is onward and upward for us. What step of faith might he be calling you to take today? Shalom!

TODAY'S READINGS
Psalm 80:1-7, 17-19 | 2 Samuel 7:1-17 | Galatians 3:23-29

Friday | DECEMBER 20

For the sake of your word and according to your will, you have done this great thing and made it known to your servant. | 2 Samuel 7:21

Your Will

The Bible says King David was "a man after God's own heart." Perhaps more than anyone else, David knew the heart of God. One of the things I love about David's relationship with God is that David didn't think the world revolved around him. "Who am I?" David asked the Lord.

We can learn from David's example. The world doesn't revolve around us. God has a plan for us and it's unfolding according to his perfect will and his impeccable timing. We just get to go along for the ride.

To that end, I believe some of our prayer time is wasted trying to get God to let us be in charge and to call the shots. It would better serve us to be searching the heart of God to know his will. Once we see what God is up to in our midst, then it's our job not to get him to do something different, but rather to fall in line with his will for our lives.

David was sure it would be a good thing to build God a temple out of cedar. But God had other plans. There are things I would prefer the Lord would do in our church, but I must be about the task of determining his will and then being obedient to his plan for my life. Nothing is more important than knowing and following his will for our lives. Today how can you know the heart of God better? Shalom!

TODAY'S READINGS
Psalm 80:1-7, 17-19 | 2 Samuel 7:18-22 | Galatians 4:1-7

Saturday | DECEMBER 21

Sovereign Lord, you are God! Your covenant is trustworthy, and you have promised these good things to your servant. | 2 Samuel 7:28

Good God

The God we serve is a good God. He will never let us down. He will always do what is right and good. It's such a blessing to know everything God does concerning us is always right. He's the perfect Father. He is not like everyone else in our lives, who all slip up now and again. He always performs perfectly in every event of our lives.

I pray you will come to this place where you can say with every fiber of your being that God is so good!!! Everything he has allowed in your life, every difficult season, every time you stepped out of your comfort zone and grew because of it, God meant it all for your good and his glory. We can trust that about him.

Find out for yourself that the Lord is good. His goodness is what he wants us to experience. He offers himself to us. His love and faithfulness are present in everything he does. Today, think about all the ways God is good to you and thank him. Shalom!

TODAY'S READINGS
Psalm 80:1-7, 17-19 | 2 Samuel 7:23-29 | John 3:31-36

Sunday | DECEMBER 22

And you also are among those Gentiles who are called to belong to Jesus Christ. | Romans 1:6

Beggar's Banquet

These words surely apply to us today. We were called from the Gentiles to belong to Jesus Christ. It's a wonderful and glorious thing that God, in his infinite wisdom, decided to bring salvation to those outside the Jewish faith. The Bible is clear that salvation has come from a Jew, Jesus Christ, to the Jewish people and then to those outside the Jewish faith. We have been grafted in like a branch attached to a tree.

It's easy in our country and culture to lose sight of the fact we were once on the outside looking in. In America today, Gentile Christians comprise the vast majority of the church. We are so numerous and dominant that it feels like we're the chosen people of God. It's right and good for us to take the time to thank God for not leaving us as we originally were, on the outside looking in.

We were once not a people but now, by the grace and power of our Lord Jesus Christ, we have become joint heirs with him for the Kingdom of God. Think about that for a moment. The dinner party was planned for the rich and powerful. But when they refused to come, God's messenger was sent out to the back alleys to find hurting people like us to join in the festivities. We should always be thankful to be beggars at the banquet. Yay God! What does it mean to you to be invited to his table as family? Shalom!

TODAY'S READINGS

Psalm 80:1-7, 17-19 | Isaiah 7:10-16 | Romans 1:1-7 | Matthew 1:18-25

Monday | DECEMBER 23

> So those who rely on faith are blessed along with Abraham,
> the man of faith. | Galatians 3:9

By Faith

I was just thinking of a song I learned 50 years ago:

> Father Abraham had many sons.
> Many sons had Father Abraham.
> I am one of them and so are you.
> So, let's just praise the Lord.

Paul wanted the non-Jewish Galatian Christians to know that, by faith, they had been grafted into the family of God. They had received their salvation by faith. Abraham believed God's promise and he was declared righteous. For those of us who believe in the saving work of Jesus Christ on the cross, we've been declared righteous too. Therefore, by faith, we're considered children of the same promise made to our Father, in faith, by Abraham. That means even though Paul was writing to predominantly Gentile converts in Galatia, he wanted them to embrace the fact they were children of the promise as well.

The same can be said for us. We are the children of the promise as the people of God. We are no longer on the outside looking in. Jesus Christ has ushered us to his banquet table. Yes, we are the children of the promise. Today, reflect on this wonderful status we enjoy as children of the promise and all the blessings that come with it. Shalom!

TODAY'S READINGS
Luke 1:46-55 | 2 Samuel 7:18, 23-29 | Galatians 3:6-14

Tuesday | DECEMBER 24

"And she gave birth to her firstborn son; and she wrapped Him in cloths, and laid Him in a manger, because there was no room for them in the inn." | Luke 2:7

God Vulnerable

I remember reading how it was common in those days to wrap up newborn babies tightly in rags to keep their little limbs secure. It was believed infants were vulnerable, immediately after birthing, to broken or dislocated bones. Swaddling is still a practice used today, providing babies with a sense of a safety and security. This reveals how the Sovereign One would choose entry into this fallen world, in the most vulnerable way. The One the Old Testament declares would be the cornerstone, upon whom all our faith would be built, began in a such a humble way, downplaying his eternal, unmatched strength.

This got me to thinking about my own desire for power. I have this built-in preprogrammed passion to avoid being vulnerable and to pursue power, at all costs. Even my prayers at times reflect this passionate pursuit of power. Any time I feel myself losing control, I quickly want to plead with the Lord to intervene on my behalf and place me back in a position of control.

Why is it that I worship the One who willingly became so vulnerable for me, but so easily dismiss that he may choose the same path of personal helplessness for me? I can see I, obviously, have a next step to take in this area. May the Lord work in me whatever is necessary to embrace the vulnerability that is so entwined with being his follower. If it was good enough for him... what heart area can you be more vulnerable with? Shalom!

TODAY'S READINGS
Psalm 97 | Isaiah 62:6-12 | Titus 3:4-7 | Luke 2:1-20

Wednesday | DECEMBER 25

and she gave birth to her firstborn, a son. She wrapped him in cloths and placed him in a manger, because there was no guest room available for them... | Luke 2:7

No Room

I wonder about all of Joseph's family. He was related to most everyone in town. He was from the family of King David. Bethlehem was David's city. The town was full of David's descendants. He must have had hundreds of aunts and uncles and cousins living there. No one had a spare mat for the couple to sleep on? We all know the phrase that there was no room in the inn. But what about all his extended family?

Could it be no one would take them in because Mary was with child before her wedding night? No one would offer hospitality to the mother with an illegitimate son? If that's true, then Jesus came into the world as an outsider. There would have been no party to celebrate his birth.

Well, I was thinking this should be a great comfort for anyone who is feeling left out this Christmas. You're in good company. Jesus knows exactly how you feel. And if you think about it, even after he claimed to be the Messiah, the Chosen One of God, he said the Son of Man had no place to lay his head. We can't go back and provide accommodations for the holy family. God is blessing you today as you reach out to make sure no one in your sphere of influence is alone this Christmas. Who can you reach out to today? Whosoever you care for, you are caring for Jesus. Shalom!

TODAY'S READINGS
Psalm 96 | Isaiah 9: 2-7 | Titus 2: 11-14 | Luke 2: 1-20

Thursday | DECEMBER 26

The beginning of wisdom is this: Get wisdom. Though it cost all you have, get understanding. | Proverbs 4:7

Get Wisdom

The beginning of wisdom is to first commit to its pursuit. In other words, if we want wisdom, we cannot expect it to magically appear—we must work for it. That's why we're disciplined in our Jesus time each day. Wisdom comes from God. He's the sole source of all wisdom. If we want to obtain wisdom, we must receive it from him. In fact, he is wisdom. And the main way he communicates with us is through his word. Anyone who is serious about gaining wisdom must intentionally pursue God daily through his holy word.

We have so many distractions competing for our attention, but only God's word brings us true wisdom. I love the fact we are to invest all our resources in the pursuit of wisdom. It is better to be penniless with wisdom than to be fabulously wealthy without it.

Jesus is our primary source of wisdom and as we pursue his presence, we receive his wisdom. Scripture is our best way into his presence. But we also can receive wisdom from godly education, through biblically based literature and wise counsel. Sound preaching is a conduit to wisdom. And finally, I also believe the Lord is revealing his wisdom through his marvelous acts of nature.

We learn the wisdom of faithfulness when the sun rises each morning. And each day we experience his blessing as we make his wisdom our number one priority. What are you willing to exchange today for godly wisdom? Shalom!

TODAY'S READINGS

Psalm 148 | Proverbs 4:7-15 | Acts 7:59–8:8

Friday | DECEMBER 27

> And the testimony is this, that God has given us eternal life,
> and this life is in His Son. | 1 John 5:11

Eternal Life

The phrase "eternal life" was used, when I was a boy, to teach me about life after death. I have learned this interpretation is lacking. Eternal life in Scripture refers to the abundant, wonderful life God has available for us, from the moment we take our first step toward his Son, Jesus Christ. He is our goal or our safe place.

As kids, we played tag for hours on end. Whenever we played, we had established a tree or some other fixed object as the official goal. As long as I hung onto that tree, I could not lose. The goal was off base for anyone who was trying to defeat me in our little game.

The obvious connection here for us is that in the game of life, Jesus Christ is our goal or safe place. As long as we are holding on to him, we can't lose. It's a rule that is both universal and eternal. So, let's run to him and hold onto our safe place as we enjoy his incomparable blessing. How can you make a conscious choice to run to him today rather than do things on your own? Shalom!

TODAY'S READINGS
Psalm 148 | Proverbs 8:22-31 | 1 John 5:1-12

Saturday | DECEMBER 28

> He called a little child to him and placed the child among them. And he said: "Truly I tell you, unless you change and become like little children, you will never enter the kingdom of heaven. | Matthew 18:2-3

Childlike

This is a familiar passage to us but is often misunderstood. The most popular interpretation of this passage is that Jesus was speaking of the "innocence" of young children. The problem I have with that interpretation is I don't find children to be innocent. They are often, by nature, selfish and self-centered and manipulative. They are sweet and beautiful and precious beyond description, but are they really innocent?

I'm convinced Jesus was referring not to their innocence but to their vulnerability. Children had no rights in that Roman culture. They existed for the pleasure of their parents. A father had total authority over his child and the government would not interfere. So, if my humble interpretation is correct, then Jesus wants his disciples to become vulnerable to his Father in heaven.

He wants us to be totally dependent upon him. As we see throughout the book of Acts, the first disciples did become like little children. They entrusted themselves to their heavenly Father's care, even to the point of death. They refused to fight back.

I have a long way to go in this area. I am a "right fighter." I need to learn to be like Jesus and entrust myself to the One who judges justly. I don't like being vulnerable. But when you look at the martyrs of the early church, they were the most vulnerable of all people. So, for me, what this looks like is simply developing a lifestyle where I refuse to defend myself and learn not to fight back. Today, how can you become more childlike before the Lord? Shalom!

TODAY'S READINGS
Psalm 148 | Isaiah 49:13-23 | Matthew 18:1-14

Sunday | DECEMBER 29

> So, Joseph got up and took the child and his mother while it was still night and left for Egypt. | Matthew 2:14

Get Up!

We don't know a great deal about Joseph. But what we do know we can surely appreciate. Scholars believe Joseph not only got up in the middle of that night and immediately obeyed the Lord's will for his life, but he embarked on a journey of more than 150 miles. He left everything he knew to go to a strange land and live among people who were strangers to him.

He's a great example for me here. Joseph did the next right, responsible thing. I've been pursuing this discipline for the last couple of years. The amazing thing I've discovered is most of the time it's not difficult to figure out what the next right, responsible thing is. The challenge is actually doing it!

So, let's just take those few things we're still not clear on and put a pin in them for a moment. Our confusion on those issues should not prevent us from obeying what we know needs to be done. Just do it! What might your next right, responsible thing be to do today? Shalom!

TODAY'S READINGS
Psalm 148 | Isaiah 63:7-9 | Hebrews 2:10-18 | Matthew 2:13-23

Monday | DECEMBER 30

> So we fix our eyes not on what is seen, but on what is unseen, since what is seen is temporary, but what is unseen is eternal. | 2 Corinthians 4:18

Eternal Perspectives

I am struggling with an earthly problem that appears to be unsolvable. Without some kind of divine intervention, it's difficult for me to see how this works out. But, as I read this verse, I realized I'm focused on what is seen. What is unseen is a God who loves me perfectly and desires the best for me. He is competent and capable and compassionate to solve my problem. He may choose to intervene and resolve my situation. Or he may, in his infinite wisdom, allow me to experience all the negative consequences.

Perhaps you're facing a similar dilemma. It may be financial or relational or work-related. Whatever the problem, we can choose to fix our eyes on the solution. The Lord is the solution to whatever troubles us. Ultimately, we can count on him to resolve our problem if we will just talk to him and release it to his care.

It may be not in this temporary life that it gets resolved. But, we are a people who are living out our lives with one eye on eternity. We know someday, hopefully soon, Jesus is coming back to make everything right. So, live in his blessing as you face today with confidence knowing the day is fast-approaching when our problems will be over forever. What problem will you trust God with today? Shalom!

TODAY'S READINGS
Psalm 20 | Isaiah 26:1-9 | 2 Corinthians 4:16-18

Tuesday | DECEMBER 31

Then they asked him, "Where is your father?" "You do not know me or my Father," Jesus replied. "If you knew me, you would know my Father also." | John 8:19

Our Everything

Absolutely everything we need to know about God in this life we can learn from observing his Son, Jesus Christ. For example, if we want to know how God feels about little children, we watch Jesus gently take them into his loving arms and bless them. Jesus is the real life, flesh and blood version of God. He is God in the flesh. His command to us is to follow him.

We are to learn to think as he thinks and act as he does. That's why we spend so much of our time studying the Gospels. They are our window into the life of the Father. Jesus is the physical revealing of all we need to know about God the Father in this life.

This is also why Jesus said he was the Way, the Truth, and the Life. He said no one comes to the Father except through him. God in his infinite wisdom has chosen to reveal himself to us through the life of Christ, as recorded in Matthew, Mark, Luke and John.

So, let's commit ourselves to knowing and loving and following Jesus as he blesses us today by revealing himself to us through his holy word. And then let's be found faithful in molding our lives to follow him. Who or what will you follow today? Shalom!

TODAY'S READINGS

Psalm 20 | 1 Kings 3:5-14 | John 8:12-19

Wednesday | JANUARY 1

> Then they will go away to eternal punishment,
> but the righteous to eternal life. | Matthew 25:46

Sheep? Goat?

I've always been troubled by this verse. It seems so final and uncompromising. We will be declared either sheep or goats and there will be no excuses. This stark statement begs the question, "How much is enough?" I mean, the need for God is overwhelming. There is no end to opportunities to find hurting people and helping them. How much is enough?

Our food pantry volunteers spend three days a week feeding the poor. Are they sheep? Do you have to be involved in all aspects of this discipline? There is feeding the poor, providing water for the thirsty, clothing the naked, visiting the sick and those in prison. The need is so great in our community. Add to that the other places around the country and world and the hurting people there—we see no limit to the suffering people who need our help.

One of the truths we already know applies here is that we can't earn our way into the Kingdom of God. We don't believe in a works-based righteousness. In other words, you can't help enough hurting people to win God's approval. But, it is clear the sheep will find hurting people and help them. The goats will not.

My conclusion is that finding hurting people and helping them is the evidence of a changed heart. We are not part of the Kingdom of God because we help hurting people. We help hurting people because we are part of the Kingdom of God. What can you do for others today that will reflect your heart for God? Shalom!

TODAY'S READINGS
Psalm 8 | Ecclesiastes 3:1-13 | Matthew 25:31-46 | Revelation 21:1-6a

Thursday | JANUARY 2

> I will bless those who bless you, and whoever curses you I will curse; and all peoples on earth will be blessed through you. | Genesis 12:3

Greatest Blessing

This is a huge promise to a man who didn't even own a piece of land. Can you just imagine God telling you he'll bless all nations on earth through you? But God did it.

He took this single, solitary 75-year-old childless man and blessed him to become a country full of millions of people too numerous to count. And out of those millions of boys to be part of Abraham's heritage, one would be the baby boy born to Joseph and Mary.

This little baby would grow up to be Jesus of Nazareth, who would take the sins of the world on his shoulders. He would do battle with both hell and death and beat the snot out of them. And now because of his redemptive work on the cross and his subsequent resurrection from the dead, "all peoples on earth" have been given an opportunity to enter the Kingdom of God. It is the greatest blessing ever conceived. And it all started with this elderly nomad who had no place to call home. It just goes to show us, God loves to use the underdog to accomplish more than anyone could hope for or imagine.

So, don't lose heart. God wasn't finished with the 75-year-old Abraham, and he's not finished with you. Ask him to show you his plans for your life. Then just watch and see how he will bless you today for your good and his glory. Shalom!

TODAY'S READINGS
Psalm 20 | Genesis 12:1-7 | Hebrews 11:1-12

Friday | JANUARY 3

When Jacob awoke from his sleep, he thought, "Surely the Lord is in this place, and I was not aware of it." | Gen 28:16

Thin Places

Irish Christians refer to "thin places." To them, a thin place is a spot where heaven and earth seemingly come together. It is a place where God is so close it feels like you can reach out and touch him.

Bethel was a thin place for Jacob. It was a special place where Jacob felt close to God. I think it's right and good for us to find our own thin places. For me, I feel closest to heaven when I am outside. There is just something about being surrounded with God's creation that makes me feel close to him.

Some people have a thin place in a special room in their home where God meets with them. For others it can be simply a favorite chair. A thin place is anywhere that we get up from and think, "Surely God is in this place."

It seems that whenever Jesus had a major decision to make or found himself in a tight spot, he would get up early in the morning and go out by himself and find a thin place where he could connect with God. I'm convinced a thin place can be anywhere we remove the obstacles that prevent us from encountering God. We just need to come to him today with a humble heart and say, "Lord, here I am." Think about where those thin places have been for you, or where you might create one set aside for communing with God. Shalom!

TODAY'S READINGS
Psalm 72 | Genesis 28:10-22 | Hebrews 11:13-22

Saturday | JANUARY 4

> Then he said, "Do not come near here; remove your sandals from your feet, for the place where you are standing is holy ground." | Exodus 3:5

Holy Ground

What an awe-filled experience that must have been for Moses! He was about to encounter the sovereign God of the universe and he would never be the same again. It was an encounter that would change the world. Even though I admit I'm a little jealous of Moses' opportunity, I also have to admit, given the same opportunity to stand on that holy ground, it might end in me having a coronary.

I never really cared for how much of the church observes high worship. I don't care for the formality. And yet in the midst of this story, there is God's instruction for Moses to take off his sandals because he was standing on holy ground.

Now, there wasn't anything special about that piece of wilderness—except for the fact God had showed up. That fact alone demanded some reverence on the part of Moses. Sometimes I wonder if perhaps I'm just a little lacking in the reverence department. Four times a day I stop to pray, but rarely am I overtaken by the awe of what I'm doing. Truth is, whenever I call upon the Lord and he shows up, the place where I'm standing is holy ground. It is made so by his mere presence. How can you become more aware today that you are standing on holy ground? Shalom!

TODAY'S READINGS
Psalm 72 | Exodus 3:1-5 | Hebrews 11:23-31

Sunday | JANUARY 5

> Then shall the young women rejoice in the dance, and the young men and the old shall be merry. I will turn their mourning into joy, I will comfort them, and give them gladness for sorrow. | Jeremiah 31:13

Promised Joy

Although this promise was given by God to his people some 2,500 years ago, it is equally precious to us today. Yes, it was originally penned for the people of God in exile to Babylon. However, in store today for all who claim the name of Christ, a date is held certain. That is the day when Christ will gather you up and your mourning will be turned to eternal joy.

It's a promise given to us from a God who cannot lie. So, regardless of where you find yourself on life's difficult path, keep one eye on that glorious day. Remember, we are just passing through here.

We are citizens of another Kingdom where Christ rules eternal. He is our hope and our future. It is in this truth we can embrace our blessing today. How can you put your eyes on things eternal today in the midst of troubles? Shalom!

TODAY'S READINGS

Psalm 147:12-20 | Jeremiah 31:7-14 | Ephesians 1:3-14 | John 1: 1-9, 10-18

Monday | JANUARY 6

When King Herod heard this he was disturbed, and all Jerusalem with him. | Matthew 2:3

Grand Design

The original word for "disturbed" is an extremely strong word. King Herod was an evil, maniacal tyrant who killed anyone who threatened his throne. In his paranoia, he even had his own family executed. When Matthew tells us Herod summoned the chief priest and the teachers of the law, he is referring to the Sanhedrin, the Jewish supreme court. They would have come running because Herod had already executed their predecessors.

So, when Matthew tells us all of Jerusalem was disturbed, we can assume they were terrified of what the evil king might do. And, sure enough, he ordered the execution of every male child two years old and younger.

Joseph and Mary and baby Jesus ended up escaping under cover of darkness. They traveled some 150 miles to Egypt. So, what is there here in this story for us today? Well, I was just thinking that although evil stood at the ready to destroy the divine plan, God's will was not thwarted. God warned Joseph in a dream to flee the area. So, the best laid plans of a most powerful and evil man were no match for God's design for this divine drama. And you are part of his grand design as well.

The same God who rescued Jesus stands at the ready to intercede on your behalf. And all the best-laid plans of evil men will not prevail against his will for your life. Ultimately, God will have his way with you, just as he did with baby Jesus. And, yes, you may suffer for a little while. You may have your journey to your own Egypt. But that doesn't mean God has lost control. When Herod killed all the baby boys around Bethlehem, he probably figured his mission was accomplished. But God had other plans for Jesus, and he does for you too. So, if you find yourself disturbed by evil today, take heart. How does it change your today knowing you are a part of God's grand, eternal plan? Shalom!

TODAY'S READINGS

Psalm 72:1-7, 10-14 | Isaiah 60:1-6 | Ephesians 3:1-12 | Matthew 2:1-12

Tuesday | JANUARY 7

> How happy your people must be! How happy your officials, who continually stand before you and hear your wisdom! | 1 Kings 10:8

How Happy

God wasn't through after he placed the wisest man who ever lived on Israel's throne. Fifteen centuries later, he sent another King, born in a manger in total obscurity. Wise monarchs from around the world failed to notice his wisdom and he died the death of a common criminal. But we know something far more glorious than they could have ever imagined.

The baby king, whose DNA is traced back to King Solomon, is also the sovereign God of the universe. And his wisdom is far superior to even the wisest man who ever lived. Jesus Christ is the sole source of all wisdom; he is wisdom personified. There is absolutely nothing wise unless it proceeds from the mouth of Jesus. And it is our amazing privilege to open up these wise words that he has entrusted to our care.

Each day, we embrace his wisdom and pray for his words to illuminate our path and give clear direction to our next step. Glory today in that blessing of unlimited wisdom given to you graciously and without measure. What pearl of wisdom can you find in the word today? Shalom!

TODAY'S READINGS
Psalm 72 | 1 Kings 10:1-13 | Ephesians 3:14-21

Wednesday | JANUARY 8

> Instead, speaking the truth in love, we will grow to become in every respect the mature body of him who is the head, that is, Christ. | Ephesians 4:15

Growing Up

Growing up is a long and arduous journey. It is not for the faint of heart. This is our everyday task. It's like doing our chores. And yes, even though there will be days when we may not feel like we are maturing, we still have our chores to do. Things like reading God's word, and praying for his direction, and being thankful, and interacting with like-minded believers, and finding hurting people, and helping them take their next step with Jesus Christ.

Then one day, hopefully soon, we will stand in front of our Lord and Savior and hear those words: "Well done, my good and faithful servant. Look how you've grown." And on that day, we will suddenly realize our blessing was hidden in our passionate, daily pursuit of the One who has called us to eternal glory. His transforming work was taking place in us all along! Despite how you may feel today, what spiritual chores can you do—and trust God to grow you up in him? Shalom!

TODAY'S READINGS
Psalm 72 | 1 Kings 10:14-25 | Ephesians 4:7, 11-16

Thursday | JANUARY 9

> "Who are you, Lord?" Saul asked. "I am Jesus, whom you are persecuting," he replied. | Acts 9:5

Who Dat?

This question Saul asked of Jesus may well be not only the most important question anyone could ever ask, but it is also the only question none of us will ever escape answering. Each morning when we rise, we open our Bibles and diligently search to know who Jesus is and what he expects from us today. It is not complicated, really. I like to pray, "Morning, Lord, it's Jay. What are you up to today? Can I be a part of it?"

Every day, like a master craftsman, Jesus slowly chips away at us and is sculpting us into the people he would have us to be. And this great work of art is taking place in your life regardless of how you feel about it.

So, take heart, dear Christian, as you search the mind of Christ and learn a little more today just who he is. Reflect on what the Lord is currently chipping away in you and how you can cooperate with him. Shalom!

TODAY'S READINGS
Psalm 29 | 1 Samuel 3:1-9 | Acts 9:1-9

Friday | JANUARY 10

> But the Lord said to Ananias, "Go! This man is my chosen instrument to proclaim my name to the Gentiles and their kings and to the people of Israel. I will show him how much he must suffer for my name." | Acts 9:15-16

Just Go!

God's ways are so often different from my own inclinations. The truth is there is no logical earthly reason for Ananias to help Saul. He was evil beyond measure. He killed Christians for a living. But the Lord had different plans.

I was also wondering why God recruited Ananias to help. He doesn't need any human intervention. He could have accomplished everything in Paul's life with or without Ananias' help.

Maybe a lesson to take with us today is that the Lord is working behind each scene in ways more complex and incredible than we could ever hope for or imagine. And when our interaction with him compels us to do something far outside our comfort zone, perhaps it would be wise for us to pause and wonder where the thought originated.

Whenever I feel led to do something I never would have come up with on my own, I'm learning to appreciate it may be divine instructions for my next step. What are you feeling compelled to do today? Shalom!

TODAY'S READINGS
Psalm 29 | 1 Samuel 3:10-4:1a | Acts 9:10-19a

Saturday | JANUARY 11

All those who heard him were astonished and asked, "Isn't he the man who raised havoc in Jerusalem among those who call on this name? And hasn't he come here to take them as prisoners to the chief priests?" | Acts 9:21

The Man

It seems God revels in using such flawed people to advance his Kingdom and demonstrate his glory. Now, one could argue the Lord chose Paul because he was a great Jewish scholar, but that misses the point. Jesus picked his greatest enemy to advance his message to the world. If you're a Christian today and you're not a Jew, you owe a portion of your journey to Paul's faithful direction.

He literally sacrificed his life to tell the world of Christ's Kingdom. And guess what? Jesus was just getting started. Even today he remains in the full-time, 24-hour-a-day business of taking flawed but hopeful knuckleheads like Paul, and you, and me, and doing in us what we could have never hoped for or imagined.

If you have a past like Paul and me, that you regret and are ashamed of, you are in excellent company. And, oh yeah, let's not be so quick to dismiss the life of another because of their past. They may be right where God wants them. And your blessing may be in walking with them for a stretch of that journey. Who have you overlooked because of their past, and who can you give a new chance and bless today? Shalom!

TODAY'S READINGS
Psalm 29 | 1 Samuel 7:3-17 | Acts 9:19b-31

Sunday | JANUARY 12

Jesus replied, "Let it be so now; it is proper for us to do this to fulfill all righteousness." Then John consented. | Matthew 3:15

Great Odds

We are in Year A of our lectionary readings. Each Sunday, we receive a reading from the Book of Matthew. Matthew is a Jew writing to Jewish Christians to confirm for them Jesus is the one the Hebrew Scriptures point to. More so than any of the other gospel accounts, we will see Matthew tying Jesus' ministry back to the prophecies, written hundreds of years earlier in what we call the Old Testament.

There are hundreds of prophecies about Jesus, written by dozens of men across the centuries! I read about an attempt to quantify the predictability of Jesus being able to fulfill even a *fraction* of the Old Testament prophecies. That number would be comparable to covering the entire state of Texas knee-deep with silver dollars, including one marked coin. And then if you were to blindfold a man and have him walk across the entire state of Texas, reach down one time and, still blindfolded, randomly pick up the marked coin—that would be the odds of one man being able to fulfill even a tiny fraction of the Old Testament prophecies about Christ. Jesus fulfilled every one of them. Today, think whether there is anything else in your life with odds like this. Shalom!

TODAY'S READINGS
Psalm 29 | Isaiah 42:1-9 | Acts 10:34-43 | Matthew 3:13-17

Monday | JANUARY 13

So they gave Jacob all the foreign gods they had and the rings in their ears, and Jacob buried them under the oak at Shechem. | Genesis 35:4

Almighty God!

It seems strange to me that Jacob allowed the false gods to find a home in his clan. It is good for us to remember the early patriarchs were working with a limited amount of information about God. God had not yet revealed himself to them as fully as he would with Moses on the mountain. One of the key principles Moses would teach them was that they should have no other gods.

So, there was always the temptation for the people to embrace the foreign gods of whichever culture they found themselves in. It's easy to be critical of them and think, "Oh, come on, they didn't know not to have other gods?" But I was thinking, even though we have centuries of God's revelations to his people, and even though we have the compiled books of the Old and New Testament, and even though we are indwelt by the Holy Spirit, we *still* are tempted to worship false gods.

Oh sure, we don't have a shrine in our bedroom dedicated to the sun god. But we *are* tempted to drift into the worshipping of false gods such as power and possessions and personal prestige. In today's terms that looks like greed for more money, wanting people to think highly of us, or even seeking security in a career. How often do we find ourselves placing the pursuit of this eternally worthless stuff ahead of our passion for Jesus Christ?

We confess with our mouths that he is the Lord of our lives, but our calendars and checkbooks and Visa bills reveal our real passion. Let's use the passage today to prompt us to do a little housekeeping. As we begin a new year, let's dedicate ourselves to have nothing come between us and our pursuit of God. Can you think of any false gods you may have embraced, even accidentally? Shalom!

TODAY'S READINGS
Psalm 89:5-37 | Genesis 35:1-13 | Acts 10:44-48

Tuesday | JANUARY 14

> "Alas, Sovereign Lord," I said, "I do not know how to speak; I am too young." | Jeremiah 1:6

Yeah But...

Jeremiah was a reluctant spokesman for God. And sadly, Jeremiah would spend the rest of his life proclaiming God's truth, only to have it fall on deaf ears.

The people didn't listen to Jeremiah, but that doesn't mean he was a failure. He was faithful to proclaim the word of God for decades. How lonely and frustrated he must have felt. He would not only be ignored for his entire adult life, but when he wasn't ignored, he was hated and even imprisoned for faithfully declaring the word of God.

Jeremiah is a great example for us to see that we're not responsible for how people react to our gospel message. They may respond favorably and embrace it. They may ignore us. Or they may even hate us for attempting to make God known. We're just called to be faithful, to find hurting people, and share the good news of Jesus Christ with them. Then after we are faithful to share, we leave the results in the sovereign hands of God. He will do with our words as he chooses.

This is a great refresher course for me because I'm always looking for measurable results from my preaching. It bothers me when I feel like people are not responding. But the lesson from Jeremiah today is that we are each being called to faithfully proclaim Jesus Christ and him crucified, and leave the rest up to God. He is faithful to perform it. What seeds can you plant today and leave to God to germinate? Shalom!

TODAY'S READINGS
Psalm 89:5-37 | Jeremiah 1:4-10 | Acts 8:4-13

Wednesday | JANUARY 15

A bruised reed he will not break, and a smoldering wick he will not snuff out, till he has brought justice through to victory. | Matthew 12:20

Strong and Gentle

Jesus didn't act like your typical warrior king. He wasn't violent. He wasn't even forceful. He was kind and gentle.

I love this gentle aspect of his character because it's something I've struggled with my whole life. I have broken my fair share of bruised reeds. And I've snuffed out flickering wicks. But Jesus wasn't like that. He always had the time and patience to help the hurting. As a matter of fact, so much of the gospel account is about him helping hurting people.

This truth should motivate us to always be strong but gentle like our Savior. We live in a culture that admires tough guys and rewards those who excel at getting things done. But Jesus didn't take the world by force. He could have been the most forceful leader who ever lived. But he refused to force himself on anyone.

The powerful hands that flung the stars in their place were known to softly hold young children. Jesus was always strong and always gentle. The only time we see the forceful side of him is when he was confronting religious leaders who were responsible for taking advantage of hurting people. Strong and gentle is the way of Christ. How can you practice those qualities today with someone who is hurting? Shalom!

TODAY'S READINGS
Psalm 89:5-37 | Isaiah 51:1-16 | Matthew 12:15-21

Thursday | JANUARY 16

> Am I now trying to win the approval of human beings, or of God?
> Or am I trying to please people? If I were still trying to please people,
> I would not be a servant of Christ. | Galatians 1:10

1,000 Sermons

This verse reminds me of one we just worked on a few days ago. Still, it kind of jumped up and slapped me in the face. I still need to do a little soul-searching on this topic. I think I'm way too concerned about trying to please people. Oh sure, in my head I know my most important audience on Sunday morning is God. But I'm by nature a people pleaser.

It bothers me too much when folks leave the church. I need to be dedicated to preaching Jesus Christ and him crucified and then let the chips fall where they may. As long as I can have confidence Jesus is pleased with my message, I should be at peace.

There is absolutely nothing I would rather do with my time than prepare and present sermons. And though I love it, I am reminded of German pastor and theologian Dietrich Bonhoeffer, who said, shortly before he was martyred for his faith in Nazi Germany, "One act of obedience is better than a thousand sermons."

So, you are faithful to proclaim the gospel of Jesus Christ in your homes and workplaces with every act of obedience. And when you do, all of heaven rejoices. Think about ways you can shift your thinking to become a God pleaser today rather than a people pleaser. Shalom!

TODAY'S READINGS
Psalm 40:1-11 | Isaiah 22:15-25 | Galatians 1:6-12

Friday | JANUARY 17

> After his suffering, he presented himself to them and gave many convincing proofs that he was alive. He appeared to them over a period of forty days and spoke about the kingdom of God. | Acts 1:1-3

He's Alive

The fact that Jesus was dead but didn't stay dead is a difficult concept for people to accept today. That shouldn't surprise us. How many of us have attended a funeral and saw the person get up from the casket and join in the service? Dead people tend to stay dead. That is a certain truth.

So, these convincing truths that bear witness to the fact many of Jesus' followers saw him alive, living and breathing after his death is a crucial aspect to our story. Chuck Colson, of the famed Watergate debacle, reveals how quickly he and his coconspirators all turned on each other within the opening moments of the investigation. But after going to prison, Chuck gave his life to Christ and is probably most famous for his intriguing question, "Who would be willing to die for a lie?" None of his buddies were even willing to be incarcerated for Nixon's lie.

The truth is, many of the people who Christ revealed himself to after his resurrection went to their grave declaring they'd seen the risen Lord. None of them were willing to back down, and they were killed for it. Would you be willing to die for the truth? It's worth thinking about. Shalom!

TODAY'S READINGS
Psalm 40:1-11 | Genesis 27:30-38 | Acts 1:1-5

Saturday | JANUARY 18

So they pulled their boats up on shore, left everything and followed him. | Luke 5:11

Gone Fishing

The disciples truly left everything to follow Jesus. To start with, they left a record catch of fish, which was like leaving a month's salary in cash on the beach. But they gave up much more than that record catch. I'm convinced when they made the decision to follow Jesus, they ended up being shunned by the Jewish leadership.

They would have been thrown out of their synagogue. And no one would be allowed any contact with them. Which meant, they could not count on their usual customers for selling their fish. Once someone was shunned, the people were no longer allowed to even approach them or touch them or speak to them for any reason.

That's why Peter would later say to Jesus, "We have left everything to follow you." It was socially and morally unacceptable for any of them to be a follower of Jesus. I wonder how many of us would choose Jesus over our careers. How many of us would be able to leave our families behind to follow the carpenter from Nazareth?

It speaks to the kind of commitment Jesus expected of his followers. And it is an encouragement to us today to follow the lead of Elisha and the apostles and focus our attention on our calling, regardless of the cost. Today, how will you choose Jesus? Shalom!

TODAY'S READINGS
Psalm 40:1-11 | 1 Kings 19:19-21 | Luke 5:1-11

Sunday | JANUARY 19

This is the one I meant when I said, 'A man who comes after me has surpassed me because he was before me.' | John 1:30

Follow Him

This is a mouthful. John the Baptist has been preaching about the Kingdom of God before Jesus had even started his ministry. John was wildly popular, and I am sure the people had great plans for this prophet of God.

But John said, "Not so fast. I am not the Messiah." Then, when Jesus showed up fresh off his wilderness temptation, John passes the mantle of leadership to Jesus. And John's theology regarding Jesus was spot-on.

Even though Jesus started his ministry after John, the baptizer knew that Jesus lived before him in eternity past. That's why he said Jesus had surpassed him because Jesus was before John. So, here we see the beginning of Jesus' ministry being ushered in by the great John the Baptist, declaring Jesus was the Lamb of God, who existed before, before. And then, I think somewhat reluctantly, John's disciples followed after Jesus.

This is important because they were content being John's disciples. But John rightfully hands them off to the care of the Savior. The lesson for us in this interaction is that Jesus Christ and he alone is the One we are called to follow. All our allegiance belongs to him. He is the One who existed in eternity past with the Father. And then, at just the right time, he came to dwell among us as the Bethlehem baby. And in that manger lay the Sovereign God of the universe, who created your babies and every baby ever conceived. God in the flesh. Behold the Lamb of God who took away our sins. How you can follow Jesus with abandon today? Shalom!

TODAY'S READINGS

Psalm 40:1-11 | Isaiah 49:1-7 | John 1:29-42

Monday | JANUARY 20

> As they traveled along the road, they came to some water and the eunuch said, "Look, here is water. What can stand in the way of my being baptized?" | Acts 8:36

Why Not?

There seems to be a sense of urgency following the eunuch's conversion. He sees some water and having given his life to Christ, he wants to be identified with him in the waters of baptism. Before he does, he asks one of the most profound questions ever asked: "What can stand in the way of my being baptized?" What a great question for a new convert to ask.

I try to present this question to anyone I lead to Christ. "What is standing in the way of you being baptized?" I want people to be baptized soon after their conversion. I think it is the normal process of the New Testament.

It's one of my greatest joys to be able to baptize someone. I love to receive their confession and then lead them into the baptismal waters. Most of the time, we use a horse-watering trough for the ceremony. Other times we will use my swimming pool. Whatever our means for getting the job done, I can't help but think the Lord is pleased with every experience. Maybe you have never been baptized. If not, what stands in your way? Shalom!

TODAY'S READINGS
Psalm 40:6-17 | Exodus 12:1-13,21-28 | Acts 8:26-40

Tuesday | JANUARY 21

> He was oppressed and afflicted, yet he did not open his mouth; he was led like a lamb to the slaughter, and as a sheep before its shearers is silent, so he did not open his mouth. | Isaiah 53:7

Zip It!

Jesus is our perfect example for how to endure unfair suffering. I think of how he was wrongly accused and innocent of all charges, yet he suffered in silence. We can learn from his sacrifice to be people of more noble character. One way we accomplish this is by simply keeping our mouths shut.

It's impossible for me to place myself in this position because I am not innocent. Even if I feel I bear no guilt in a specific situation, I have plenty of other actions I am guilty for. But whenever I am wrongly accused, I can't seem to stop running my mouth about it; I think it's up to me and me alone to set the record straight.

I want to learn to suffer in silence, to have the quiet strength of Christ. Perhaps in doing so, in a strange yet beautiful way, we are sharing in the suffering of Christ. So, let's not be so concerned about how others perceive us.

Jesus was seen as a vile criminal and a laughingstock. He was the greatest communicator who ever lived and yet when wrongly accused, he kept his mouth shut and suffered in silence. Today, think about times when you might have chosen the quiet strength of silence and let that draw you closer to Christ. Shalom!

TODAY'S READINGS
Psalm 40:6-17 | Isaiah 53:1-12 | Hebrews 10:1-4

Wednesday | JANUARY 22

> Then John's disciples came and asked him, "How is it that we and the Pharisees fast often, but your disciples do not fast?" | Matthew 9:14-17

Nunya

How glad I am church people no longer ever question the actions and motives of other believers. I am, of course, being facetious. Fasting was a common practice held in high regard by the religious elite of Jesus' day. It was a natural thing to notice Christ's disciples were not following the rules. But the truth is, what Jesus did and how he led his followers was none of their business.

I have adopted the word NUNYA for this application. We love to encourage others with three important truths whenever we find ourselves sticking our noses in the business of others:

1) We don't know what they know.

2) We don't know what God knows.

3) We don't even know what we know.

The truth is, God's ways are not our own. And it's quite possible he is working in others' lives, in ways we're just not privy to. Why? Because it's NUNYA. It is none of our business. We have enough work to do today determining our own next step without evaluating others' hearts and ministries that are not our responsibility. Think about ways you've been overly concerned about how others are living out their faith, and see if there's something God wants to reveal about your own heart. Shalom!

TODAY'S READINGS
Psalm 40:6-17 | Isaiah 48:12-21 | Matthew 9:14-17

Thursday | JANUARY 23

> The Lord is my light and my salvation—whom shall I fear? The Lord is the stronghold of my life—of whom shall I be afraid? | Psalm 27:1

No Fear

I'm assuming this is one of David's psalms. He spent much of his early adult life dodging the assassin's sword. He literally hid out in different caves each night, moving repeatedly to stay a step ahead of King Saul and his henchmen.

Each night, when he would lie down to sleep, he must have wondered if this would be the fated night. Yet, in the midst of his constant terror, David looked to the Lord for his strength and safety. He knew without the Lord's intervention he was no match for Saul's army.

Yet when David prays these beautiful psalms, we see his quiet confidence in the One he believed would sustain him. At every 12-step recovery meeting it is said, "There is One who has all power, that One is God, may you find him now."

So even if, or especially if, you are up against insurmountable odds today, take heart, Christian! You have an advocate who promises to intercede on your behalf. He is far more powerful than all the forces of evil that would try to destroy you. The Bible claims, "Greater is he who is in me than he who is in the world." The Lord is the stronghold of your life—of whom shall you be afraid? Think today on what challenges you face and allow the truth of this verse to comfort you. Shalom!

TODAY'S READINGS
Psalm 27: 1-6 | 1 Samuel 1:1-20 | Galatians 1:11-24

Friday | JANUARY 24

> One thing I ask from the Lord, this only do I seek: that I may dwell in the house of the Lord all the days of my life, to gaze on the beauty of the Lord and to seek him in his temple. | Psalm 27:4

Beautiful Lord

I am so thankful we are no longer required to go to the temple to interact with God. Christ's work on the cross has cleared the way for us to have unfettered access to God, wherever we may be. It is still crucial for us to go to him. Now we have a connection with him every time we open his word and read about his desire for our lives.

I do think there is a temple-like experience each time we get together as a church and offer up our sacrifice of praises to God. When our worship band leads us, I like to close my eyes and imagine I'm in God's throne room worshipping at his feet.

I'm also convinced something special happens during our preaching event. God uses flawed servants like me to proclaim the very truths of his will for our lives. So, let's remember when we get together on Sunday morning to worship God; this is his perfect plan for our worshipping life.

We aren't in Jerusalem at the temple, and many of us are not in a large cathedral, but we are in the very presence of God. And that is our perfect opportunity to gaze on the beauty of the Lord.

Think about your favorite worship experience until you feel the positive emotions again, and let that put you in God's presence again as you encounter him. Shalom!

TODAY'S READINGS
Psalm 27:1-6 | 1 Samuel 9:27-10:8 | Galatians 2:1-10

Saturday | JANUARY 25

Jesus answered them, "It is not the healthy who need a doctor, but the sick. I have not come to call the righteous, but sinners to repentance." | Luke 5:31

Doctor Please

Jesus was always on the lookout for the flawed but hopeful. He could have endeared himself to the religious elite and would have had a position of great power in the Jewish community. Instead they all ended up hating him and were responsible for his death. The tragic irony is the flawed but hopeful became the leaders of the early church, while most of the religious elite dedicated themselves to destroying the church. Ironically, in the end it was the religious elite who were exposed as sick and in need of a doctor while the flawed but hopeful became the ones of great influence in the fledgling church.

That's why I've always used the flawed but hopeful as my target audience. What I've learned is that it's not the best way to quickly build a big church. It is easier to grow a church by focusing on the religious people in the community and tending to their needs. But Jesus didn't do that—nor will I.

His target audience was those who were sick and in need. He was always ready to provide them with hope. So, we will keep reaching out to the hurting. Will you think about who in your life may need the hope and life of Jesus today, and seek them out? Shalom!

TODAY'S READINGS
Psalm 27:1-6 | 1 Samuel 15:34-16:13 | Luke 5:27-32

Sunday | JANUARY 26

> Leaving Nazareth, he went and lived in Capernaum, which was by the lake in the area of Zebulun and Naphtali—to fulfill what was said through the prophet Isaiah: | Matthew 4:13-14

Biggest Loser

When the twelve tribes of Israel were given the Promised Land, God ordered them to eradicate the people living there. The Israelite tribes of Zebulon and Naphtali disobeyed God. They settled with the indigenous people and intermarried and adopted their evil ways. So, they were the first of the northern tribes to be defeated. God punished them by allowing them to be conquered by the Assyrians. Isaiah predicted it would happen and when the time was right, they were either killed or taken captive.

The geographical area was on the western side of the Sea of Galilee. Nazareth, where Jesus was raised, and Capernaum, where he settled during his ministry, were located in these two territories. But centuries earlier, these territories were seen as cursed by the Jews in the south. That's probably why Nathaniel, when told Jesus was from there, asked, "Nazareth, can anything good come from there?"

Isn't it just like God to use the very territory seen as cursed to usher in the Kingdom of God? It's a wonderful example of how God's sovereign plan is always unfolding for us, his children, for our good and his ultimate glory. Think, how has God's sovereign plan in your life unfolded for your good and his glory today? Shalom!

TODAY'S READINGS
Psalm 27:1, 4-9 | Isaiah 9:1-4 | Matthew 4:12-23

Monday | JANUARY 27

Therefore, do not be partners with them. | Ephesians 5:7

Wake Up!

This is a straightforward command. Don't partner with the disobedient. Someone has said, "Show me your friends and I'll tell you your future." When I think back on many of the actions in my life that I regret, I can't help but notice most of the time when I'm outside of the will of God, I'm involved with someone who doesn't share my passion for the Lord.

We shouldn't be surprised when people outside the Lord's influence choose evil. It's naïve to assume people who have no relationship with God will choose to honor him with their lives. Whenever they're doing deeds of darkness, they're just doing what they're supposed to be doing.

Our task isn't to get non-Christians to modify their behavior. Our job is to present Jesus Christ and him crucified with everything we do and say. Jesus said we are the light of the world. Light and darkness cannot co-exist together. When light is presented to darkness, dark becomes light. Light always illuminates darkness.

We should not share in those deeds of darkness. So, who is it in your life that is pulling you away from the Lord? Commit yourself today to make the necessary changes to no longer partner with them. Shalom!

TODAY'S READINGS
Psalm 27:7-14 | Judges 6:11-24 | Ephesians 5:6-14

Tuesday | JANUARY 28

...for it is God who works in you to will and to act in order to fulfill his good purpose... | Philippians 2:13

Sit Still

I was just thinking about my alone time with God each day, sitting quietly in his presence. The blessings we receive are amazing when we empty our minds and rest in this time with him. To sit and allow God to work his will in us reveals his perfect plan for our lives.

It is not easy at first. We are full of thoughts and banter. Our minds are easily distracted. We are used to a busy world around us and it's difficult to just sit in silent reflection.

However, each day by adding a little more time and starting to train our minds to empty and listen, we begin to sense his presence. It is difficult for him to talk to us when our minds are full of music and reading and thinking. I am not saying this will be easy, but I promise you it will be worth it.

As your thoughts center more and more on him, your trust in who he is will take the place of your worries and fears. The more time we spend with him increases our trust in him, and our natural tendencies—our default mode—will change to automatically call on his name in all that we do. As we saturate our minds with Scripture, he will show us how to spend our time and where to place our energies. We will feel his love saturate our lives and flow over onto all we do and say. Practice being still today, and see what he will say to you. Shalom!

TODAY'S READINGS
Psalm 27:7-14 | Judges 7:12-22 | Philippians 2:12-18

Wednesday | JANUARY 29

> I remain confident of this: I will see the goodness of the Lord in the land of the living. Wait for the Lord; be strong and take heart and wait for the Lord. | Psalm 27:13-14

Waiting Room

It is right and good for us to remember the Lord desires good for us. Yes, he will allow us to go through difficult times, and he will use those times to strengthen us. But if we wait for him, he will always come through for us.

Our job is to control our fears and to embrace this truth: we serve a God who has ultimate control over everything that happens to us. I remember when God allowed Judah to be carried off by the Babylonians into captivity, his words for the people were to wait for him. He said, "I know the plans I have for you, plans to prosper you and not to harm you, plans to give you hope and a future."

This is why, as followers of God, we can face today regardless of how difficult it may be. Because we have a kind and loving and all-powerful God who is telling us, "Wait for me." And we have confidence that when the time is right, he will intercede on our behalf and we will see the goodness of the Lord! What are you waiting for the Lord to reveal to you today? Shalom!

TODAY'S READINGS
Psalm 27:7-14 | Genesis 49:1-26 | Luke 1:67-79

Thursday | JANUARY 30

They must turn from evil and do good; they must seek peace and pursue it. | 1 Peter 3:11

Pursuing Peace

Pursuing peace is more than just minding our own business. Jesus said, "Blessed are the peace MAKERS." It is easy to misinterpret this to mean that if we avoid trouble, we are peacemakers. Peter learned well at Jesus' feet and exhorts the church to pursue peace. That means at times an intentional effort to bring peace to a volatile situation.

So, when people aren't getting along, we do more than stay out of it and mind our own business. That is avoiding the conflict, but it is not pursuing peace. I believe the reason pursuing the peace was so important to Jesus and his apostles was because wherever there is peace there is evidence of the Kingdom of God. And when people truly experience the Kingdom of God, then God's reputation is enhanced.

When our friends are fighting about religion or politics, it's our responsibility to pursue peace in that situation. And the only way I know how to do that is to check our egos at the door and, in complete humility, pursue the path of peace. When everyone around us is in conflict and we're calmly and humbly pursuing peace, we shine like a beacon in the dark.

The next time you find yourself in a volatile situation, pray to God to make you a humble servant in pursuit of his perfect peace for that conflict. And then allow the Holy Spirit to speak words of love and grace through you. Think about how you can actively pursue peace today. Shalom!

TODAY'S READINGS
Psalm 15 | Deuteronomy 16:18-20 | 1 Peter 3:8-12

Friday | JANUARY 31

Remember, the sins of some people are obvious, leading them to certain judgment. But there are others whose sins will not be revealed until later. | 1 Timothy 5:24

Our Three Lives

Someone wisely said that we all have three lives: our public life, our private life and our secret life. For most of my life, my experience in church has been getting together with a bunch of other upwardly mobile folks doing their best to appear fine on the outside in a desperate attempt to keep everyone else from knowing what was really going on. It is indeed a sad commentary how, although Jesus established his church to find hurting people and help them take their next step with him, it has morphed into a social gathering of great pretenders.

I'm convinced someday we'll all stand before Christ and give an account, and none of us will be concerned at all about the struggles of our neighbors. I have a sneaky suspicion we'll all feel equally inadequate. So, I say, why don't we get a head start on the process and accept one another just where we are, with all our flaws—public or private or even secret. Each time we choose that step, we're doing our part in answering Jesus' prayer he taught us to pray when he asked the Father, "Your Kingdom come, your will be done, on earth as it is in heaven." Who are you standing in judgment over today? Who is Holy Spirit prompting you to be vulnerable with today? Shalom!

TODAY'S READINGS
Psalm 15 | Deuteronomy 24:17-25: 4:1 | 1 Timothy 5:17-24

Saturday | FEBRUARY 1

"A new command I give you: Love one another. As I have loved you, so, you must love one another..." | John 13:34

Jesus-Like Love

These are parting words from Jesus. He is preparing to be arrested and crucified. He could have told them any number of things like, "Keep track of the treasury." Or he could have told them to recruit others to join with them. But his final words for them were to love one another. They'd been taught to love one another since they were old enough to talk. But Jesus claims this is a new command.

What was new about it? They were to love one another like he loved them—which meant they were to be kind and patient and long-suffering and forgiving of each other. Not only that, they were to display this kind of unusual love even for the unlovable.

It was new because Jesus had demonstrated a love that went beyond simply loving those who were good to them. His kind of love extended even to those who would do them harm. He had taught them to love one another in such a way the world would take notice.

Yes, this was a new command. And, I was thinking it's probably the most important command for ensuring a healthy church. Let it be said of us that we love each other passionately, that we forgive each other's faults faithfully, and that we always overlook one another's weaknesses, for God's glory and our ultimate good. How will you love like Jesus today? Shalom!

TODAY'S READINGS
Psalm 15 | Micah 3:1-4 | John 13:31-35

Sunday | FEBRUARY 2

Brothers and sisters, think of what you were when you were called. Not many of you were wise by human standards; not many were influential; not many were of noble birth. | 1 Corinthians 1:26

Flawed But Hopeful

Paul could have been writing this letter with us in mind. I can't think of one person I know who is influential or of noble birth. We truly are the flawed but hopeful. So, we join our ranks with the first century Church, which according to casual observers, was made up of losers and lunatics. The Christian worldview, when practiced correctly, always acts as a magnet for hurting people who are carrying a lot of excess baggage. It has always been my passion to shepherd a flock of people who are not influential by human standards.

Our flawed but hopeful people are our treasures, which we will present to Christ on the day of his coming, without fault and with great joy. How do you see yourself in the light of God's love for you? Think today about the reasons for the hope you have no matter how flawed you are. Christ in you, the hope of glory. Shalom!

TQDAY'S READINGS

Psalm 15 | Micah 6:1-8 | Matthew 5:1-12

Monday | FEBRUARY 3

"Who are you?" he asked. "I am your servant Ruth," she said. "Spread the corner of your garment over me, since you are a guardian-redeemer of our family." | Ruth 3:9

Guardian Redeemer

The guardian redeemer back in the day was a near relative of a man who had died and left his widow in dire straits. It was a biblical command for the man to buy back the farm she had lost after his death. And then to marry his deceased relative's widow and father a son with her, to be raised with the express purpose of carrying on the family name.

It was an incredibly generous offer, given the fact the redeemer was sacrificing greatly for something he wouldn't gain from. Although the custom was wonderful and the story of Ruth is amazing, the grand purpose is to point us to the ultimate guardian redeemer, Jesus Christ.

Each of us discovered we too were left hopeless and in need of someone to rescue us. And to our great joy, we discover, at just the right time, Jesus showed up and paid the total price for our redemption. Because of that glorious truth, we stand before God today as the bride of Christ. Today, meditate on the gift we have been given as the bride of Christ and let thankfulness usher you into his presence. Shalom!

TODAY'S READINGS
Psalm 37:1-17 | Ruth 3:1-13; 4:13-22 | Luke 6:17-26

Tuesday | FEBRUARY 4

"May the Lord repay you for what you have done. May you be richly rewarded by the Lord, the God of Israel, under whose wings you have come to take refuge." | Ruth 2:12

Take Cover

The phrase "under whose wings you have come to take refuge" is a pivotal phrase in the book of Ruth. The story is all about Ruth being covered for her well-being and protection. The word picture painted here is that of a hen spreading her wings to cover and shield her little chicks in a storm. Like the mother hen protects her young, Boaz prays that God will cover Ruth.

I read that during a barn fire, hens have been known to drape their wings over their young and give up their lives to save their chicks. In chapter three, Ruth will boldly approach Boaz and ask him to cover her with his garment. The spreading of his garment over her symbolized Boaz's desire to protect Ruth.

It is beautiful imagery. Boaz prays God will protect her and then he answers his own prayer. He chooses to become Ruth's kinsman redeemer. And she will be richly rewarded, as she finds care and protection under his strong arms.

I love this story because it reminds me of how we have found refuge in our Kinsman Redeemer, Jesus Christ. He stretched out his arms and covered us with his blood and sealed his protection on us for all eternity. Yay, God! How do you feel when you allow yourself to take refuge in Jesus' arms? Shalom!

TODAY'S READINGS
Psalm 37:1-17 | Ruth 2:1-16 | James 5:1-6

Wednesday | FEBRUARY 5

But the meek will inherit the land and enjoy peace and prosperity. | Psalm 37:11

Spiritual Heroes

Our culture simply refuses to value meekness. Our heroes in film and literature are not meek but vengeful. My favorite movies are those featuring a hero who spends the entire movie trying to get even with the bad guy. Then the climax of the film is when the hero destroys him. Those are the kind of movies and books that sell.

We've been programmed to cheer for the one who fights back. But the Bible says it's not the violent who will inherit the land; it is the meek who will be rewarded. I still need to develop in this area. I want to learn to value the meek and to see the meek as being blessed by God.

Jesus is our prime example. He refused to fight back. Even when he was wrongly accused, he suffered in silence. His strength was quiet yet powerful. The apostles were meek as well. You never see them fighting back. And the early Church followed their lead, suffering martyrdom without lifting a hand or saying a vengeful word.

They suffered and went to their graves without inheriting the land. So, the inheritance must come in the next life, and the peace and prosperity will be fully experienced upon Christ's return.

May God grant us the courage and strength to have the same attitude as Jesus and the apostles and may he empower us to suffer in silence. May it be said of us that we earned the right to inherit the land. Who in our culture embodies this meekness? Let us think today on them and honor them and seek to be more like Jesus in this. Shalom!

TODAY'S READINGS
Psalm 37:1-17 | Ruth 1:1-18 | Philemon 1:1-25

Thursday | FEBRUARY 6

Only be careful and watch yourselves closely so that you do not forget the things your eyes have seen or let them fade from your heart as long as you live. Teach them to your children and to their children after them. | Deuteronomy 4:9

Kid Stubb

I love to see our children worshipping with us on Sundays. I see them scurry off to their class and I know our staff has prepared an excellent teaching for them. It's so precious to see them receive communion with their grandparents. Then when the children bring their food to the altar and make their donation as we pray with them, it gets me all choked up.

But my favorite part is when they help me do the benediction. As they hold their little hands in the air and I pronounce God's blessing on the congregation, everything just seems right and good to me.

It's encouraging for me that we have Scripture urging we teach the ways of God to our children. There is absolutely nothing we do all week long as important as helping our children understand the Lord's ways for their lives. We're influencing them in such a profound way, it will have a lasting effect for generations to come. Who are the precious children God is calling you to serve? Shalom!

TODAY'S READINGS
Psalm 112:1-10 | Deuteronomy 4:1-14 | 1 John 5:1-5

Friday | FEBRUARY 7

> Who is wise and understanding among you? Let them show it by their good life, by deeds done in the humility that comes from wisdom. | James 3:13

Wise Guys

I love the way wisdom and humility are tied together here. One of the aspects I love about the 12 steps community is each step is born from humility. I've grown to believe humility is the key to a contented, successful life. It doesn't seem to me humility is valued in our culture the way it is in Scripture. Humble people in our culture are often viewed as weak.

The Bible says our attitude should be the same as that of Christ Jesus. Even though he was God in the flesh, he made himself nothing and became obedient to death, even death on a cross.

Humility is an act of the will. If we want to take our next step toward Jesus, it begins by seeing ourselves as a servant—not just a servant to God, but a servant to others. This is why James talks about the good life as being one where deeds are done in humility. It means we become the humble servant when we help in a food pantry or soup kitchen.

It's possible to feed thousands of people and do it all without humility; it's a heart posture we choose that makes the difference to God. Who is wise among us? It is the one who serves others in humility. Is your heart in the right place? Think about humility as a choice in your life today. Shalom!

TODAY'S READINGS

Psalm 112:1-10 | Isaiah 29:1-12 | James 3:13-18

Saturday | FEBRUARY 8

> You have let go of the commands of God and are holding on to human traditions." | Mark 7:8

Vain Worship

This obsession with the washing of hands was a developed tradition. I think it's interesting, when it came time for Jesus to perform his first miracle, it was all about this ritualistic washing. It was the water in these large clay pots used for washing that Jesus turned to wine. It was a tradition the religious leaders were passionate about and Jesus used it to make something great. It wasn't just wine—it was the *best* wine.

In this first miracle, Jesus confronted the religious tradition, and in doing so, he made some of the people very unhappy—those who were bound by the religious spirit. But others he made very happy—those who were desiring the true person and power of God, not just religion.

Before we're too hard on the religious leaders in Jesus' day, we need to ask ourselves, "Are there any traditions we're holding onto that are displacing the commands of God?" Traditions can be good. We use them to teach our children and grandchildren. But how do we know if we are clinging to man-made traditions that are a poor substitute for the real thing?

One of the tests is to simply ask ourselves, "Does Scripture deal with this topic?" I find it's usually beneficial to remain silent about traditions not addressed in the Bible. The rule is that if Scripture is silent on a subject, then so are we. Think, have any rituals or traditions taken over your desire to simply be with Jesus? Shalom!

TODAY'S READINGS
Psalm 112:1-10 | Isaiah 29:13-16 | Mark 7:1-8

Sunday | FEBRUARY 9

They will have no fear of bad news; their hearts are steadfast, trusting in the Lord. | Psalm 112:7

A Wise Old Saying

This is classified as wisdom literature. That means we read it differently than other genres. In wisdom literature, we commonly see bold statements like this are generally true.

Generally speaking, the righteous do not fear bad news. But it's not universally true. For example, Job was the most righteous of men and he received news he was bankrupt and all his children had died.

So, we can say the righteous do receive bad news. That doesn't mean this statement is false. It's simply critical for us to receive it as wisdom literature. We have the same principle in our American wisdom literature. For example, we say, "Look before you leap." Generally speaking, this is a true proverb. A person who is thoughtful and cautious will often avoid unnecessary trouble. We also have an American proverb that says, "He who hesitates is lost." That can also be true. If we get bogged down in indecision, we can miss a once-in-a-lifetime opportunity.

Which one of these proverbs applies? It always depends on the context. So, we can learn to identify the type of biblical literature we're reading. It may be a narrative that's simply retelling a story or perhaps it's poetry that has its own rules and tendencies. Prophetic literature and the Gospels have their own rules.

The letters toward the end of the New Testament are meant to be read and interpreted as documents written by an individual with a specific audience in mind. And finally, the apocalyptic or "end time" literature needs to be read with its own discipline. There's no need to get bogged down in this. We don't have to be scholars to appreciate these different modes of communication. We live in our own ways of expression every day without giving it much thought. Read today's verses and see the different ways the authors of the Bible reveal God's message of hope. Shalom!

TODAY'S READINGS

Psalm 112:1-10 | Isaiah 58:1-12 | Matthew 5:13-20 | 1 Corinthians 2:1-16

Monday | FEBRUARY 10

Your word is a lamp for my feet, a light on my path. | Psalm 119:105

The Clear Path

I was thinking how important God's word is to our survival. We read in our Old Testament lesson for today that there was a time in Israel's (Judah's) history where they existed for generations without God's word to guide them. The result was they worshipped false gods. It seems we will always worship someone or something.

For us, it's of the utmost importance that we hold Scripture in high regard. We are to use it to guide us along the path of life. I think it's so exciting absolutely everything we will ever need to know about how to manage our lives has been written down for us in this amazing book!

This isn't some outdated document that no longer applies to our lives. It's a living, breathing, active force that will always shed light on our situation. We just simply have to show up each day and see what God has to say to us.

So, let's continue to read his word for our lives with the full assurance that God will use it to reveal our next step toward our Lord and Savior, Jesus Christ. As you read today's verses, see how God will highlight something to spark revelation for you. He loves to hide gems for us to find. Shalom!

TODAY'S READINGS
Psalm 119:10: 5-112 | 2 Kings 22:3-2 | Romans 11:2-10

Tuesday | FEBRUARY 11

> Neither before nor after Josiah was there a king like him who turned to the Lord as he did—with all his heart and with all his soul and with all his strength, in accordance with all the Law of Moses. | 2 Kings 23:25

Give It All You Got

Josiah is a great example for us. I love the fact that once he was given God's word, he dedicated himself and the country to obeying its precepts. Josiah existed in a very worldly culture that was heavily influenced by other worldviews. I find it so interesting he didn't listen to the Law of Moses to see if it matched the thoughts of his contemporaries, or even if he agreed with it. He basically said, "We are going to listen to the Law of Moses and obey it to the letter of the law." And then Josiah ruled his country in accordance to the Law.

I love the fact that he said the words on the scroll were God's instruction for his people and then set policies to simply obey what the Law said. It was simple, but it surely was not easy. He must have faced a great deal of opposition from those who wanted to continue worshipping the false gods and pursue the cultural norms.

The lesson for us is to rededicate our lives each day to knowing and obeying God's holy word, and then to remove any obstacles that might keep us from being the people God called us to be.

What are some cultural beliefs you may be clinging to that do not come from Scripture? How can you let go of these today and replace them with God's word? Shalom!

TODAY'S READINGS
Psalm 119:105-112 | 2 Kings 23:1-8, 21-25 | 2 Corinthians 4:1-12

Wednesday | FEBRUARY 12

I told you that you would die in your sins; if you do not believe that I am He, you will indeed die in your sins." | John 8:24

Our Only Hope

For Christians, everything pivots on the life of the carpenter from Nazareth. It's not about religion, but it is always about a relationship. These men who Jesus was warning were some of the most religious people you can imagine. They had the religious part down pat, but they were sorely lacking in the relationship department.

So, the warning for us today is to focus on our relationship with Jesus Christ. We need to give ourselves wholly and completely to the lover of our soul. We must dedicate ourselves to knowing and loving and following Jesus Christ.

We accomplish that through prayer and study and worship and service. We should look at every day as an opportunity to know and love and serve Jesus more than we did the day before. Jesus said to the religious leaders of his day, "You don't know me!"

Another time, Jesus warned there would be those who come before him on the Day of Judgment who will be surprised to hear him say, "Get away from me! I never knew you!" Let it be said of us, in our flawed but hopeful way, that we were folks who were passionate about knowing and loving and serving our Lord and Savior, Jesus Christ. The crazy part is, Jesus wants to know us even more than we desire him! Let that sink in today as you come to him with intention and dedication. Shalom!

TODAY'S READINGS
Psalm 119:105-112: 105 | Proverbs 6:6-23 | John 8:12-30

Thursday | FEBRUARY 13

Blessed is the one who perseveres under trial because, having stood the test, that person will receive the crown of life that the Lord has promised to those who love him. | James 1:12

Never, Never Give Up

Standing up to the test during trials is an opportunity to demonstrate our faith in God. While most people will panic in the midst of a trial, we can calmly persevere because we know the One who holds the future securely in his strong hands.

So, how do we persevere when things are bad? How do we endure under financial or relational or emotional attack? One of the important keys for us amid an attack is simply to be faithful to our disciplines of prayer and meditation and study and worship and service to others.

First things first, get in his presence. Whenever we find ourselves in a crisis, the easiest thing to do is to allow the crisis to steal away our time with God. We fret and worry and take matters into our own hands. Even when we're struggling—especially when we're struggling—it's essential we maintain our discipline and be open to God's leading. And all that means is to simply do the next responsible thing.

If it's time to do our devotions, we give our attention to God's word. When we don't feel like worshipping on Sunday morning, we get up and go anyway. Then, probably the most critical thing is that we get out of our own head long enough to help someone else take their "next step" with Jesus. The best way to persevere under trials is to remain disciplined with the One who calms the storm. What are you going through right now that you can overcome with the promises of the Lord? Shalom!

TODAY'S READINGS
Psalm 119:1-8 | Genesis 26:1-5 | James 1:12-16

Friday | FEBRUARY 14

Blessed are those whose ways are blameless, who walk according to the law of the Lord...
I will obey your decrees; do not utterly forsake me. | Psalm 119:1-8

The Blessed Life

I studied this psalm in depth last year. It's the longest psalm and smack dab in the middle of the Bible. It is written in 22 sections, and each section corresponds with a letter of the Hebrew alphabet. Each section has eight verses in it. I love how each verse gives us another reason to read and study the word and then adds ways to respond to it.

Many of the verses we grew up memorizing are in Psalm 119. This particular one triggers some red flags, like "How can I keep the law?" I want to be on the right side of those judgments.

One of the things we learn from trying to obey the Law of Moses is that no one has ever been able to faithfully keep them. Paul and David say it's a standard we can't meet. Remember the verse, "There is none righteous, not even one..."

So, how am I to be one of those "blessed" people who keep God's laws? Thanks be to God: Jesus kept the Law and took my punishment for breaking it. Because of Jesus' perfect obedience, including his willing sacrifice on the cross, we can each give thanks to him for his saving grace that covers all our sin and keeps us in an ongoing state of his glorious blessing. Where today can you ask for grace to walk according to God's law and enjoy his blessing? Shalom!

TODAY'S READINGS
Leviticus 26:34-46 | 1 John 2:7-17 | Psalm 119:1-8:1

Saturday | FEBRUARY 15

And he answered them and said to them, "Why do you yourselves transgress the commandments of God for the sake of your traditions?" | Matthew 15:3

Traditions

I'm so relieved the church today never goes overboard in our traditions! But seriously, this teaching has caused me to question absolutely everything. I've had enough experience, both good and bad regarding the traditions of men, to approach everything with a wary eye.

What I've learned is if I'm willing to search the Lord's heart on any topic through the study of Scripture and prayerfully pursue his will, he is faithful to show me the way. Therefore, whenever someone is upset with my teaching or my leading and wants to discuss it with me, I always encourage them to come and talk but to bring their Bible.

I always want to be in pursuit of the truth—God's truth. I'm not so arrogant to believe I'm always right, but I never want to exchange my man-made tradition for someone else's false teaching. So, let's be willing today to question everything we believe and all we've been taught and, for our efforts, receive the peace of God that surpasses all understanding. What beliefs in traditions do you hold tightly to that could use reexamining in light of God's truth? Shalom!

TODAY'S READINGS
Psalm 119:1-8 | Deuteronomy 30:1-9a | Matthew 15:1-9

Sunday | FEBRUARY 16

...leave your gift there in front of the altar. First go and be reconciled to them; then come and offer your gift. | Matthew 5:24

A Heart Ready for Worship

A little context may be helpful here. Jesus is speaking to people while in the northern territory of Galilee. The altar was in the temple a few days away in Jerusalem. So, the word picture he's painting for us is that of a traveler who has made the trek to Jerusalem to offer a sacrifice.

It would have been incredibly inconvenient for someone to find a place to tie up their sheep and leave it unattended at the altar. Then trudge all the way back to Galilee to make amends. And then, having made things right with the offended brother, to return once again to Jerusalem to offer up the sheep on the altar.

The whole process would have taken several days, maybe as much as a week. What Jesus is commanding here is a big deal. It shows how vitally important he felt it was to live at peace with everyone, regardless of the circumstance.

I think this should give us pause. How many of us are at odds with someone? Let's not let another week go by without reconciling—or another day. When we are wrong, we need to promptly admit it. As far as it depends on us, we need to live at peace with everyone. And then, after making things right, we're prepared to offer our sacrifice of praise in the house of the Lord.

Think, who do you need to reconcile with? What step can you take today? Let no debt be left outstanding, except to love. Shalom!

TODAY'S READINGS

Psalm 119:1-8 | Deuteronomy 30:15-20 | Matthew 5:21-37 | 1 Corinthians 3:1-9

Monday | FEBRUARY 17

I have hidden your word in my heart that I might not sin against you. | Psalm 119:11

God In Us

This is a comforting verse for me. Every morning I get up early and read the Scripture that has been prepared for us. When I do, I know God is working in me for his glory and my good. I'm so thankful these scriptures are prepared for me, and all I have to do is show up and read them and allow God to have his way with me for a little while.

I believe if we hide his word in our hearts, he'll change us. And as he does his part, we will become more like Jesus. Every day, a little bit at a time, the miracle is taking place. The process is so slow and methodical, we barely notice he is transforming us.

We are different than we were last year, and we will continue to grow in knowledge and wisdom. All we must do is keep showing up. God will do all the heavy lifting. May it be said of us that we were passionate and persistent to hide God's word in our hearts so we might not sin against him. To God be the glory for his blessing on our lives today! Let us show up today and present ourselves to God as we enjoy his transforming work in us. Shalom!

TODAY'S READINGS
Psalm 119:9-16 | Exodus 20:1-21 | James 1:2-8

Tuesday | FEBRUARY 18

My brothers and sisters, believers in our glorious Lord Jesus Christ must not show favoritism | James 2:1

Picking Favorites

This is why, as a pastor, I go out of my way to not know how much money people give to our church. I never want to be accused of showing favoritism. It's common in small churches like ours for the largest givers to have greater influence on the leadership. It's a tricky subject, because leaders in the church should be faithful givers. We shouldn't encourage the faithful to give while leadership holds back.

People often vote with their checkbooks, so if they're unhappy with the direction of the church, they'll withhold their tithe. But I think we do a commendable job of not showing favoritism to those who are more financially secure.

Poor people can be very faithful in their giving while not donating a large sum of money. Wealthy people can give more than others while still not being faithful. So, over the years I've learned it's best if I simply don't know how much individuals give. I have had people tell me God has led them to be faithful to the tithe, but I've never checked how much they're giving. I hope this policy has kept me from showing favoritism. Today, examine your methods and motives to see if there's any way you may be showing favoritism, and let God guide you in his way. Shalom!

TODAY'S READINGS

Psalm 119:9-16 | Deuteronomy 23:21-24, 4:10-15 | James 2:1-13

Wednesday | FEBRUARY 19

"So, they are no longer two but one flesh. What therefore God has joined together, let no man separate | Matthew 19:6

One Flesh

This verse has served me well, helping me stay focused on my marriage counseling. I've witnessed and been part of many divorces over my career. They're always painful. My temptation is to get caught up in the dispute and then I inevitably choose a side. But I find my peace in the phrase by Jesus, "Let no man separate."

To that end, my job is to simply do everything within my God-granted ability to preserve marriage. I have my opinion on divorce but much of it is just that—my opinion. If I stay focused in encouraging couples to fight for their marriage, I feel I'm on a firm scriptural foundation.

I try not to stand in judgment over those who choose divorce, and I'm faithful to provide a safe place for them to worship and take their next step from there with Christ. However, I'm in the marriage-saving business. I find my peace there and I pray you might do the same today. Think about the marriages in your sphere of influence and how you can encourage unity today. Shalom!

TODAY'S READINGS
Psalm 119:9-16 | Proverbs 2:1-15 | Matthew 19:1-12

Thursday | FEBRUARY 20

Moses reported this to the Israelites, but they did not listen to him because of their discouragement and harsh labor. | Exodus 6:9

When The Going Gets Tough

I wonder how often we've been unable to hear God's good news for our life because we were in crisis? Think about it. Moses was promised, directly from the Lord, they were going to be freed from slavery, escorted by God to the land filled with milk and honey, and given that land as a free gift for all of them. It was an incredible, life-changing, earth-shattering announcement, but they couldn't see past their current crisis to embrace the fact that God was indeed going to be their God.

Who or what are you allowing to drown out the promises of God in your life today? God said, "I know the plans I have for you; plans to prosper you and not to harm you; plans to give you hope and a future."

We can cling to the promises of God in every crisis regardless of the pain. Yes, amid a heart-breaking divorce, or even at the tiny grave of our newborn baby.

Through all of life's highs and lows there is the overarching protection of the promises of God to sustain us. Though we may struggle here for a little while, our Promised Land awaits us as well.

So, despite whatever crisis we find ourselves in today, let's stand up and wipe the tears from our eyes, raise our hands in the air and give glory to the God who continues to sustain us with his eternal blessing. What promises of God can you think on today to sustain you in what you're facing right now? Shalom!

TODAY'S READINGS

Psalm 2 | Exodus 6:2-9 | Hebrews 8:1-7

Friday | FEBRUARY 21

By faith Moses' parents hid him for three months after he was born, because... | Hebrews 11:23-28

Peering Past the Darkness

What is faith? According to the beginning of this Hebrews chapter, faith is the substance of things hoped for, the evidence of things not seen. This verse tells us faith is assurance that we will receive the things we hope for. Faith is the assurance we will receive the promises God gives. Faith is also the evidence, or proof, of what we cannot see or what we have yet to see.

By faith we know God made the universe, even though we can't see God and we weren't present at creation. This Scripture about Moses is a great example of faith. There are many examples of faith in Scripture, just like this story about Moses, that are so important to us because, if we have faith, we know God can work miracles in our lives.

We can know he can and will sustain us, even through the most difficult times of our lives. He will always provide for us absolutely everything we need at the right time. But most important, by faith he will develop his holy, righteous character in us, so we can continue to grow as an intricate part of his holy family. Faith is our part in receiving the blessing of God on our lives today. And by the faith *of* the son of God, it will be accomplished. Think on that. Shalom!

TODAY'S READINGS
Psalm 2 | Exodus 19:9-25 | Hebrews 11:23-28

Saturday | FEBRUARY 22

> They kept the matter to themselves, discussing what
> "rising from the dead" meant. | Mark 9:10

Children of the Resurrection

All our lives pivot on this singular truth: God raised Jesus from the dead. He was alive and then they killed him and next he was alive again.

If that were to be said of any other famous historical figure, we would say, "Nonsense." But, since it's the story of Jesus Christ, we embrace it with all our heart, mind, soul, and strength. And we exist to proclaim to all who will listen that God raised Jesus from the dead.

The Bible says if Jesus had not been raised from the dead, then we should be the most pitied of all people. Why? Because if Jesus is still sealed up in a tomb outside of Jerusalem, then we're all living a lie.

If he's not alive, he can't sustain us in our current trials. If he's not alive, he can't return in all of his glory to rapture his church. If he's not alive, he won't sovereignly rule over us for all of eternity. But he can, and does, and will do all these things, to the glory of God the Father.

So, no matter what we're facing today, we can do it with the full confidence of a risen Savior who has our back. And for that blessing we shout out together, "Yay, God!!!" Take time to celebrate your life as a child of the resurrection by meditating on Jesus in your life today. Shalom!

TODAY'S READINGS
Psalm 2 | 1 Kings 21:20-29 | Mark 9:9-13

Sunday | FEBRUARY 23

For prophecy never had its origin in the human will, but prophets, though human, spoke from God as they were carried along by the Holy Spirit. | 2 Peter 1:21

Our Divine Anchor

This verse really gets my juices flowing. Absolutely every word conveyed by the prophets of God was done under his sovereign care, direction, and protection. We receive, through them, the very words of God.

I don't think that means their eyes rolled back in their heads or they were overtaken by a supernatural force. I also don't think that as they were carried along their own personalities were suppressed. God used these men to convey present, past, and future truths regarding the Kingdom of God, through their own God-given personalities.

What's important for us to embrace is that every word they put their pen to was God-breathed and was birthed in the mind of God. I further believe God protected these writings for the people of God's posterity.

So, he has not left us flailing in the breeze. We are anchored secure to his holy word for our good and his glory. Let's remember that and be thankful today. What infallible truth from God's word will be your anchor for today? Shalom!

TODAY'S READINGS

Psalm 2 | Exodus 24:12-18 | Matthew 17:1-9 | 2 Peter 1:16-21

Monday | FEBRUARY 24

> Then the Lord said to him, 'Take off your sandals, for the place where you are standing is holy ground. | Acts 7:33

Our Holy Ground

God talks to Moses through the burning bush and commands Moses to take off his sandals because he is on holy ground. It seems like a weird request. Why would God ask Moses to do that?

I think God was reminding Moses to enter his presence with a humble heart. When you take off your shoes, you are touching the earth. The earth is part of creation. Therefore, taking off your sandals is a way of humbly identifying yourself as part of creation, not the creator. Or another way to say it is "being grounded" in humility and reverence for God.

We must remember God is God and we are not. We need to have the right perspective by never allowing anything in our lives to get in the way of our relationship with the Lord. The presence of God is our holy ground—not work, ambition, security, money, family, friends, or anything else.

God may not ask us to take off our shoes, but he does ask us to always approach him with a humble heart and holy awe. Remember to receive God's blessing today as you humble yourself in his holy presence. Today, be mindful as your approach God's word and humbly "take off your sandals" to enter his presence in prayer. Shalom!

TODAY'S READINGS
Psalm 78:17-20, 52-55 | Exodus 33:7-23 | Acts 7:30-34

Tuesday | FEBRUARY 25

So too, at the present time there is a remnant chosen by grace | Romans 11:5

Preserved by Grace

No matter how far out of control things seem to be shifting, God still holds all of it in the palm of his sovereign hand. The words of the great apostle thunder through the centuries and remain a constant reminder that God is in control. "There is a remnant chosen by grace." And we are a glorious part of that flawed but hopeful remnant.

As we consider the state of our own country and the moral swamp we find ourselves in, we can cling to this truth. In the final analysis, it's not a question of whether or not ours or any nation is more or less evil. Those who do not belong to Christ will always serve their master well.

No, what remains to be answered is whether we, the remnant, will be found faithful to do our part. Will we be that shining city on a hill, a light for all the world to see?

This Sunday, as you are worshipping with friends and family, thank God for the remnant and that through his unmerited favor you have been chosen. Then let us turn our thoughts away from the evil surrounding us, and focus our attention on the task at hand. Just like Elijah, we have plenty of work to do. It isn't easy being part of the remnant chosen by grace…but it sure is good! Today, will you be aware of the part you are called to play in this unfolding story of grace? Shalom!

TODAY'S READINGS
Psalm 78:17-20, 52-55 | 1 Kings 19:9-18 | Romans 11:1-6

Wednesday | FEBRUARY 26

Rather, as servants of God we commend ourselves in every way: in great endurance; in troubles, hardships and distresses... | 2 Corinthians 6:4

Cheap Grace?

Today is Ash Wednesday. Tonight, we will all gather together at the church and impose ashes on one another, to remind ourselves we have been bought and paid for with a price—the terrible price of Christ's death on the cross.

It's customary during this season of Lent to abstain from something we enjoy, like soda pop or ice cream or chocolate. But when I read the words of the apostle Paul, I can't help but think that somehow I'm missing the point. While I'm thinking chocolate and soda pop, Paul speaks of beatings and imprisonment.

This makes me think maybe, just maybe, God is calling me to take my next step as I share in the suffering of his Son, Jesus Christ. I'm not suggesting we all go out and get arrested, but there has to be something more to this than refusing to indulge ourselves for a few weeks.

How much has our faith cost us? And if you're like me and can only answer, "not much," why is that? Is that cost so low to match the commitment? I have some serious soul-searching to do in this area. I don't want to have a faith that costs me nothing. May Ash Wednesday bless you with insight to the true value of our faith. As you receive the ashes today, be mindful of what Christ gave and what he may be calling you to sacrifice. Shalom!

TODAY'S READINGS
Psalm 78:17-20, 52-55 | Joel 2:1-2, 12-17 | Matthew 6:1-6, 16-21
2 Corinthians 5:20-6:10

Thursday | FEBRUARY 27

Create in me a clean heart, O God, and renew a steadfast spirit with in me. | Psalm 51:10

Clean Heart

On first glance, this psalm appears to advocate that, to receive the clean heart most of us desire, we must begin with being aware we need some tending to. My recovery from the terror of alcoholism began with my willingness to admit I had a problem. I was just like David here in the psalm. My life had become unmanageable. The key to recovering from alcoholism, or any sinful activity, is to conclude the heart we currently possess needs to be changed for the glory of God.

The surest way to remain in our addiction or sin is to want to hold on desperately with one hand to the heart we're familiar with, while at the same time asking God to change it. He'll never force a clean heart on us.

So, what is it in your heart today that you desire God to change? Are you willing to let go of that which is familiar to receive that which is fantastic? If you say yes, you'll soon discover God is doing for you what you cannot do for yourself. What would you be willing to let go of today to let God purify? Shalom!

TODAY'S READINGS
Psalm 51 | Jonah 3:1-10 | Romans 1:1-7

Friday | FEBRUARY 28

Create in me a pure heart, O God, and renew a steadfast spirit within me. | Psalm 51:10

All the Right Stuff

Isn't this what we all want? I long for a pure heart. My heart at times seems so contaminated by the surrounding evil, it feels anything but pure. However, when it comes down to where the rubber meets the road, my heart is as pure as the stuff I put in it.

This verse reminded me of the adage, we don't think our way to right acting, but we act our way to right thinking. In other words, simply wishing our hearts were pure will not accomplish the task. We must take action to see to it that we're exposing our hearts to all the right stuff and blocking entry of the wrong stuff.

It means we're faithful to pray and do our daily devotions, that we're consistent in weekly worship, and we're hiding God's word in our hearts. But it also means we become proactive about what we expose our hearts to, from radio to television to books and movies. Much of what is being sold today as entertainment will not help create a pure heart.

Finally, we participate in gaining a pure heart by surrounding ourselves with other Christians who are in hot pursuit of the ways of the Lord. And as we enjoy the blessing of God on our lives today, slowly but surely his Spirit is purifying our hearts. Today, how will you participate with God in the purification of your heart? What will you mindfully let in and what will you intentionally keep out? Shalom!

TODAY'S READINGS
Psalm 51 | Jonah 4:1-11 | Romans 1:8-17

Saturday | FEBRUARY 29

> Therefore, whoever takes the lowly position of this child is the greatest in the kingdom of heaven. | Matthew 18:4

Vulnerable

A child had no rights in first century culture. Today in America our children are protected by the Constitution. We have a myriad of laws on the books designed to increase their protection. But that wasn't true in Jesus' day.

Children were viewed as property back then. From the moment of birth, a baby could even be discarded and left to the elements at a father's discretion, simply because she was a girl. Children were the most vulnerable in that society. But Jesus stuns his disciples by declaring that whoever takes the lowly, vulnerable position of a child will be exalted in the Kingdom of Heaven.

So, what does this look like today? Well, it must mean Jesus isn't looking for "self-made men and women." He is looking for those who will humbly take their place in the Kingdom of God and allow God to have his way with them. It means being malleable and easy to shape for the glory of God. It means to willingly give up control of our lives so that Jesus Christ can call the shots.

He is the potter. We are the clay, ready to be made into whatever he desires. Our response as we live in his blessing today should simply be, "Yes, Father, your will be done in my life." In what ways today can you humbly give up control to our Father? Shalom!

TODAY'S READINGS
Psalm 51 | Isaiah 58:1-12 | Matthew 18:1-7

Sunday | MARCH 1

"...but God did say, 'You must not eat fruit from the tree that is in the middle of the garden, and you must not touch it, or you will die.'" | Genesis 3:3

Stretching The Truth

Eve's recall of God's words to her aren't quite accurate. I don't think God said anything about touching the fruit. She added that to the command to make it seem more unreasonable. I wonder how often we do that in our interaction with God?

God gives us clear and concise directives through his word, and we distort it to make it seem unreasonable. Once we've made up our minds his command is unreasonable, it's a very short step to disobedience. We call it "justified."

God's commands are always reasonable, with our wellbeing in mind. He never picks out a rule to add to our misery. The psalmist said today, "I will instruct you and teach you in the way you should go; I will counsel you with my loving eye on you." Every command is bathed in his unfailing love.

So, when he instructs us not to do something, it is never to withhold good from us. Disobeying, Eve would eat from the fruit and give some to Adam and it would set in motion a series of events that would have devastating effects to mankind for all of history.

Let's dedicate ourselves to knowing God's will for our lives. And then let's pray for the discipline to carry it out. Think about ways in which you might alter God's commands a bit to justify certain behaviors. How can you embrace his loving word today in its fullness? Shalom!

TODAY'S READINGS
Psalm 32 | Genesis 2:15-17; 3:1-7 | Matthew 4:1-11 | Romans 5:12-19

Monday | MARCH 2

> You are my hiding place; You will protect me from trouble and surround me with songs of deliverance. | Psalm 32:7

Our Hiding Place

David could have written this psalm. He spent a good deal of his young adulthood running and hiding from King Saul.

For years David was busy each day finding a hiding place for the night to stay a step ahead of the evil King Saul. And although we may not have anyone in hot pursuit of our lives, it's comforting to know God gives us a hiding place. In fact, he is our hiding place as the psalmist says. He is a safe place where the enemy cannot get to us.

I love the imagery of God standing guard over us and singing warrior songs of deliverance. Or perhaps we're surrounded by angels and they're all singing over us a song of victory. We are hidden in him and untouchable to the enemy. So, take a moment today and just be in your hiding place.

Feel the strength and protection of the Lord and his mighty army surrounding you. And think about the divine blessing that absolutely nothing can harm you as you remain in your hiding place. Imagine yourself taking refuge in God. What is he saying to you? Shalom!

TODAY'S READINGS
Psalm 32 | 1 Kings 19:1-8 | Hebrews 2:10-18

Tuesday | MARCH 3

Blessed is the one whose transgressions are forgiven, whose sins are covered. | Psalm 32:1

Free to Go!

Think about it… our sins are covered with God's grace. Jesus did all the work for us at the cross.

Our part is coming to him with our sin and pain and asking for forgiveness. Imagine having been arrested for a crime you committed. Now, you're standing in a courtroom as the judge waits to read the jury's verdict. The word "guilty" echoes through the cold hall. You brace yourself for the sentencing and are stunned to hear the judge say to you, "Your sentence is time served. You are free to go."

What? But wait, how can this be? You are absolutely found guilty, but your sentence has been erased. Now, think how that would make you feel. Instead of a lifetime of incarceration and separation from everything you love and hold dear, you've been given a new lease on life. Can you imagine how that would feel? I hope so!

Every believer, who has been freed by the love of Christ, ought to know this feeling. David knew how it felt! He knew forgiveness is a blessing and it brings happiness to each of us. God forgives completely, not because of anything we have done, but because of what Jesus did on the cross.

When God forgives our sins and declares us free, we're truly free to go. Now, who in their right mind would choose to remain in prison for a crime they've been found guilty of but have been forgiven for? What do you say we go out today and live under the blessing of Christ, who has declared us free to go and live out our abundant life for the glory of God? Today, what step can you take to embrace forgiveness and walk in the freedom that is yours in Christ? Shalom!

TODAY'S READINGS

Psalm 32 | Genesis 4:1-16 | Hebrews 4:14-16

Wednesday | MARCH 4

"See that you do not despise one of these little ones. For I tell you that their angels in heaven always see the face of my Father in heaven. | Matthew 18:10

Child Care

I love our little ones at church. They're one of the positive things that keeps me going whenever I'm discouraged.

I'm not exactly sure what Jesus means in this verse, but it sounds as though our children have angels in heaven who are in the very presence of God the Father. Just think about that for a moment. If Jesus puts that much priority on caring for the children, it should be a priority for us as well.

I pray every child who comes through our doors will know the unconditional love of Christ. I pray they will grow and be strengthened in their relationship with him. And I pray wherever we are called to serve, it will be a safe and happy place.

I love it when I see our kids running around and having fun in the Lord's house. I'm thankful for all of our volunteers, who work so tirelessly to see to it we're burying the word of God deep in the hearts of our children. I'm convinced there's nothing we could do with our time that will have more of a lasting impact on the Kingdom of God than to love our children well. Today, pray for the children in your life to take their next step with Jesus. Shalom!

TODAY'S READINGS

Psalm 32 | Exodus 34:1-9, 27-28 | Matthew 18:10-14

Thursday | MARCH 5

> For the Spirit God gave us does not make us timid, but gives us power, love and self-discipline. | 2 Timothy 1:7

The Power of the Empty Tomb

Paul talks about this "power" in his opening letter to the Ephesians. He prays the eyes of their heart might be enlightened. Then he draws attention to the fact that they have the same power living in them that raised Christ from the dead.

Now he writes to his beloved Timothy that the power makes us so we are not timid, but instead it emboldens us to live lives of power and love and self-discipline. Timothy was a young man in a position of leadership that was reserved almost exclusively for older men. But Paul knew God had called young Timothy to be a leader and Paul wanted him to lead with power and love and self-discipline.

This is a great verse for those of us who feel like we've been called to a great task. It ultimately isn't our skill or our intellect that enables us to be faithful leaders for the Lord. It is God's power, the same power that raised Christ from the dead. So, we can accept our role as Sunday school director or teen leader or teach a Bible study, not because we're all that and a bag of chips, but because we go forward with power today, through the blessing of God. Because the One who called us is faithful. Think, what is God calling you to that you need to rely on his amazing strength and power to bring it to pass? Shalom!

TODAY'S READINGS
Psalm 121 | Isaiah 51:1-3 | 2 Timothy 1:3-7

Friday | MARCH 6

You will again have compassion on us; you will tread our sins underfoot and hurl all our iniquities into the depths of the sea | Micah 7:19

Leaving It All Behind

These can be some of the most comforting words in all of Scripture. I love this word picture of Christ hurling my sins into the depth of the sea, never again to be held against me.

I have a difficult time letting go of some of my most memorable sins. I give them to God and gratefully allow him to bury them in the depths of the sea—and then I go fishing for them.

I was thinking that my attitude is actually a little arrogant. I'm convinced God removes our repented sins as far as the east is from the west. But for some reason, I think there's something unique about my sins that I need to hold onto them, they're just so big. When I stop and think about it like that, I can't help but wonder, *What is so special about my sin?* I mean, God can take care of everyone's sin but mine?

So, let's take our sins to Jesus and lay them at the foot of the cross—really leave them there—and allow him to have his way with them. Don't waste time and energy with regrets; he doesn't. Let it go and get on with what God has in store for you next. He doesn't want you bogged down in the past. What sins are you having a hard time letting go of? What can you release to God today and not look back? Shalom!

TODAY'S READINGS

Psalm 121 | Micah 7:18-20 | Romans 3:21-31

Saturday | MARCH 7

When Jesus heard this, he was amazed at him, and turning to the crowd following him, he said, "I tell you, I have not found such great faith even in Israel... | Luke 7:9

Chain of Command

It caught me a little off guard when I read Jesus was amazed. I mean, after all, he is the Son of God. Doesn't he know everything?

There are some instances in the Gospels where we see Jesus predicting future events. Yet there are other examples when it appears he did not possess foreknowledge. God in his infinite wisdom revealed truths to Jesus as he would to anyone who's living a life tuned in perfectly to the Father's will. In this case, Jesus discovered great faith in another. I love that he was always looking for men and women of faith.

The centurion demonstrated his faith by testifying that his servant's well-being rested in the hands of a perfectly loving Savior. The centurion knew Jesus had the same power over every single person as he did over his own soldiers. All Jesus had to do was give the word and his servant would be healed.

It does us good to remember we serve a God who's wholly and completely in control of the details of our lives. We can always trust he has the capacity and the compassion to bring about healing for his glory and our good. Although we know from experience he doesn't always intercede the way we hope, it's essential we embrace the blessed fact that he stands sovereign over every situation in our lives. What situation can you lay down before Jesus today in absolute trust that he hears, knows, cares, and wants to intercede for you? Shalom!

TODAY'S READINGS
Psalm 121 | Isaiah 51:4-8 | Luke 7:1-10

Sunday | MARCH 8

> I will make you into a great nation, and I will bless you; I will make your name great, and you will be a blessing. | Genesis 12:2

The Faith of Abraham

Abram was a lonely old man when God made this covenant with him. How many of us at 75 years of age, with no children, would believe that even God could make us into a great nation? Yet the Bible says Abraham believed God and it was credited to him as righteousness. Was Abraham a perfect example for us?

No, but I love the way God took the flawed but hopeful faith of one old man and built upon it. From that mustard seed of faith, God built Abraham's offspring into a great nation. Whenever his faith would begin to fail, God would intercede in a most miraculous way and enable Abraham to take his next step toward Almighty God.

What do these promises have to do with us? Well, the Bible teaches that we who believe in Abraham's God are children through faith. This means we are heirs to the promise given him as well.

Just like Abraham, if we believe God then it is credited to us as righteousness. We can live out this life today with full assurance we are children of the promise, chosen by God to be a blessing to the nations. It's a promise from a God who cannot lie. Think about what it means to be an heir to God's promises, just as Abraham was. If God did it for him, he will do it for you. Shalom!

TODAY'S READINGS
Psalm 121 | Genesis 12:1-4 | John 3:1-17

Monday | MARCH 9

…fix your thoughts on Jesus… | Hebrews 3:1b

A Mother's Grief

Pastor Lynn Breeden, a dear saint of God and contributor to this book, has taught me more about this verse than anyone I've ever known. She learned this lesson at the feet of Jesus during the most difficult time of her life. In her own words:

We celebrated my son's fifth birthday at Riley Children's Hospital on September 30, 1987. We didn't know at the time it would be his last birthday. I woke up very early that morning. I was panicked to think about all that would take place that day. Was he up to the celebrations? He was a very sick little boy. I found myself in the bathroom crying, overwhelmed, scared, and sad. I was on my knees unsure of how to do this day. I cried to Jesus to help me. The verse he gave me that morning has stayed with me every day since. "I can do all things through Jesus, who gives me all the strength I need" (Philippians 4:13). I was able to fix my eyes back on him, the one who had already gotten me through so many things in my young 28 years. In a split second I dried my eyes, washed my face, and opened the door to a lovely birthday celebrating my precious child.

There are many times in Scripture where God interrupted someone's life to shift their perspective from the earthly to the heavenly, from fear to trust, despair to hope, anguish to joy; they experienced the hand of God at work in their midst, like I did that day in that hospital room where God reminded me that in my weakness he is strong. My eyes needed to be fixed back onto him. I needed him to make an intentional shift in my perspective. There on my knees on that cold bathroom floor I made a choice to fix my eyes on Jesus, the author and perfecter of my faith. Then miraculously God provided in ways more marvelous than I could ever ask for or imagine. It did not take away one ounce of my pain, but it did provide me with an eternal perspective that has changed my life forever.

Let Lynn's story inspire you to fix your eyes on Jesus today in whatever situation you may be going through. How will you cry out to him today? Shalom!

TODAY'S READING

Psalm 128 | Numbers 21:4-9 | Hebrews 3:1-6

Tuesday | MARCH 10

> The wolf and the lamb will feed together,
> and the lion will eat straw like the ox… | Isaiah 65:25

Living In Peace

I can hardly wait for the world to be at complete peace and harmony. Just think about it. God will put an end to all conflict.

There will be no murders or rapes or assaults of any kind. The natural order will be that all the world will live at peace. Even the predatory actions of animals will cease. The wolf and the lamb will feed together.

What implication does this future reality have on us today? If in the next life there is no conflict, then when we pray "Your Kingdom come," we are reaching up and grabbing our own little piece of heaven and pulling it down to earth. Every time we find ourselves in conflict, we have the opportunity and the responsibility to bring peace and reconciliation to the situation. We do not have to live at odds with others. It's why we pray, "On earth as it is in heaven."

We can choose to turn the other cheek and go that extra mile. Whenever we do, I'm convinced we're advancing the Kingdom of God. We tend to look at big conflicts like war and terrorism. But what I would like us to think about for the moment is what situation in your life needs to be reconciled? Who are you in conflict with today? Be immersed in the blessing of God as you faithfully give them a call or send them a note. As far as it depends on you, may you live at peace with everyone. Shalom!

TODAY'S READINGS
Psalm 128 | Isaiah 65:17-25 | Romans 4:6-13

Wednesday | MARCH 11

Blessed are all who fear the Lord, who walk in obedience to him. | Psalm 128:1

Trust and Obey

Why is it so important to walk in obedience?

This psalm is all about the blessings we receive when we are following God. God desires us to serve him and to show our love for him by being obedient to his word. I think of the Scripture in John 14 that says, "If you love me, you will obey what I command."

Jesus never had his own agenda. He was always about pleasing the Father in the work he did here on earth. It makes me think about the call on our lives. Are we being obedient to that?

God chose you perfectly to love the people in your life. It isn't by chance you have the relatives, friends, job, and church family that you do. God led you to where you are for a reason.

When we walk in obedience we will be blessed. This psalm is all about showing you the blessings when you walk in the center of his will. Are you walking in obedience out of obligation or joy of pleasing the Lord? What might he be calling you to do today? Shalom!

TODAY'S READINGS
Psalm 128 | Ezekiel 36:22-32 | John 7:53 – 8:11

Thursday | MARCH 12

He is before all things, and in him all things hold together | Colossians 1:17

Stuck Like Glue

I find this verse very comforting. The One who personally watches over us flung the stars into their place. He stood at the edge of the ocean and commanded, "You can go this far and no farther."

He created the tiny creatures that are too small to see and the large ferocious animals that walk in the jungle. He did it all, and you know what? It wasn't hard. It was easy for him to make all our eyes behold.

Now, to talk about the creation of this vast universe is one thing, but Paul says not only did he create it all but, "In him all things are held together." That means that, not only did he start spinning our solar system in all its complexities, but his hands are responsible for its complex maintenance as well. Without his constant breath of life, it would all fall apart!

He can sustain the vast universe as we know it, yet he still has time to tend to whatever problem we lay at his feet. He's an incredible God, capable of far more than we can ever hope for or imagine.

I'm so thrilled to get to know him, even if it is in this limited fashion. So, today let's give all praise and honor and glory to the One who created us and who lovingly cares for us with his sustained blessing. Today will you meditate on and praise our beautiful glorious God for all he has done and is yet to do in your life? Shalom!

TODAY'S READINGS
Psalm 95 | Exodus 16:1-8 | Colossians 1:15-23

Friday | MARCH 13

Each morning everyone gathered as much as they needed, and when the sun grew hot, it melted away. | Exodus 16:21

Jehovah Jireh

It's just like God to use the provision of the manna as a life lesson. Each day he would deliver to his people just what they needed for that day—no more, no less. Tomorrow, he would provide for that day in the same manner. God was teaching them a facet of his character that is Jehovah Jireh, meaning "God will provide."

For their entire desert experience, each morning they awoke to see his abundant provision. He wanted the people of God to learn he'd provide absolutely everything for them they needed. That they would never need to worry about tomorrow.

So, what is the lesson for us today? Jehovah Jireh! God will supply absolutely everything we need to live a victorious Christian life. We can be like God's ancient people and grumble for more variety or complain because we want to fill our barns with excess. However, God knows what is best for us. He never makes a mistake. He always shows up with exactly what we need and at just the perfect time.

So, let's be joyful and thankful today that Jehovah Jireh God always provides. And let's learn to trust his blessing today for absolutely all we need. What provision can you hand over to God's care and trust for him to provide? Shalom!

TODAY'S READINGS

Psalm 95 | Exodus 16:19-21 | Ephesians 2:11-22

Saturday | MARCH 14

> Now he had to go through Samaria. | John 4:4

On The Lookout

This story in the Bible is a little peculiar to me.

The vast majority of Jews traveling from Judea to Galilee would avoid or bypass Samaria by taking the route east of the Jordan River. The Jews viewed the Samaritans as ceremonially unclean. They avoided any form of contact with them. That's why this statement that Jesus had to go through Samaria is quite odd.

It was the Holy Spirit who compelled Jesus to travel through Samaria. He ended up teaching there for a few days and reaped a great harvest. The Samaritans were ready to hear the gospel message. They would have been the last people the disciples would have been interested in teaching. But the Bible says Jesus *had to go through Samaria.*

So, this made me think, perhaps we're missing out on our own Samaritan experience. It's easy to discount someone as not being ready to hear the gospel. It's convenient to think they wouldn't be receptive anyway, so let's avoid them. Yet we don't know what God knows. All along God may have been preparing their hearts for an encounter with us. We need to have a listening heart to allow Holy Spirit to compel us where he *have to go.*

Let's be open-minded about where God may be leading us. Let's be alert to the fact that his ways are not our ways. Today, be sensitive to that nudge. Be consciously aware and on the lookout for the blessing of your Samaritan experience. Follow his lead and go. Shalom!

TODAY'S READINGS
Psalm 95 | Exodus 16:27-35 | John 4:1-6

Sunday | MARCH 15

"...but whoever drinks the water I give them will never thirst. Indeed, the water I give them will become in them a spring of water welling up to eternal life." | John 4:14

Living Water

I imagine it was a scorching day around noon. Jesus was probably hot from traveling when our unnamed woman shows up with a clay jar in hand at the well. Jesus asks a very simple request, "Will you give me a drink?"

There are a few things wrong here. Jews are not supposed to talk to Samaritans. Men did not address women without their husbands present. And, rabbis didn't talk to women like this one. Jesus is obviously willing to toss out the rules, but our woman at the well isn't. She reminds him, "You are a Jew and I am a Samaritan woman. How can you ask me for a drink?"

I think it's interesting we don't get to know her name. Jesus talked to her for quite a while. She shared about her five husbands, the water jar. We can picture the scene, we hear her personality in the story. She is real and her encounter with Christ is one of the most powerful in Scripture. I think without her name, we're able to step into her story even more fully.

We can write our own names in the margin of our Bibles. Her story is our story. We are just as broken and full of doubt as she was. Yet, I believe God gets us just like he understood this woman and her journey perfectly. She returned to town with an empty water jar still at the well, but her heart was overflowing with the Good News of Jesus! Today will you imagine yourself in this story and quench your thirst for the living water Jesus offers to you? Shalom!

TODAY'S READINGS

Psalm 9 | Exodus 17:1-7 | John 4:5-42 | Romans 5:1-11

Monday | MARCH 16

So, I gave them over to their stubborn hearts to follow their own devices. | Psalm 81:12

Stubborn Hearts

This may well be the worst position to find oneself in.

It is a most dreadful thing for the Lord to turn his back on you. But he wasn't quick to abandon Israel. He gave them countless chances, but they kept refusing to submit to his will.

Do you think God is still letting people reap what they sow? When you stop and think about it, it's happening all the time. For example, the first time someone steals something, the sense of guilt is overwhelming. But the next time it becomes a little easier, and the next easier still, until finally the person can rob at will and suffer no guilt. I believe that's because God has given him over to his own stubborn heart to suffer the full effect of the consequences of his sin.

Is there an area in your life that no longer has God's hand of protection over it? Is there something you've been doing for so long now that, even though in your mind you know it's wrong, in your heart you have become numb? God said, "If my people would only listen to me." Give it to God and let him do his incredible work on it today. Shalom!

TODAY'S READINGS
Psalm 81 | Genesis 24:1-27 | 2 John 1:1-13

Tuesday | MARCH 17

Sing for joy to God our strength; shout aloud to the God of Jacob! | Psalm 81:1

A Joyful Noise

Over the last few years there has been a lot of controversy over traditional and contemporary music in worship.

This Scripture doesn't seem to care what you sing as long as you're singing praise to God our strength. Shout aloud to the God of Jacob! Singing to God is not only what we do out loud, but what we're doing inside our hearts. He doesn't care what type of song you sing; it could be a hymn of old or a contemporary song that was just written.

This psalm opens with the word "Sing!" God designed singing to be a heartfelt expression of praise to him. This means we should sing with volume, feel alive, shout it out! Make a joyful noise. Our hearts as we sing should be overflowing with joy—a joy that comes from the knowledge of knowing our God and praising him and his good works.

I am in love with this psalm. I love to sing, even though only God can appreciate it. He doesn't care if it's pleasing to others' ears, only that it's from our hearts in honor of him. Sing loud today to the God of Jacob, sing for joy to God our strength! Make music in your heart today and sing to the Lord with joy and gladness. Shalom!

TODAY'S READINGS

Psalm 81 | Genesis 29:1-14 | 1 Corinthians 10:1-4

Wednesday | MARCH 18

"Therefore I bring charges against you again," declares the Lord. "And I will bring charges against your children's children. | Jeremiah 2:9

A Living Legacy

Jeremiah's task was to show the people of God how far they'd wandered from his perfect will. It seems his warnings fell on deaf ears. They refused to listen. And their disobedience had repercussions for their children and grandchildren.

This made me think about the fact that we're always in the process of building a legacy for our children and grandchildren. The choices we make will leave a lasting impression on our kids.

Now, we're not guilty of worshiping false gods—or are we? Any time we give anyone or anything priority over God, we're involved in false worship. Our gods are not Baal and the like, but we worship fame and fortune and long for lives that may be different than what God has planned for us.

Speaking of our legacy, how much time do we spend poring over homework with our kids and diligently working for a better education that will ensure them a more affluent life? And then how little time do we spend teaching them the ways of the Lord?

Let's make a commitment today to invest in our children's and grandchildren's legacy as we teach them the ways of the Lord. Let it be said of us that we received the glorious blessings of God as we made our children's and grandchildren's spiritual legacy our number one priority.

Think, how can you be intentional about the example you set today? What will you model in your choices today for young eyes watching you? Shalom!

TODAY'S READINGS
Psalm 81 | Jeremiah 2:4-13 | John 7:14-31, 37-39

Thursday | MARCH 19

The Lord is my shepherd, I lack nothing. | Psalm 23:1

An Abundant Life

It is crucial for us to remember that God has graciously provided for all our needs. Think about that for a moment. Absolutely everything we need is ours by the grace of God.

It's easy to get our "needs" confused with our "wants." The psalmist does not say God gives me everything I want. Whenever I'm asked to pray in public over a common meal, I like to pray, "Lord, thank you for always giving us everything we need, including this meal." It is right and good, especially for those of us who've been brought up with plenty, to be reminded we lack nothing.

One of the problems with living in a consumer-driven culture is we're always tempted to compare what we have to what others have. When I visit Haiti, I can't help but feel they're not burdened with this attitude. Each day is a struggle to put food on the table. And if it wasn't for God providing food through Haitian Support Ministry, thousands of children would go to bed hungry.

But he does provide for them. And they're eternally grateful. So, let's take a moment today and thank God that he always gives us everything we need. Think today on all that you have, all the ways God has provided what you need, and let thanks and praise lead you into his presence. Shalom!

TODAY'S READINGS
Psalm 23 | 1 Samuel 15:10-2 | Ephesians 4:25-32

Friday | MARCH 20

The Lord is my shepherd, I lack nothing | Psalm 23:1

Never Over Matched

This is a universal truth for all God's people that has stuck with me for a couple of days now. Regardless of how frightened we become, we have been blessed by God with absolutely everything we need for a victorious life in Christ.

One of the overarching themes in this beautiful psalm is that we are safe and secure and sufficiently supplied for by the God who created us. He knows well our every need and he is constantly about the business of tending to those needs. He is never caught off guard. He does not slumber or sleep. He doesn't wake up one day and look down upon us and say, "Wow! I never saw that coming."

We serve a God who is in complete control of every detail of our lives. That's why we can face everything, including the valley of death, with great confidence because we have a promise from a God who cannot lie, that he will never leave us or forsake us.

So let this cold, cruel world throw its very worst at us. It's okay because God is never over-matched. Thank God that his goodness and love will follow us all the days of our lives. And no matter how bleak our circumstances may appear, we shift our focus to the spiritual truth of who we belong to, and draw strength from his abiding presence. What stressful circumstances in your life today can you get a new heavenly perspective on? Shalom!

TODAY'S READINGS
Psalm 23 | 1 Samuel 15:22-31 | Ephesians 5:1-9

Saturday | MARCH 21

He was with God in the beginning. | John 1:2

In the Beginning

I love how John begins his Gospel account. Scholars believe John was the last of the four Gospel writers to put pen to papyrus. As a matter of fact, it's widely held John wrote his Gospel decades after the other three. By the time he got around to writing it, the church had existed for sixty some years.

By then there was a lot of false teaching circulating about Jesus. One of the issues with the false teachers was the deity of Christ. John is perfectly clear that the Bethlehem baby existed co-equal to the Father before the beginning of time.

It's like John is saying, "Look here. Before you think of Jesus as a tiny baby lying in a manger, first remember Jesus created your baby and every baby that has ever been conceived. And before you think of Jesus as that 12-year-old boy who sat in the temple and asked and answered questions with wisdom beyond his years, first remember Jesus Christ is the sole source of wisdom. And finally, before you think of Jesus as a victim of the Roman executioner, first remember if he wanted to, he could have called 10,000 angels to rescue him."

John would have us know it was Jesus' voice that boomed across the chaotic darkness, "Let there be light." We serve a Savior who has existed from eternity past. So, as we read through the Gospels this year, let's always live in the blessing that Jesus Christ co-existed with God before the beginning of time. Think on Jesus today not only as one who is here now but who always was and is, your rock and redeemer. How is he speaking to you from his eternal throne? Shalom!

TODAY'S READINGS
Psalm 23 | 1 Samuel 15:32-34 | John 1:1-9

Sunday | MARCH 22

> But the Lord said to Samuel, "Do not consider his appearance or his height, for I have rejected him. The Lord does not look at the things people look at. People look at the outward appearance, but the Lord looks at the heart." | 1 Samuel 16:7

An Examination of the Heart

This proves it; the Lord prefers short people. But seriously, what this text does teach us is that the Lord is not impressed by our outer appearance. He's concerned with the inner man.

Wow! When you stop and think about that for a moment, it's staggering. We primarily judge people by their looks. I'm convinced handsome men and pretty women have a natural advantage in our culture. We place a high premium on looks. But the Lord looks at the heart.

This should be a great encouragement to us. We are not limited by our physical appearance. Nor are we loved by that measure. It's not that the Lord makes exceptions for unattractive people. This passage teaches us that we cannot cover up our spiritual blemishes with make-up or loose clothing. Knowing the Lord looks only at the heart should compel us to constantly be attentive to what's happening in both our heart and his.

We should be compelled to fill ourselves with the heart of God as we abstain from those activities that cause our hearts to be ugly and hurry to the things of the Lord. Let's commit ourselves today to have pure hearts that chase after the heart of God. He has chosen us just as he did David. We are sons and daughters of the Most High God. Let's act like it. Think, when have you been tempted to act in accordance with someone's appearance? Or when have you tried to make yourself appear a certain way out of pride? Let God lead your heart to what matters today. Shalom!

TODAY'S READINGS
Psalm 23 | 1 Samuel 16:1-13 | John 9:1-41

Monday | MARCH 23

> For he has rescued us from the dominion of darkness and brought us into the kingdom of the Son he loves... | Colossians 1:13

From Death to Life

Regardless of what we are struggling with today, we need to remember we were once enemies of God, separated from him because of our willful disobedience. But now, we have been rescued from the darkness and ushered into the Kingdom of Light. And for that fact we are forever grateful.

I remember listening to a WWII vet at a Bible study talking about the Pacific campaign. He was telling of storming an island beach in small boats under heavy gunfire. His voice began to crack as he remembered the awful day and how so many of his friends and comrades had died in that invasion. Then, through his tears, he said, "I don't know why all those young men died and I was allowed to live my life."

You could tell some fifty years removed from that awful incident that it was still the motivating event in his life. He's a retired school principal and a trusted and respected man in the community. And he had lived out those fifty years dedicated to making his life count. Finally, he said, "I feel the same way about Jesus saving me. I have been rescued from the battle and brought from certain death to life with my king. Praise God for his goodness." It is good and right today to think on how God has rescued us from darkness and brought us into his marvelous light. How far have you come with him? Shalom!

TODAY'S READINGS
Psalm 146 | Isaiah 42:14-21 | Colossians 1:9-14

Tuesday | MARCH 24

Immediately, something like scales fell from Saul's eyes, and he could see again. He got up and was baptized... | Acts 9:18

A Story of Hope

Saul's conversion to Paul is nothing short of a miracle.

God spoke to this man who was doing so much damage to the followers of Christ and gave him an opportunity to change it all and become a man who would do so much good in the name of Jesus. Today we celebrate this conversion and it also reminds us of our own.

Saul turned his dark heart over to God. Sometimes our conversions are big like Saul's. There have definitely been times in my life where I needed a wake-up call. But, conversion can also be small moments where God gently calls our attention, wanting to reveal something to us.

The whole point is, how do we respond? Do we open our eyes and hearts, accepting whatever might come from him, asking God where he can use me today?

Saul/Paul's story is a story of hope for us. We fall and fail, a lot, but we can be grateful to a God who in his mercy continues to give us the opportunities to respond to his grace as he faithfully turns our hearts back to him. Some of his greatest miracles are an inside job, still blessing us today. How does God turn our hearts to him daily? Where can you see him revealing truth to you today and shedding his light, even in the smallest of things? Shalom!

TODAY'S READINGS
Psalm 146 | Isaiah 59:9-19 | Acts 9:1-20

Wednesday | MARCH 25

"...and their sight was restored. Jesus warned them sternly, "See that no one knows about this." | Matthew 9:30

Shhhh!

Having just experienced an incredible miraculous healing, what were they supposed to do—keep walking around like they were still blind? Although they disobeyed Jesus, it was still a kind of cool thing they couldn't help telling the good news of their newfound sight with everyone who would listen. They are a good example for us.

When he found us we were all blind to the spiritual reality of Jesus Christ and him crucified. But he wasn't willing to leave us in that sad condition. He reached down and opened our spiritual vision to the reality of his death, burial, and resurrection.

That's why I quit my job, so I could devote all my time to learning and preaching the word of God. It's why we do children's ministry, and teens, and help the hurting, and Bible study, and every other ministry in our churches, because we can't help but to share with others what Christ has done in our lives. Jesus wanted these men who he'd healed to be quiet because the time wasn't right for a showdown with the Jewish establishment.

As far as we're concerned, he wants us to use ourselves up telling everyone who'll listen about his love for us all. Think, who can you share your healing with today? Let the Good News bubble up inside you and tell someone who needs to hear it. Shalom!

TODAY'S READINGS
Psalm 146 | Isaiah 60:17-22 | Matthew 9:27-34

Thursday | MARCH 26

> I wait for the Lord more than watchmen wait for the morning,
> more than watchmen wait for the morning. | Psalm 130:6

Divine Waiting

I'm trying to learn to be one who waits on the Lord. It is hard for me.

I'm much more comfortable getting out ahead of God and then praying for him to come and clean up my mess. I've never been good at waiting on anyone or anything. But waiting on the Lord is different, because waiting on him comes with a promise.

As far as the devil is concerned, I think he's content to have us do anything, as long as we're not waiting on the Lord. Because he's well aware those who wait on the Lord are given God's perspective on their issues. So, we will learn to wait.

We will sit quietly and wait for the Lord to speak to us. We will not grow weary in waiting, even when the answers come back slowly. We will discipline ourselves so every day we will incorporate a time for us not to read and not to ask and not to sing but to simply wait for God to come to us. We'll place our hope in the Lord and his unfailing love, as we wait for him like watchmen waiting for the sun to rise. Because we know he's even more faithful than the sun.

Will you spend time today waiting quietly on the Lord and let him speak to you how he wishes? Shalom!

TODAY'S READINGS

Psalm 130 | Ezekiel 1:1-3; 2:8-3:3 | Revelation 10:1-11

Friday | MARCH 27

I wait for the Lord, my soul does wait, and in His word do I hope. | Psalm 130:5

Soul Waiting

This concept of soul waiting is a tough one. If I can be purely transparent with you, the Lord is usually too slow for my liking. Even in this moment, I feel like he is intentionally making me wait for what to write next. I'm anxious! Why is it so difficult to let my soul rest? I need to keep doing, being productive.

Every day he makes me wait. But what if what I see as inefficient and frustrating, he sees as his perfect plan being played out in my soul?

For now, I'll just think about these divine words he revealed to me today, and sit and wait in his presence for his blessing. What's eating at your soul right now and will you make a conscious step to slow down and wait for the Lord today? Shalom!

TODAY'S READINGS

Psalm 130 | Ezekiel 33:10-16 | Revelation 11:15-19

Saturday | MARCH 28

> When he had led them out to the vicinity of Bethany,
> he lifted up his hands and blessed them. | Luke 24:50

Go In Peace

I love the fact that the last experience the disciples had with Jesus before he returned to his Father was a blessing. In our worship service we call it a benediction. It's not only a sending forth to the upcoming week, but it's a weekly reminder that we're not going it alone. The one who has called us is faithful. We go in his power and his strength to be his people in our homes and schools and work places.

I always remind my folks at the close of each Sunday service that the blessing will rest on them for the week until we gather together again next Sunday. I guess you could call it a seven-day blessing. But Christ's blessing for all of us who are taking our next step with him has endured now for 2,000 years with no sign of ever diminishing.

May God richly bless you today as you go out and serve him with all your heart and all your mind and all your strength and all your soul. Go in peace. In the name of the Father and the Son and the Holy Spirit. Amen. Enjoy and remember your blessings today as a child of God. Shalom!

TODAY'S READINGS
Psalm 130 | Ezekiel 36:8-15 | Luke 24:44-53

Sunday | MARCH 29

Jesus wept. | John 11:35

The Tears of God

Every time I speak at a funeral I'm reminded of this verse. Why is Jesus crying?

It was God's punishment for sin that brought on death. He was aware of it. You could even say it was his idea. He chose to allow Lazarus to die instead of hurrying to Bethany and curing him of whatever caused his death.

When you think about it, Jesus was all up in the middle of death in general, and this death in particular. So, why is he crying? I think it's because he hates death. Death was not part of his original plan for us. Adam and Eve were created by him to live forever.

When he saw the pain death had caused Mary and Martha, he was heartbroken. Out of compassion, he made his way to Lazarus' tomb with tears in his eyes. Then he had them roll away the massive stone that sealed off that dark dungeon of death.

I wonder if, as he stared death in the face, he couldn't help but think of his own death, now just days away. Then he yelled, "Lazarus, come out of there!" I've always thought he named Lazarus specifically because he didn't want everyone else in that cemetery to walk out as well! Not yet anyway… Today, think on what Jesus must have been feeling and why he wept. Remember him as a human and a savior. Shalom!

TODAY'S READINGS
Psalm 130 | Ezekiel 37:1-14 | John 11:1-45 | Romans 8:6-11

Monday | MARCH 30

Teach me to do your will, for you are my God… | Psalm 143:10

A Holy Workout

A dear friend of mine just started working out for the first time. Listen to her story: "I recently joined the YMCA and it has all these new weight machines, bikes, treadmills, and elliptical machines. I'm overwhelmed with them. I tried a few and they were hard to maneuver. So, today I asked for instructions on how to use them. Guess what? They are still hard. Do you remember the first time you learned to ride a bike? It was so hard, and so was the ground. But, the reward was great. And so will the benefits I get for learning the weight machines. I will get stronger, my blood pressure will lower, my stress will lower, and I will generally feel better.

"Some days I too feel like God has a new bike ready for me to learn to ride. As you read over Psalm 143, picture yourself in David's place. And then turn your eyes to verse 10 again. God has something to teach us. 'Teach me to do your will, for you are my God…'

"There is bound to be trouble in our lives. Failure is just part of life. Not exactly what we want to hear. We only want to hear that it's going to be okay. But life is full of hard stuff. I believe it's through the hard stuff that God teaches us to be more like him. The only way to learn the will of God is to be connected to God. To listen and discern as you read Scripture. To ask for his wisdom, the wisdom that only comes from the Holy Spirit, and then to understand what you're learning. God will show you the way. He promises to teach you all you need to know to trust Him each day."

Are you open to learning what God's will is for your life? Wil you ask him today to help you know his will? Shalom!

TODAY'S READINGS
Psalm 143 | 1 Kings 17:17-24 | Acts 20:7-12

Tuesday | MARCH 31

For we are God's handiwork, created in Christ Jesus to do good works, which God prepared in advance for us to do. | Ephesians 2:10

A Work of Art

If my memory serves, the Greek word here for "handiwork" is "poemo" from where we get our English word "poem."

So, it's like Paul is saying each of us is an original work of art and our life flows out of the hand of the author of our faith. An encounter shared with me by a friend illustrates this point so beautifully: She was reading the story of Moses and the stone tablets with the commandments "written by God's hand" as the Bible says. She got to thinking about this and asked God curiously, "What does your *actual* signature look like?" She says God instantly and beautifully answered her: "Your life is my handwriting. Everything you do and say, the way you live your life is my handwriting."

Know that God's spirit is alive in you and lived out through you. You are his poem, his song, his work of art as you live and breathe and act out his love in your life, doing the things he has prepared for you in advance that serve and glorify him.

Let's face the day with this fact in mind: God has already prepared the way. Everything we say and do is part of his divine plan. You are the pen in his hand. And how we live it out is like poetry to his ears. How will you let his life flow through you today? Shalom!

TODAY'S READINGS
Psalm 143 | 2 Kings 4:18-37 | Ephesians 2:1-10

Wednesday | APRIL 1

> ...so I bought the field at Anathoth from my cousin Hanamel and weighed out for him seventeen shekels of silver. | Jeremiah 32:9

A Pig in a Poke

Most people would say Jeremiah bought a pig in a poke. Judah was under siege by the mighty Babylonians. It was just a matter of time before they would either be killed or carried into exile.

For the next seventy years that field would be utterly useless. But God is always promising a future for his people. Yes, Judah would be conquered and those with skills would be carried off into exile. But Jeremiah knew the day would come when God would bring back those in exile and return the Promised Land to the people of God. Jeremiah bought the field in anticipation of what God had promised.

The lesson for us is that we serve a God who has plans for us, plans to prosper us and not to harm us, plans to give us a hope and a future. That means no matter how dire your circumstances, know God loves you and he promises to never leave you or forsake you. After you've suffered for a little while, the Bible promises you will receive eternity in heaven with Jesus where there will be no more crying and no more tears. Come quickly, Lord. But while you remain, how can you take a step toward God's plan and promises for your life today? Shalom!

TODAY'S READINGS
Psalm 143 | Jeremiah 32:1-9, 36-41 | Matthew 22:23-33

Thursday | APRIL 2

because of your partnership in the gospel from the first day until now | Philippians 1:5

Howdy, Partner

I love this verse. It's very comforting to know it's God who is acting on our behalf to grow us into the men and women he would have us be.

Now you may be wondering, if God is doing the growing, what is our part in all this? The answer is simply that we show up. If we will be faithful to do our Bible study and pray and worship and fellowship with other Christians while we're doing works of service, God will do his part. We must show up and be available to him.

I remember a t-shirt from years ago that said, "Be patient with me. God is not through with me yet." I think it serves us well to remember we are all a work in progress. We all have our own junk that we bring to the table, caused by our own poor choices and the pain done to us by others.

So, if you find yourself struggling today, first stop beating yourself up. God's not through with you yet. Second, get back into the game. By now you know what you should be doing with your time to prepare for the day of Christ Jesus. Just do it and let God do the rest. Think today how God is partnering with you to bring his gospel to those in your circle of influence. How can you yield to his plan today? Shalom!

TQDAY'S READINGS
Psalm 31:9-16 | 1 Samuel 16:11-13 | Philippians 1:1-11

Friday | APRIL 3

For to me, to live is Christ and to die is gain. | Philippians 1:21

Tunnel Vision

Paul said everything that needs to be said here. Those who hated him and wanted him to stop his preaching about Jesus just didn't know what to do with him.

They told Paul if he didn't stop speaking about Christ, they'd have him executed. To which he responded that would be fine with him, so then he could go and be with Jesus. Seeing as Paul welcomed death, they decided to let him live.

Paul's response was that as long as he had breath in his body, he couldn't help but speak about Jesus. "For me to live is Christ and to die is gain." Once one comes to that point in one's life, everything except Christ fades into the background.

Can you, like the great apostle, say that to live is Christ and to die is gain? Are you resolved to share Jesus Christ and him crucified with whomever will listen? Is your greatest passion to go be with the Lord? Are you committed that as long as he leaves you here, you'll proclaim the Good News of his life and death and resurrection?

Let's live in the blessing of God as we double down today in our efforts to share Jesus with everyone God places in our path. Indeed, to live is Christ and to die is gain. How will you live purposefully today? Shalom!

TODAY'S READINGS
Psalm 31:9-16 | Job 13:13-19 | Philippians 1:21-30

Saturday | APRIL 4

They will mock him and spit on him, and scourge him, and kill him and three days later he will rise again. | Mark 10:34

Christ's Day Planner

I've spent a great deal of time and energy wondering how my life is going to play out. I can't help but feel much of what I'm trying to accomplish in the church is dependent on other people, who often have a different agenda than mine.

So, I get up most mornings and fret over what obstacle will be placed in my way today. Then when the inevitable happens, I'm sad and depressed and withdrawn.

But Jesus, on the other hand, knew exactly how his day was about to go and it wasn't good. As a matter of fact, it was horrible, and I hang my head in shame when I compare my trials to his.

Our Old Testament writing today was from the pen of Jeremiah. God called him as a young man to speak for him to the people of God for the next four or five decades. God told him, "Oh, by the way, they will never listen to you. They will treat you with disinterest and will abuse you at every turn. But you just keep on faithfully proclaiming my word to them." Can you see your life today in light of Jesus' great suffering and sacrifice? Today, can you meditate on and be thankful for even the trials in your life, and turn your complaints and worries to praise and prayer? Shalom!

TODAY'S READINGS
Psalm 31:9-16 | Lamentations 3:55-66 | Mark 10:32-34

Sunday | APRIL 5

> Because the Sovereign Lord helps me, I will not be disgraced. Therefore, have I set my face like flint, and I know I will not be put to shame. | Isaiah 50:7

A Face Like Flint

When you read through today's gospel lesson you can't help but to be amazed by Christ's determination. This is a prophecy about Jesus.

Think about it—the very people he had created were bent on destroying him. But he didn't falter. He carried God's plan through perfectly for his own death. He set his face like flint, determined to carry out his Father's will.

This tragic event can be a great encouragement to us. When we are faced with a difficult Kingdom task, we too should set our face like flint. Once we are convinced we're in the center of the Father's will, we should proceed with confident determination. We know the One who calls us is faithful. He will not let our efforts serving him be in vain.

Regardless of the personal cost to us, let's serve our great God and King with supernatural determination. Because we know that after we've suffered for a little while, the One who suffered in our place will call us to glory. Grant us the determination to proceed with your plan, regardless of any personal cost. Today, take the opportunity to renew your resolve toward the Father's will for you, even if you're unsure and doubt. Make a new stand and set yourself in his direction. Shalom!

TODAY'S READINGS
Psalm 31:9-16 | Isaiah 50:4-9 | Matthew 26:14-27 | Philippians 2:5-11

Monday | APRIL 6

"Leave her alone," Jesus replied. "It was intended that she should save this perfume for the day of my burial. | John 12:7

Back Off

Jesus, just a few short days away from his crucifixion, experiences a lavish gift from Mary. I think the anointing brought him a little comfort.

As he faces the arrest and torture and makes his way to Golgotha, the fragrance of that beautiful perfume would linger on his body. Perhaps it reminded him that he had been anointed for the task of saving the world.

I can't imagine how horrible the anticipation of that distressing event must have been. By this time he must have known his death would separate him from the Father. He'd spent all of eternity co-existing with the Father.

I'm convinced the terror of knowing what horrific thing was about to happen would have caused any man other than Jesus to run and hide. But he didn't. Covered with that beautiful perfume he gave his face to be punched, his beard to be spit upon, and his back to the whip. The torture would have been unbearable. Yet he did not flinch. He willingly took the punishment that was reserved for you and me. As you contemplate his sacrifice today, let the weight of it move your heart to praise and worship him. He is worthy to be praised. Shalom!

TODAY'S READINGS
Psalm 36:5-11 | Isaiah 42:1-9 | John 12:1-11 | Hebrews 9:11-15

Tuesday | APRIL 7

> Brothers and sisters, think of what you were when you were called.
> Not many of you were wise by human standards; not many were influential;
> not many were of noble birth. | 1 Corinthians 1:26

Christ's Nobodies

Paul could have been writing directly to you and me. Not many of us are wise or influential or come from powerful families.

People in the world don't look on us with great envy. They see a group struggling to get by, just like the Church at Corinth. Even now that we've given our lives to Christ, we're not very influential. We have no one from the powerful or elite among us.

Paul is writing to folks without power or influence and yet God chose them anyway. So, if you're feeling nobody recognizes you or you feel unworthy, rejoice! Because as a Christian, power and influence aren't necessary to be greatly used by God.

That doesn't mean God won't use people of status or stature. He does, but I think only when they are humbled and realize what they have or who they are is all because of God. The Lord works in different ways from us mortals. What men put stock in and emphasize as important is often put completely aside by God.

Jesus, you are calling us to be your children and giving us our own seat at the banquet table. Think about your position seated with Christ today and what that really means for your identity as a believer. Shalom!

TODAY'S READINGS
Psalm 71:1-14 | Isaiah 49:1-7 | John 12:20-36 | 1 Corinthians 1:18-31

Wednesday | APRIL 8

Hasten, O God, to save me; come quickly, Lord, to help me. | Psalm 70:1

Just in Time

I was just thinking about how David opens this psalm.

He seems frantic, pleading with God to come quickly and help him. It seems when we're in crisis, we're always wanting God to hurry up and help us. God rarely operates on our timetable.

He has the power to bring everything into his plan at any moment he wants. God is on his own time. We find that difficult to understand because we're always placing time constraints on ourselves of one kind or another. What seems to be a time-sensitive crisis here on earth may not be an emergency at all from an eternal perspective. It reminds me of the popular business meme that says, "Poor planning on your part does not constitute an emergency on my part."

It's hard sometimes to wait and allow God to act on our behalf in his own time. But the truth is, God is always on time… every time! Let's rest patiently in the blessing of God today as we slow down and wait on him to act for our good and his glory. Consider any areas where you've been impatient for God to act and how you might give those up to him today. Shalom!

TODAY'S READINGS
Psalm 70 | Isaiah 50:4-9 | John 13:21-32 | Hebrews 12:1-3

Thursday | APRIL 9

I have set you an example that you should do as I have done for you. | John 13:15

A Servant to All

Foot washing was reserved for the lowest of all servants in the Jewish culture of the day. That's why, I assume, none of the disciples volunteered. It was beneath them to wash their friends' dirty feet.

So, Jesus did it. Why? To demonstrate to them that each should be servant of all. How does that translate to our culture? Some folks literally do a "foot washing" service each year on this day.

While it's hard to argue with doing exactly what Jesus said, we don't necessarily need to have our feet washed. I think what Jesus wanted to teach them in this moment is that he knew the apostles would only be as successful as their willingness to serve one another. While they were busy arguing over who would be greater in the coming Kingdom, Jesus was perfectly demonstrating the act of willing service to others.

So, that should translate to the way we get along with each other. We should go out of our way to prayerfully consider how we may serve one another. Then we need to be about the business of taking our "next step." This doesn't only entail our love for those in our inner circle, but we should treat our guests and strangers with servants' hearts as well.

Whenever a visitor comes to our churches, whether it's to worship or be served by our helping ministries, everyone needs to submit to them with a servant's heart. Ask Holy Spirit who you can reach out to and serve today. Look for those nudges in the spirit and follow his lead. Shalom!

TODAY'S READINGS
Psalm 116:1-2, 12-19 | Exodus 12:1-14 | John 13:1-17, 31b-35
1 Corinthians 11:23-26

Friday | APRIL 10

Just as there were many who were appalled at him—his appearance was so disfigured beyond that of any human being and his form marred beyond human likeness. | Isaiah 52:14

What's So Good About It?

They beat Jesus so badly he didn't even look human. I've always wondered if that's why no one recognized him after his resurrection.

I hate that he suffered so badly. It must have been terribly painful as well as humiliating to endure that brutal torture. The ugliness reminds me of what my sins have caused. It is right and good, especially on this Friday, for us to wrestle with the pain our sin caused Christ.

The Bible says he was pierced for our transgressions. I don't like to think of his death that way. It's easier for me to blame the evil Jewish authorities, or the Romans with whom they conspired. But to know it was my sin that caused him all that pain and anguish is almost more than I can take. And we all know the rest of the story.

He died but he didn't stay dead. Praise God! But for today and tomorrow and its night as well, we are tasked with the responsibility of imagining what life would be like if there were no glorious Easter morning. What if his torture and death was the end of a sad, sad story? Today, think about the sin that caused Jesus pain and, knowing that connection, praise him for his mercy and love. Shalom!

TODAY'S READINGS

Psalm 22 | Isaiah 52:13-53:12 | John 18:1-19:42 | Hebrews 10:16-25

Saturday | APRIL 11

> Because of the Lord's great love we are not consumed, for his compassions never fail. They are new every morning; great is your faithfulness. | Lamentations 3:22-23

Sunday's Coming

Writing this lament must surely have changed the writer's perspective. He was distraught and dejected, beside himself with grief and in agony. Yet he refused to allow his dire circumstance to distort his view of God.

Regardless of what he was experiencing, he clung to the truth that the Lord is good. He paints a pathetic picture of a man who is being punished by God and shut off from his goodness. Yet by the end of his prayer, he is offering praise to a God he believes will not ultimately abandon him.

This is a great example for us. We too have gone through experiences where we've felt abandoned by God, and yes, even punished by him. But we take refuge in the fact that our God is a good God. And despite what we may suffer, we have a promise from a God who cannot lie that he will never leave us or forsake us. Indeed, his mercy is new for us this morning. Cling to his mercy. Embrace his love. He is more dependable than the rising sun. Jesus knows exactly how we feel. Sunday's coming! If you have ever felt abandoned, can you relate to the author of this verse? Can you praise him and find your way back to God's goodness no matter what? Shalom!

TODAY'S READINGS

Psalm 31:1-4, 15-16 | Lamentations 3:1-9, 19-24 | John 19:38-42 | 1 Peter 4:1-8

Sunday | APRIL 12

They asked each other, "Were not our hearts burning within us while he talked with us on the road and opened the Scriptures to us? | Luke 24:32

Hearts on Fire

Jesus really is incredible, isn't he? He's always and only about spreading the Kingdom of God. And isn't it just like him to go to two disciples we don't even know to announce his resurrection? As he spoke to them their hearts were burning within them.

What must it have been like to realize the Jesus they were mourning, the One the Jews had crucified, was right there with them, alive, living and breathing? What a privilege to have seen the risen Christ! That experience must have motivated them to serve God for the rest of their lives.

So what about us? I've never had the honor of physically touching the risen Christ. But Jesus said we are in his presence now every time we feed the hungry, or give water to those who thirst, or visit the sick and those in prison. I'm convinced when we approach those situations with a pure heart, we too are strangely warmed.

Just like that first Easter morning, he is right there in front of us. All we must do is open our eyes, and our hearts will be burning within us. What amazing truth about Jesus makes your heart burn within you today? What words bear witness in your heart? Shalom!

TODAY'S READINGS
Psalm 114 | Isaiah 25:6-9 | Luke 24:13-49 | 1 Corinthians 5:6-8

Monday | APRIL 13

Give thanks to the Lord, for he is good; his love endures forever. | Psalm 118:1

Gratitude

Gratitude. This is my word for the year, and I've been spending a bit of time immersed in this word and what Scripture has to say about it.

A grateful heart sees each day as a gift from God. When you focus on what you don't have, you miss the blessings you do have. A grateful heart is always looking for reasons to be grateful.

In the book *One Thousand Gifts*, the author writes in her journal, all day, every day, all the things she's thankful for. As we express gratitude daily to God, we're always looking for where we are blessed. What a positive way to live our lives.

Gratitude gets us through the hard stuff in life. It takes away our worry and anxiety. It connects us daily with the God who provides for us and loves us deeply. "Give thanks to the Lord, for he is good…" Let's give a big "YAY GOD" today and recall our blessings. Shalom!

TODAY'S READINGS

Psalm 118:1-2, 14-24 | Exodus 14:10-31; 15:20-21 | Colossians 3:5-11

Tuesday | APRIL 14

And whatever you do, whether in word or deed, do it all in the name of the Lord Jesus, giving thanks to God the Father through him. | Colossians 3:17

Living Thankfully

I think this would be a good verse to display at our work stations or desks. It serves to remind us we're bondservants of the Lord our God. And because of that, we are to submit our will to his.

Fact is, if we're building a house, or manufacturing a product, or raising our kids, we are working for the Lord. And it's for his glory we put our hands to any task. While we do it, we give thanks to God through Christ.

If I'm reading this verse correctly, the service we perform or the product we produce is our thanks to him for what he has graciously done for us. If that's true, then we should be the top employees in our respective companies. No one should outperform us, because we're working for the Lord.

Did you notice this verse includes the words we speak as well? That means every conversation, every phone call, every story we repeat is uttered in the name of the Lord. Have you ever realized the words you choose are your way of showing Jesus how much you love him and how grateful you are for what he has sacrificed on your behalf? Consider all the ways in which you can give God glory today in every word and deed. Shalom!

TODAY'S READINGS
Psalm 118:1-2, 14-24 | Exodus 15:1-18 | Colossians 3:12-17

Wednesday | APRIL 15

> Joshua said to the Israelites, "Come here and listen to the words of the Lord your God. | Joshua 3:9

The Still, Small Voice

I want to hear God telling me the way I should go. Don't you?

I often say I just want a banner to appear in the sky when I'm trying to know God's will for my life. I want to hear his audible voice speak to me. But, how do we hear God's voice? Is he really speaking? I believe God is a great communicator!

He created the gift to communicate, so he must do it really well! That means he does speak, and we do have the ability to hear him and respond to his voice. If God is speaking, we should do everything in our power to hear his voice and listen! I think that is the key though…listening. I think most of us are lacking in that listening part.

So, how does God speak to us? He speaks through his word. He has revealed so much of his will and the plans for us through the word of God. Spending time reading his word is one of the strongest ways we can hear directly from him. I believe God sometimes speaks in whispers. He will speak softly to our spirits and instruct us through our circumstances and can direct our thoughts to his plans.

God also speaks through his people. I've had God speak through other Christians in the form of encouragement, correction, or guidance. My prayer for you today is that you can be still and listen and focus on his voice. I promise if you do, you won't be sorry you did! Spend time being still before God today without an agenda and listen for what he wants to say to you. He wants to talk to you more than we know! Shalom!

TODAY'S READINGS
Psalm 118:1-2, 14-24 | Joshua 3:1-17 | Matthew 28:1-10

Thursday | APRIL 16

> Be wise in the way you act toward outsiders;
> make the most of every opportunity. | Colossians 4:5

Wise Guys

This is a good reminder for us, again today, to be attentive toward our guests on Sundays. We need to continue to be on the lookout for visitors.

It's easy to be kind and loving toward one another and think that we're a friendly church. The real test of our friendship is how we treat the folks we don't know. So, we should all have our hearts open toward for visitors.

Greet them before the service. Invite them to stick around after church and go have lunch with you. A good rule of thumb that intentionally friendly churches adopt is to remind every member not to speak with its own members for the first 10 minutes after the service; instead focus that time on the guests. This habit disciplines us to be on the lookout for "outsiders."

There will be plenty of time to spend with friends later. Paul reminds us we need to be wise in the way we act toward outsiders. To me, this means we each need to be intentional about the way we treat our guests. If we are wise, God will honor that and will bless our ministry. But it takes everyone being actively involved, looking for and greeting and befriending outsiders.

So, resolve and plan ahead of time to be intentional about being friendly to outsiders this week. Remember—the true test of a friendly church is not the way we love each other. Even non-Christians do that. The real test of our friendliness is the way we treat outsiders. How can you be intentional today about being inclusive with outsiders? Who needs to be welcomed with Christ's love today? Shalom!

TODAY'S READINGS

Psalm 16 | Song of Solomon 2:8-15 | Colossians 4:2-5

Friday | APRIL 17

...and last of all he appeared to me also, as to one abnormally born. | 1 Corinthians 15:8

I Am What I Am

Paul is re-emphasizing his apostolic authority. By this time there were many men claiming to represent Christ. But only the apostles were taught by Jesus personally.

Paul was not a follower of his during Christ's earthly ministry. As a matter of fact, Paul was an enemy of the church in his younger days. It was his life's ambition to persecute and even to arrest and murder the followers of Jesus. After Christ had returned to heaven, Paul was instrumental in the death of Stephen, who was martyred for his faith. But one day, as Paul was traveling to Damascus to arrest more Christians, the Lord encountered him along the way.

Once Paul came face to face with Jesus, he became a follower of the Way. Then, in some miraculous way, the Lord began to personally instruct Paul on the truths of Christianity. Paul was never the same again. He became Christ's leading spokesman to the Gentiles and was responsible for spreading the Good News of Jesus Christ throughout the Roman Empire. Paul was excellent at his calling and eventually gave his life for the cause.

We've been given the high honor of having Paul's words to encourage us in the faith. He wrote the majority of the New Testament and we are forever indebted to Jesus Christ for Paul's masterful work. But for those of us who read the words of Paul, it's easy to fall into complacency. So, let's take a moment today to give praise to God for men like Paul who blazed the trail for us to follow. It is because of God working through men like Paul that we have the privilege of learning everything we'll ever need to know about Jesus Christ in this lifetime. As you read the New Testament today, consider the blessing we have been given through Paul's words and meditate on God's mercy and power to change a heart so radically against him. Think on this power to transform your own heart. Shalom!

TODAY'S READINGS
Psalm 16 | Song of Solomon 5:9-6:3 | 1 Corinthians 15:1-11

Saturday | APRIL 18

...because you will not abandon me to the realm of the dead, nor will you let your faithful one see decay. | Psalm 16:10

Eternal Pleasures

This is a prophetic psalm. The psalmist probably doesn't know it, but he's writing about Jesus as well as himself.

This psalm reminds us that in all our lives God gets the final say. What Satan must have thought would be his greatest victory ended in utter defeat. That should be a boundless encouragement to any of us facing trials and tribulations. Ultimately, God will have the final say in each of our situations.

This is so comforting for me because the older I get, the more I feel I'm no match for the enemy. Yet the Bible claims, "Greater is he who is in me than he that is in the world." So, we can stare down the most awful trial with the full assurance that God never intends to leave us twisting in the wind. We already have the victory.

God didn't abandon Jesus in his hour of need and he will be there for us as well. Therefore, our hearts are glad, and our tongues rejoice and our bodies rest secure today in the eternal blessing of Christ Jesus, our Lord. What struggle can you release today into God's hands, knowing the victory is his? Will you press in to the battle again and not give up, knowing God fights for you? Shalom!

TODAY'S READINGS
Psalm 16 | Song of Solomon 8: 6-7 | John 20:11-20

Sunday | APRIL 19

Though you have not seen him, you love him; and even though you do not see him now, you believe in him and are filled with an inexpressible and glorious joy... | 1 Peter 1:8

Sight Unseen

We have never actually seen Jesus, but we love him and believe in him.

Peter and John each speak about being eyewitnesses to the Resurrection. That would have been an incredible encounter, to experience Jesus risen from the dead. But Jesus said to Thomas, "Blessed are you because you have seen and believed but even more blessed are those who believe and haven't seen."

Hey, that's us! So we can joyfully approach this day because we believe in a risen Lord who promises to never leave us or forsake us. Peter says we are filled with inexpressible and glorious joy. For those of us who've been trudging this path of faith for years now, it's easy to develop a lackluster attitude to our faith.

Let's remind each other today that we're filled with inexpressible and glorious joy because we have been saved from our selfish and sinful life and ushered into the wonderful Kingdom of God. Consider how you can trust the unknown future to a known God today. Think on such things and rejoice in a God we can know intimately through faith. Shalom!

TODAY'S READINGS
Psalm 16 | John 20:19-31 | Acts 2:14, 22-32 | 1 Peter 1:3-9

Monday | APRIL 20

> And if Christ has not been raised, your faith is futile;
> you are still in your sins. | 1 Corinthians 15:17

I Pity the Fool

In this verse, that is one big if. As a matter of fact, you could say it's the biggest IF.

Our entire future well-being rests on the fact that God raised Jesus from the dead. It's why Paul wrote that if the resurrection is not true, then we professing Christians are to be the most pitied of all people. But praise God, Christ has been raised.

Death couldn't keep him, hell couldn't handle him, and the grave couldn't hold him. Just like Jonah and the great fish, after three days Jesus walked out of that deep dungeon of death, never to die again. So, we are not to be pitied.

Quite the contrary, we are to be envied above all people. We serve a risen Savior. He is in the world today. I know he is living, whatever men may say. Let's go out and live today as children of the Resurrection. We are alive in Christ. And because death couldn't handle him, we too can live with the greatest confidence. Praise God! He's alive! What does the truth of the Resurrection mean for you today? Shalom!

TODAY'S READINGS

Psalm 114 | Judges 6:36-40 | 1 Corinthians 15:12-20

Tuesday | APRIL 21

The last enemy to be destroyed is death | 1 Corinthians 15:26

Just Passing Through

What it will be like when death is destroyed? Fascinating to ponder…

I miss my mom and dad so much. They're never far from my mind. What joy it will be to see them again!

Just think what it will be like to have the despair of death removed from our lives. No more tears, no more sadness. Then we will get to spend every moment of every day, for the rest of our lives, with the people we love. Just imagine what it will be like to be reunited with the people we love.

I wonder if people age after their death? Will everyone be the same age as when they died? I hope there will be small children for us to enjoy. It's going to be wonderful when Jesus makes everything right.

So, let's live today as people who are just passing through this place. Whatever sorrow we may be enduring is temporary. Jesus is coming soon! And when he gets here we will experience unending joy! I can't wait! What emotions do you feel when you imagine the day of God's Kingdom, of eternal life in God's presence? How does that change the way you think and feel and live today? Shalom!

TODAY'S READINGS
Psalm 114 | Jonah 1:1-17 | 1 Corinthians 15:19-28

Wednesday | APRIL 22

"When my life was ebbing away, I remembered you, Lord, and my prayer rose to you, to your holy temple..." | Jonah 2:7

A Whale of a Story

Sometimes God must resort to pretty dramatic things to get our attention. He certainly got Jonah's attention when he was tossed into the sea. He must have felt his life was at an end, but God wasn't willing to let him get away so quickly. As he was trapped in the belly of that fish, he couldn't run away any more. He was stuck. I bet he couldn't even sleep in the yucky belly of that great fish. He had some time to come to his senses and pray.

His prayer reveals he knew he'd come to the end of his rope and all he had left was to submit to God's authority, "When my life was ebbing away, I remembered you, Oh Lord, my prayer rose to you." He knew only God could help him now. Earlier it says, "From deep in the realm of the dead I called for help, and you listened to my cry." When he was saved from death, he sure appreciated the grace God gave him. "...those who cling to idols—or those who trust in other things, instead of God—forfeit the grace that could be theirs and turn away from his love." I can only imagine the relief Jonah felt when he realized God had not turned him away. At the end, he sings a song and can hardly wait 'til the day he can be at the temple again to praise God.

I want us to think today about the many out there who are living lives without knowing God personally. So many of us feel we're in a mess we can't get out of. Like Jonah, we're making choices that lead us further and further away from the Lord. I pray as we meditate over Jonah's story today, we will have compassion for those who are struggling. The cost of running away from God is great. God offers a relationship with him that is already covered with his grace. All it takes is to receive this free gift, seek forgiveness, and our lives will be restored. Like it says in one of my favorite verses, "Whosoever believes in him shall not perish but have everlasting life." Pray today for loved ones who are running from God, that they meet God at the end of their ropes. Shalom!

TODAY'S READINGS

Psalm 114 | Jonah 2: 1-10 | Matthew 12: 38-42

Thursday | APRIL 23

What shall I return to the Lord for all his goodness to me? | Psalm 116:12

My Over-Running Cup

My sponsor in AA makes a nightly gratitude list. Another one of my accountability partners sends out one thank-you letter for each day of the year. I think I could use some work in this area. I mean, I know God understands I'm grateful for all he's done for me, but he probably would like to hear it every day.

It's so easy to get wrapped up in the business of each day that we forget to say thank you. And I also think it's important to serve those who are less fortunate than we are. We live such a privileged life.

God has blessed us 21st century Americans in ways our ancestors literally could not have imagined. So, let's take time today to return thanks to the Lord for all the goodness he has shown us. And after we have thanked him for his goodness to us, let's go out and help someone who could use a hand. Today, as an act of thanksgiving, bless those who God puts in your path.

Think of ways to put some hands and feet on your gratitude. Shalom!

TODAY'S READINGS
Psalm 116:1-4, 12-19 | Isaiah 25:1-5 | 1 Peter 1:8-12

Friday | APRIL 24

What shall I return to the Lord for all his goodness to me? | Psalm 116:12

Past Due

This is a great question to ask ourselves. "What shall I return to the Lord?"

He's given us more than we could have expected. We have eternal life with him. It's a life that began the day we gave our heart to him. And he gave us himself. And not just for the time being—but forever.

He reached down and rescued us from a self-centered, selfish existence and brought us into his glorious Kingdom. So, what exactly should we return to him? It's really quite simple.

Everything. We owe him everything. If we spent every waking moment for the rest of eternity serving him, we would still come up short. What shall we return to the Lord? Well, he gave us our lives so we need to return the favor and give our lives back to him.

I'm not just talking about donating a little more time to Christian service. I'm speaking of giving ourselves wholly and completely to him. That means giving him access to our heart, all the hidden areas, all the time. We've been bought and paid for with the price of his death on the cross. We owe him all of us back. What part of yourself have you withheld from God and how can you return it to him today? Shalom!

TODAY'S READINGS
Psalm 116:1-4, 12-19 | Isaiah 26:1-4 | 1 Peter 1:13-16

Saturday | APRIL 25

> But when you give a banquet, invite the poor, the crippled, the lame, the blind... | Luke 14:13

Party Time

This idea flew in the face of common practice. People were inclined to invite the wealthy, hoping they would return the favor.

The poor, the crippled, the lame and the blind weren't in any position to have a banquet, so there was never anyone to return the favor. Jesus is always looking out for the disadvantaged. He has a soft spot in his heart for the marginalized. He did 2,000 years ago during his earthly ministry and he does today as well.

That's why I believe we should be intentional to ALWAYS be reaching out to the poor and disadvantaged. When we do, we're modeling our ministry after Jesus. I'm convinced nothing pleases him more than seeing our churches finding hurting people and helping them take their "next step" toward him. May they have a home with us today. And may we experience the blessed love of Christ Jesus because they do. Today, look around you, past the well dressed and clean. Seek out and entertain someone who would never be able to return the favor. Shalom!

TODAY'S READINGS
Psalm 116:1-4, 12-19 | Isaiah 25:6-9 | Luke 14:12-14

Sunday | APRIL 26

Because he turned his ear to me, …I will call on him… as long as I live. Then …I called on the name of the Lord…: "Lord, save me!" I will lift up the cup of salvation and …call on the name of the Lord… | Psalm 116:2,4,13

Hello, God

In this passage in Psalms we hear the author calling out three times on the name of the Lord.

The Bible tells many stories of prayers where his people called on the name of the Lord. Why do we hear this over and over again? I think maybe it's because God wants us to see the victory that comes through him when we pray, when we call on his name in prayer.

God wants us to be encouraged by the prayers of his people. People like Moses, David, Hannah and Solomon and so many more. People who pray are more like Christ. People who pray understand Scripture better. People who pray are more loving. Why? Because prayer puts it all together for us.

Paul says, pray at all times, with all kinds of prayers. It is at the heart of God. Today we still pour our hearts out to God in prayer. We can share our burdens and disappointments with him. We confess our mistakes and our failures. We share our dreams—the very dreams he placed in our hearts—and ask him to bless our families and ministries. We express our gratitude to him for every blessing that comes from above. And we worship him with praise and song. What a blessing that we may call on him at any place or any time! Exercise your freedom to call on him today. Thank him for the grace and mercy that makes him so accessible to us whenever we call. Shalom!

TODAY'S READINGS
Psalm 116:1-4, 12-19 | Acts 2:14, 36-41 | Luke 24:13-35 | 1 Peter 1:17-23

Monday | APRIL 27

Is anything too hard for the Lord? I will return to you at the appointed time next year, and Sarah will have a son. | Genesis 18:14

It's a Boy

What a great question this is for us to ask ourselves and each other.

Is there anything too hard for the Lord? God would, at just the perfect time, take this 100-year-old man and his 90-year-old wife and bless them with a baby. And this wasn't an adopted baby; Sarah would become pregnant through the natural process and carry a baby boy to full term. Wow! What a story!

We're so accustomed to hearing it that it no longer amazes us. But God had promised Abraham a son a decade earlier and then made him wait for the miracle. I think that's one of the important messages this story teaches.

In AA we're fond of saying, "Don't give up just before the miracle happens." We've learned the God we serve is faithful and he always keeps his promises. And, if we're patient and wait on him today, he'll bless us by doing for us what we cannot do for ourselves. Pray, Lord, bless me with the patience to wait on you today. Meditate on the promises he has kept for you in the past and what that means for your future. Shalom!

TODAY'S READINGS
Psalm 134 | Genesis 18:1-14 | 1 Peter 1:23-25

Tuesday | APRIL 28

For those who find me find life and receive favor from the Lord. | Proverbs 8:35

Hot Pursuit

The writer of Proverbs encourages us to invest all we have to find wisdom. Our primary source of that wisdom is God's holy word.

So that makes our study of Scripture to be one of our most crucial daily tasks. Nothing we do is more important and more valuable than to think rightly about God. So we make the reading and studying of God's word a priority in our lives. We'll never regret the time and effort we spend in pursuit of godly wisdom.

I've presided over more funerals than I can count. I don't remember even once hearing someone share on their death bed that they wished they hadn't wasted so much time reading God's word. Our time is spent focusing on the trivial instead of the eternal. It is right and good that we spur one another on to be good students of the word of God.

The enemy will have us to believe we're too busy to spend time searching the mind of Christ. And if that doesn't work, he'll try and convince us we can't understand it. But we know he's a liar—the father of lies. So, let's recommit ourselves to receiving the blessings of God today by pursuing his glorious wisdom. How will you pursue him today? What resistance (lies) do you need to overcome? Shalom!

TODAY'S READINGS
Psalm 134 | Proverbs 8:32-9:6 | 1 Peter 2:1-3

Wednesday | APRIL 29

Lift up your hands in the sanctuary and praise the Lord. | Psalm 134:2

Hands Up

This reminds me of our worship together on Sundays. I love to sing along with our worship leaders. I don't sing very well, but the Bible doesn't say to sing pretty. It says to make a joyful noise in your heart to the Lord.

I like to close my eyes and imagine I'm in the throne room of heaven in the very presence of God. When I do that, everything else just seems to fade away. It's as if I've been transported to glory and have been given the opportunity to tell God how much I love him. When we all are doing that together at the same time it's a beautiful thing.

It makes me wonder and anticipate what it will be like when we all get to heaven together. It's going to be the most glorious experience ever. We'll be there together singing praises to our great God and King, Jesus Christ. And all of humanity will declare his glory.

The Bible says "then every knee will bow and every tongue confess that Jesus is Lord, to the glory of God the Father." I can't wait. Come quickly, Lord. Do any worship songs bring you into his presence especially well? Today make music to him and enjoy him with song. Shalom!

TODAY'S READINGS
Psalm 134 | Exodus 24:1-11 | John 21:1-14

Thursday | APRIL 30

Once you were not a people, but now you are the people of God; once you had not received mercy, but now you have received mercy | 1 Peter 2:1

God's Peeps

Peter's words apply to us today as well.

Being a part of the Kingdom of God gives us our identity. No matter what our heritage or who our parents are, the most important aspect of our lives is that we are followers of Jesus Christ and heirs to his Kingdom. He has showered his amazing mercy on us and he has rescued us from our own selfish desires.

Peter is writing to a group of people who are strangers in a foreign land. They know well what it means to be an outsider. And now, he would have all of us, regardless of where we're living, to live like we don't really belong here.

We're just passing through here. It serves us well to remember as people of God that earth is not our home. Our identity lies in our citizenry in heaven. We're not to get caught up in the doings of the people who surround us, because we are a chosen people and a royal priesthood.

When Peter calls us a holy nation, he's reminding us we're to be holy or separate from the people we live among. So, let's focus our attention today on the fact that we do not belong here. Heaven is our home. We are only here to proclaim with our lives the glory of God. Go in peace. Think, what does it look like to get your identity established in heaven? To know you are a child of God and heir to his Kingdom? How does that affect how you live your life and impact those around you? Shalom!

TODAY'S READINGS
Psalm 23 | Exodus 2:15-25 | 1 Peter 2:9-12

Friday | MAY 1

Live as free people, but do not use your freedom as a cover-up for evil; live as God's slaves. | 1 Peter 2:16

Free Slaves

Peter would have us identify first and foremost as slaves to God. For people who are steeped in our "American Freedom" and, in particular, who embrace our individual civil rights, this phrase, "live as God's slaves," seems foreign to us.

We are, above everything else, free men and women. That is our American perspective. After all, there has been so much blood and treasure spent on that precious freedom. But if Peter could write specifically to American Christians, he might emphasize our primary duty is to willingly submit as slaves to God.

When you read the Gospels, you can't help but think Peter would have been a good American. His rugged individualism is evident. But he learned at the feet of Jesus to submit himself first to the authority of God.

This was demonstrated to him perfectly by Christ's humble submission to the will of the Father. So, first, every day and in every way, we are slaves of God! It is our primary duty to know and to submit to his will for our lives. We've been bought with a price. Our lives are no longer our own. I have some room for growth here. Today, pause to think about how you can be a slave to something honorable, a submission that makes you free. Shalom!

TODAY'S READINGS
Psalm 23 | Exodus 3:16-22; 4:18-20 | 1 Peter 2:13-17

Saturday | MAY 2

But the Pharisees and the teachers of the law muttered, "This man welcomes sinners and eats with them." | Luke 15:2

Mind Your Manners

When it came to his dining companions, Jesus submitted to the will of the Father. It was important for him to help the people on the fringe of society understand the Kingdom of God was for them as well.

This was huge because they'd been excluded from their fellow Jews. No one would have anything to do with them, much less eat with them. To share a meal with someone in that culture was a big deal. One would only eat with those they liked or those who were like them. But Jesus always ate with those who the Father liked.

It is important in our lives whom we choose to break bread with. That is why our fellowship meal after every church service is so vital to our ministry. I'm always thrilled when I see folks eating with a visitor. It often means more to them than people know. It's one thing to randomly be seated next to someone in worship. It's wonderful to choose to sit with someone for a meal.

Whenever we do that, we're imitating Christ and submitting to the will of the Father. Although our service is over, our eating time together may be our purest form of worship. Be blessed in it. Praise God! Who is the Lord calling you to share a meal with today? Shalom!

TODAY'S READINGS
Psalm 23 | Ezekiel 34:1-16 | Luke 15:1-7

Sunday | MAY 3

They devoted themselves to the apostles' teaching and to fellowship, to the breaking of bread and to prayer. | Acts 2:42

Like a Dog on a Bone

This is a good verse for us to memorize. For twenty centuries the Church has used this verse to remind us of not only how the early Christians lived out their lives, but what we need to be about today.

First, I have shared with you whenever this word "devoted" comes up that it originally meant "to tenaciously cling to." I always use the word picture of a dog with a bone in its teeth, fighting to keep someone from taking it away. It wasn't that the early church went about the business of adhering to the apostles' teaching. But they clung to it like a dog on a bone.

So, we too should be obsessed with what the apostles taught about Jesus Christ and him crucified. But they didn't stop with learning about Jesus. They also tenaciously clung to the fellowship and the observance of communion and a lifestyle of prayer. That is how God used them to grow his church and to literally change the world for the glory of God. These are the same disciplines you are charged with observing today. This is a great opportunity for self-examination and to ask how you are tenaciously clinging to those four areas. Today, what is your next step in tenaciously clinging to the things of God? What area can you strengthen? Shalom!

TODAY'S READINGS
Psalm 23 | Acts 2:42-47 | John 10:1-10 | 1 Peter 2:19-25

Monday | MAY 4

"…All of you, clothe yourselves with humility toward one another, because, "God opposes the proud but shows favor to the humble." | 1 Peter 5:5b

Life in the Trenches

I was thinking about a young veteran friend of mine. He was a special forces soldier in the Middle East wars. Mark would talk about being in the trenches. He always said when you're in the trenches, all are equal. They're all just brothers, looking out for each other, protecting each other without prejudice. Despite politics, religion, race, or background, their unit served as one. I think this is what selflessness and humility might look like.

Humility is the opposite of pride, arrogance and ego. I read somewhere humility is mentioned around 100 times in the Bible and is perfectly demonstrated in the life of Jesus. He didn't come to be served; he came to serve. Living humbly affects our attitudes and how we treat everyone we encounter in our lives, how we treat people through our actions and our words.

Yes, we too have been drafted in a war. It is a battle for men's souls. Much of our success will be determined by our humble commitment to the soldiers God has placed alongside of us in the trenches. Our blessing is hidden in our humility. Who can you humbly reach out to today? Who can you take interest in and place above yourself? Shalom!

TODAY'S READINGS
Psalm 100 | Ezekiel 34:17-23 | 1 Peter 5:1-5

Tuesday | MAY 5

For the Lord is good and his love endures forever; his faithfulness continues through all generations. | Psalm 100:5

Perfectly Faithful

Jesus Christ is the same yesterday, today and forever. He never changes.

Although this psalm was probably written some 3,500 years ago, God remains the same faithful God. Even his life and death and resurrection have not affected his faithfulness to us. He will always do what his holy word says he will do.

We never have to worry if he will provide for us and protect us like a good shepherd. When the timing was perfect, he laid down his life for us. We never have to question his fabulous love for us. No matter what we do or how we respond to his love—or fail to respond to it—he remains the same faithful God. There is no one else like that in our lives.

His love for us is not conditional upon our reaction to him. His love for us is conditional only upon his own flawless character. That's why his faithfulness can continue through all generations. What has God's faithfulness meant to you? Think, how has he come through for you and what does knowing this truth about him mean to you? Shalom!

TODAY'S READINGS

Psalm 100 | Ezekiel 34:23-31 | Hebrews 13:20-21

Wednesday | MAY 6

Know that the Lord is God. It is he who made us, and we are his; we are his people, the sheep of his pasture. | Psalm 100:3

God's Flock

It is good to know who we are, but it's also good to know *whose* we are. We were created *by* him and *for* him.

You could argue God has an even greater claim on us than the people of God who the psalmist is writing to. We have not only been created by God, but when we strayed from him like lost sheep, God brought us back.

Then he bought us with the terrible price of his sacrificed Son. He owns us lock, stock and barrel. We truly are his sheep.

There's something comforting in that for me. It's good to know where we belong. And it's good to know the Good Shepherd is looking out for us. He didn't just buy us back and then leave us to fend for ourselves. He is intimately involved in the details of our everyday lives, just like a shepherd is with the sheep he loves. We are so blessed to have a Savior who loves us perfectly. What more could we ask for? Think, how does the Good Shepherd watch over you? Shalom!

TODAY'S READINGS
Psalm 100 | Jeremiah 23:1-8 | Matthew 20:17-28

Thursday | MAY 7

> but God did say, 'You must not eat fruit from the tree that is in the middle of the garden, and you must not touch it, or you will die." | Genesis 3:3

Say What?

The Lord seems to be bringing this topic to my heart again so it must be important. Eve was getting creative with the Lord's command regarding the tree in the middle of the garden. We have no record of God saying they couldn't touch the fruit from that tree. It caused me to wonder how often we're guilty of misquoting God.

We need to be diligent about knowing God's perfect form of communicating to us, which is the Bible! Whenever we misquote God, we risk misrepresenting his character. The command to Adam and Eve, as far as we know, was to not eat the fruit. When Eve added, "and you may not touch it," it made God appear to be an unrealistic taskmaster.

The danger with this is it's easier to disobey when it appears God isn't being fair. We can justify our disobedience much easier. So, let's commit ourselves to knowing and accurately quoting God's word. And let's love each other enough to hold one another accountable in this area.

The God we serve is perfectly reasonable in his expectations of us. I'm thankful he never demands anything of us that is too burdensome. The Bible is chock full of reminders that he is always reasonable in his commands. Think, are there any Scriptures where you may have taken liberties interpreting what God said to give yourself room to sin? Shalom!

TODAY'S READINGS
Psalm 31:1-5, 15-16 | Genesis 3:1-12 | Acts 6:8-15

Friday | MAY 8

Keep me free from the trap that is set for me, for you are my refuge | Psalm 31:4

It's a Trap

This verse makes me think about the temptations Satan puts before us.

When you stop and think about a trap, your mind goes to something that's alluring. I'm currently trapping racoons that have taken over my little hermitage in the woods. I'm using peanut butter to lure them. To the racoon, it looks safe enough, just a nice little snack. Nothing wrong with having a snack! But once it enters my trap and places its foot on the lever, the door slams closed and it's mine to do with as I please.

Satan's traps are a lot like that. They appear harmless, sometime even beautiful or good. We're lulled into a sense of thinking there's no harm here. But once we take the bait, he has us vulnerable and can have his way with us.

Temptations are never easy, but God promises to be there to walk through it with us. He loves when we choose him over temptation. He loves our obedience when we say no to sin. Just like our verse today, "Keep me free from the trap that is set for me, for you are my refuge." Today, can you think of anywhere in your life there may be a tempting trap set for you? Know your surroundings, have a plan for escape, and know God will be faithful to rescue you. Shalom!

TODAY'S READINGS
Psalm 31:1-5, 15-16 | Exodus 3:1-12 | Acts 7:1-16

Saturday | MAY 9

"Very truly I tell you," Jesus answered, "before Abraham was born, I am!" | John 8:58

I Am

Jesus is claiming to be the same God who Moses saw in the burning bush. No wonder that they wanted to stone him to death. God told Moses to tell the people that "I Am" sent you.

Now Jesus is saying that he is the "Great I Am." The Jewish teachers, instead of searching for stones to kill Jesus, should have fallen on their faces and worshipped him. I suppose whenever any man claims to be God in the flesh you have a choice of calling for psychiatric help or worshipping him as the God of the Universe. Those are the two options that he has left open for us.

He was more than a good man and a moral teacher. He was the one who flung the stars into space and said to the ocean, "You can go this far and no farther." Yes, they should have fallen on their faces and worshipped him. Instead they tried to kill him and eventually they would succeed.

How about us? What are we going to do? I say we all get together with our friends tomorrow morning and sing praises to our great God and King, Jesus of Nazareth. Shalom!

TODAY'S READINGS
Psalm 31:1-5, 15-16 | Jeremiah 26:20-24 | John 8:48-59

Sunday | MAY 10

Then he fell on his knees and cried out, "Lord, do not hold this sin against them." When he had said this, he fell asleep. | Acts 7:60

Father, Forgive Them

Having the privilege of seeing Jesus in heaven standing at the right hand of the Father had a powerful effect on Stephen. The revelation of that experience led to his death.

However, it also revealed perfectly that Stephen's relationship with Jesus had become so strong he was anxious to forgive—even to forgive the very same people who were killing him. This is significant because Stephen's reaction reveals the unusual way a person responds to evil when they're connected to the risen Christ.

Evidently when one's relationship with Jesus is in order, then one is blessed with a forgiving heart. Stephen was actively taking his next step toward the risen Christ and the result was forgiveness in the face of the most evil attack. What could be more personal than to have a large group hate you so much they feel compelled to end your life? Yet Stephen, full of the Holy Spirit, prayed the same prayer Jesus prayed as they were executing him.

Wow! This accounting of Stephen's death reveals a great deal on how we might respond to evil when we're taking our next step toward Christ. It gives me great hope for a higher way. Even in the face of cruelty and hatred, who can you forgive today? Shalom!

TODAY'S READINGS
Psalm 31:1-5, 15-16 | Acts 7:55-60 | John 14:1-14 | 1 Peter 2:2-10

Monday | MAY 11

> Now when Pharaoh let the people go, God did not lead them by the way of the land of the Philistines, even though it was near… | Exodus 3:17a

The Long Way Home

Even today, the Lord is still leading us the long way home. We never seem to stop praying for shortcuts, but just like God's people in the days of Moses, he still prefers the long way home for us.

There's something profoundly beautiful about getting up each day and taking our next step with Jesus. Slowly but surely, one step at a time, the Lord is leading us to our forever home with him. Even when the road is rough and our journey is difficult, we can take great comfort in the fact he is taking us down the right path.

We are reminded today of the verse that says, "There is a way that seems right to a man [the shortest, easiest way], but in the end it leads to destruction. Have you been down a difficult road? Think, why does God take you the long way? How is he transforming you along the way? Shalom!

TODAY'S READINGS
Psalm 102:1-17 | Exodus 13:17-22 | Acts 7:17-40

Tuesday | MAY 12

Do not be wise in your own eyes; fear the Lord and shun evil. | Proverbs 3:7

The Fear of the Lord

The writer of Proverbs announces the fear of the Lord is the beginning of wisdom. In other words, if we want real wisdom, not simply worldly knowledge, we begin by learning to have a healthy fear of the Lord.

"Fear" in this context is referring to a strong sense of respect. He doesn't mean we are to be cowering in fear of God. He means to be about the business of faithfully following the Lord, we must first believe he is so great he deserves our utmost respect. It's out of that awe we can make the decision—our number one priority in life—to know and follow the will of God.

He doesn't want us thinking too highly of our own worldly knowledge or thinking we're smart in the eyes of the world. Because, to be effective in the Kingdom, we must first value godly wisdom.

That wisdom, the kind that leads to a productive, peaceful life in the Kingdom of God, begins when we value and desire the Lord's wisdom over absolutely anything this world has to offer. Only those who have successfully submitted their will to the Lord and whose hearts and minds are connected to his are truly wise. Consider, how healthy is your fear of the Lord? Are you in constant reverent awe? Do you desire his wisdom above all else? Shalom!

TODAY'S READINGS
Psalm 102:1-17 | Proverbs 3:5-12 | Acts 7:44-56

Wednesday | MAY 13

Jesus replied, "Very truly I tell you, everyone who sins is a slave to sin | John 8:34

A Slave to Sin

I was raiding the fridge this morning around 2 a.m., found a snack and ate it. I said to myself, "Now my tummy is happy." And then it dawned on me—my tummy is a spoiled brat.

I have an unhealthy relationship with food. My stomach is my master and I am its slave. I no more than finish one meal than I begin to plan and fret about the next. And God forbid I ever miss a feeding. I need to learn to apply the same discipline to my desire for food as I'm trying to do with the other areas of my life.

Jesus said that we cannot serve two masters. We will love the one and despise the other. Please pray for me that I'll stop serving my stomach and turn to the Lord instead.

Well, that's my story; what is yours? What area of your life do you need to bring under the lordship of Jesus Christ? Give it to him today and come up with a plan to go forward. He has promised to walk with you every step of the way. Shalom!

TODAY'S READINGS
Psalm 102:1-17 | Proverbs 3:13-18 | John 8:31-38

Thursday | MAY 14

> Praise be to God, who has not rejected my prayer or withheld his love from me! | Psalm 66:20

A Sure Bet

The psalmist here is talking about his own personal life and how God has interacted with the people of God.

Is this psalm merely descriptive for his life or is it also descriptive for our lives too? Can we claim with the psalmist that God has not rejected our prayers nor withheld his love from us? Sometimes I wonder…

There are days when I feel extremely close to God and I'm washed in his presence. Other days, I feel disconnected from him and his love. So, what are we to do on those days?

Well, I think God would have us get up out of bed anyway. And on those days, we open up his word and feed upon it, and we say our prayers amid our frustration. He is our rock and our fortress. He doesn't have bad days where he feels disconnected from us. He's always in the full-time 24 hours a day business of loving us perfectly.

This is true on our good days and our bad. So, yes, praise God, regardless of how we may feel, for he has not rejected our prayers today and he has not withheld his love from us. Think, when you feel rejected or abandoned or excluded, how can you apply truth to your situation and move in the direction of God anyway, knowing he is faithful? Shalom!

TODAY'S READINGS
Psalm 66:8-20 | Genesis 6:5-22 | Acts 27:1-12

Friday | MAY 15

Praise our God, all peoples, let the sound of his praise be heard | Psalm 66:8

A Beautiful Sound

To what extent does this verse describe your life this week? Psalm 66 is one of a few psalms that calls upon the whole earth, ALL peoples, to praise God! God Almighty, the sovereign God of all creation, Lord of all the earth. All the earth should and someday will praise him!

The Bible declares the day is coming when every head will bow, every knee will bend and every tongue will confess Jesus is Lord, to the glory of God the Father. That means we've been given a head start on everyone else. What a privilege and honor!

To that end, let's just go ahead and treat today, regardless of what we're going through, like this is the day when the whole world declares his glory. Who knows, maybe someone will join in our joy. What kind of sound are you making today? Will you praise him today? Sing psalms and make music to him today! He inhabits the praises of his people. Shalom!

TODAY'S READINGS
Psalm 66:8-20 | Genesis 7:1-24 | Acts 27:13-38

Saturday | MAY 16

> Peace I leave with you; my peace I give you. I do not give to you as the world gives. Do not let your hearts be troubled and do not be afraid. | John 14:27

No Fear

I read this text at every funeral service I'm asked to preside over.

They're some of the most comforting words in all of Scripture. Jesus shared it with his disciples amid their great fear and confusion shortly before he was arrested. He knew what they were about to experience would be the greatest crisis of their lives. He was going to be killed. Then, just when it appeared like everything was going to be okay after his resurrection, suddenly he would leave them again, frightened and confused.

So, he offered them a blessing of supernatural peace—one that would transcend anything they'd ever experienced on earth. "I don't give as the world gives," he said. This passage is a lifeline for us anytime we're left frightened and confused. We can stand amid our despair with a peace that passes understanding because we belong to the One who is far greater than our current situation.

This means, regardless of what we're going through, we hold unswervingly to the hope we profess. Jesus Christ is our Lord! We will not be afraid!

How today will you claim this peace for yourself and your loved ones? Will you allow Christ's peace to transcend your circumstances? Shalom!

TODAY'S READINGS
Psalm 66:8-20 | Genesis 8:13-19 | John 14:27-29

Sunday | MAY 17

In that day you will know that I am in my father and you in me, and I in you. | John 14:20

Mixed Up

Think about how immersed the lives of the Father and Son and Holy Spirit are; it is difficult to clearly define who is who.

Similarly, the divine plan for your life is to be entwined with all God is and all he desires for you. So, we think like him and act like him and feel what he feels. That's a life that has, at least for this moment, let go of all our human insecurities so we can be mixed up in him.

Sometimes when I preside over a wedding, the bride and groom choose to do the "sand service." They will each take their own separate jar of sand made of two distinct colors and then pour them together into one vase. The two once separate offerings are blended together in a way that can never be sorted out.

You, my friend, are the bride of Christ today. And as your perfect Bridegroom, Jesus is calling you to get so mixed up in his life you can't ever be separated from his amazing love. So joined together that no one knows where your identity ends and his begins. Today, lose yourself in his grace and experience the glorious blessing of being all mixed up in his love. Shalom!

TODAY'S READINGS

Psalm 66:8-20 | Acts 17:22-31 | 1 Peter 3:13-22 | John 14:15-21

Monday | MAY 18

> I have set my rainbow in the clouds, and it will be the sign of the covenant between me and the earth. | Genesis 9:13

A Rainbow Promise

I was thinking about what scholars call an unconditional covenant. Most covenants or contracts are conditional on the part of the agreeing parties.

There are payments to be made and goods or services to be provided in many cases. And if each party in the covenant maintains their part of the bargain, the covenant remains in place. But if one party is unable or unwilling to perform their part of the covenant, then the agreement is null and void.

God's covenant with the world is of a different nature. This amazing covenant is unconditional. There is only one performing party and he is the Sovereign One. This agreement made by God is conditional only upon his flawless character. And he never reneges on a deal.

There will be many more covenants God makes that will be conditional on our performance. We will fail to keep up our end of the bargain in each case. That's what I think about whenever I see the rainbow.

I'm painfully aware of how often I've failed to live up to the commitments I've made with Noah's God. But my unfaithfulness does not affect his enduring promise to never destroy us all again. I love to think about the fact that God always delivers what he promises. Thank you, God, for never breaking your promise to us. Today journal about God's faithfulness and what his unchanging nature means to you. Shalom!

TODAY'S READINGS

Psalm 93 | Genesis 9:8-17 | Acts 27:39-44

Tuesday | MAY 19

For, "Whoever would love life and see good days must keep their tongue from evil and their lips from deceitful speech. | 1 Peter 3:10

Good Times

There is, according to Peter, a way to please God that involves far more than avoiding conflict.

He is describing for us here an active pursuit of peace. In other words, wherever there is conflict, it's our job to find a way to insert peace into the situation. We are to find the path to peace amid turmoil.

This means there will be volatile situations we would prefer to avoid when we have the God-given responsibility to bring godly peace. I liked it better when I thought my job was to simply mind my own business! Think about what an impact we could have on our families, our workplace, and our churches if we always sought peace and pursued it.

What I believe Peter is advocating is that we intercede where there is conflict and interject the peace of God. This seems to be dangerous to me because we run the risk of being attacked for interfering. Today, please pray about this and meditate upon it. What circumstance is available to you to provide godly peace? Shalom!

TODAY'S READINGS
Psalm 93 | Deuteronomy 5:22-33 | 1 Peter 3:8-12

Wednesday | MAY 20

Very truly I tell you, you will weep and mourn while the world rejoices. You will grieve, but your grief will turn to joy. | John 16:20

Suffering in Silence

Jesus is so amazing. He endured the suffering and degradation of his crucifixion knowing the world would celebrate his death.

I mean, it would be difficult enough to understand a man willingly enduring a hero's death, but he was abandoned by his friends while the world treated him like HE was the worst of all criminals. This passage reveals he knew that was the way it was going to happen. He would suffer and die while the world rejoiced.

What incredible discipline this required. What amazing love motivated it! I wonder if his mind goes back to that terrible day whenever we complain about how we're being "mistreated"?

This should inspire us to take the bumps and bruises that come with ministry with quiet confidence because we know even in some small way, we're sharing in the suffering of Christ. It is an honor to serve our Commander in Chief and to follow in his footsteps no matter the cost.

Today, challenge yourself to learn to quietly share in the suffering of Christ. Shalom!

TODAY'S READINGS

Psalm 93 | Deuteronomy 31:1-13 | John 16:16-24

Thursday | MAY 21

> I pray that the eyes of your heart may be enlightened in order that you may know the hope to which he has called you, the riches of his glorious inheritance in his holy people, and his incomparably great power for us who believe. That power is the same as the mighty strength he exerted when he raised Christ from the dead… | Ephesians 1:18-20a

The Eyes of Your Heart

As Christians, we possess the same power in us that God used to raise Christ from the dead.

Wow! That will do just fine. I try to remember, whenever I'm praying for strength, to ask God to enlighten the eyes of my heart so I realize I already have residing in me the same power that raised Christ from the dead.

If I'm interpreting this correctly, it's not that I need more power. It's that I need to realize the power I have already received. This has always been very exciting for me. There is no need or reason, for that matter, for me to walk around wishing I had more power. But, isn't it just like God to provide us with absolutely everything we need to live victorious lives? He always provides for us. He is a great God!

So, let's stop feeling sorry for ourselves and worrying about our circumstances. We have the same power residing in us that raised Christ from the dead! Think about the power of Christ risen and then imagine that same power in you. That you may know this by faith! Shalom!

TODAY'S READINGS
Psalm 93 | Acts 1:1-11 | Luke 24:44-53 | Ephesians 1:15-23

Friday | MAY 22

As for you, you were dead in your transgressions and sins... | Ephesians 2:1

Life and Death

Paul points a bleak picture here. Was there something uniquely wrong with the people of Ephesus? Were they particularly evil?

No, the only difference was now they had put on Christ and had trusted him for their salvation. For Paul, you were either alive in Christ or dead in your sin. Did you notice how he said all of us were busy gratifying the cravings of our flesh and following its desires and thoughts? He included himself in that group.

What struck me here is that Paul has left no more room for anyone to ride the fence. Like Paul, we may have been devoutly religious, but we were dead in our transgression and sins. But thanks be to God, he did not leave us in that awful state. He offered us a way to pass from death to life in Christ.

So, we should live each day of our lives with the full knowledge that we have escaped that awful condition. Now we have been tasked with the job of proclaiming the glory of God with our words and deeds. Everything we say and do should reflect our gratitude to Christ for what he has done for us. So, let the world know we are alive in Christ. How will you reflect God's grace in your life today? How did he bring you back to life from sin and death? Shalom!

TODAY'S READINGS
Psalm 93 | 2 Kings 2:1-12 | Ephesians 2:1-7

Saturday | MAY 23

> The one who sent me is with me; he has not left me alone, for I always do what pleases him. | John 8:29

God Pleasers

This would be a good prayer for each of us. It begins with a promise that God is always with us. That's very comforting and when you think about it, this promise provides the power for the second part.

Our lives and our mission are simple—extremely difficult but incredibly simple. We should always do what pleases the Father. The challenge for us is two-fold.

First, to always do what pleases him, we need to know what that is. And the way we understand what pleases him is to immerse ourselves in his word. He has provided for us, in the holy Scriptures, everything we need to know about pleasing him in this lifetime. Once we know what pleases him, through private and corporate Bible study, the second challenge is to *do* what we know is pleasing to him.

As we know, this can be quite the task. I'd say most of the time when I'm displeasing God, it's not a lack of godly wisdom; it's plainly my blatant refusal to do what I know is right. This is where the disciplines of prayer and meditation become so vital.

We must spend time alone in silent solitude talking to him and listening for his still, small voice. Then we're able, a little more each day, sometimes quickly, sometimes slowly, to take our next step. And with each step we take, we're closer and closer to always pleasing him. So, give yourself daily to those disciplines. Show up with your body, and your mind will follow. Today, be silent and listen for the still, small voice, and write down what you hear. Shalom!

TODAY'S READINGS
Psalm 93 | 2 Kings 2:13-15 | John 8:21-30

Sunday | MAY 24

> Humble yourselves, therefore, under God's mighty hand, that he may lift you up in due time. | 1 Peter 5:6

Need a Lift?

This is a two-fold process. In the first, we are active and in the second we are passive.

Peter would have us humble ourselves. That says to me the Lord isn't going to do it for us. This is where some scholars would say our free will comes in. God will not force us to humble ourselves. We can live out our entire lives doing things our way. Scripture teaches us plainly that someday every knee will bow and every tongue confess that Jesus Christ is Lord. Or in other words, it's not an issue of *if* we will all be humbled—it's an issue of *when*.

Evidently everyone will be humbled, but not everyone will be lifted up. The only way we can be lifted up, or exalted by God, is if we humble ourselves. Now, being lifted up is a glorious thing. For all who humble themselves, God will lift them up and make them joint heirs with Christ. I am not completely sure what all that will entail, but I love the possibility of ruling with the Lord Jesus Christ.

Okay. What does humbling ourselves look like? I believe it is to decide to turn our will and life over to Christ. That means to the best of our ability we say, "Lord, I tried life my way and didn't do so well. I am going to begin today to live for your honor and glory and not for mine. Show me my next step and I will take it." How will you humbly submit to God's will today? What is that next step he is asking you to take in obedience? Shalom!

TODAY'S READINGS

Psalm 68:1-10, 32-35 | Acts 1:6-14 | John 17:1-11 | 1 Peter 4:12-14; 5:6-11

Monday | MAY 25

> Exalt the Lord our God and worship at his holy mountain,
> for the Lord our God is holy. | Psalm 99:9

Holy, Holy, Holy

What does the word holiness mean to you?

My earliest memory of that word is from the song, "Holy, Holy, Holy, Lord God Almighty." I was pretty young, and I loved singing it in church. It's still one of my favorites. Recently my connection to this word is my fascination with the Scripture found throughout the Bible that says, "…be Holy for I am Holy…"

I've thought a lot about the meaning of this coming from God. I believe God's forgiveness is not only about receiving him as our Lord and Savior and his grace that covers our sins, but it's also about transforming us to make us holy, just as he is holy. Imagine this holy, amazing God saying, "I have cleansed you for holiness." Can you imagine?

He wants us to be like him, holy. He's saying, I have done what you cannot so you can have this opportunity to be holy like me. What?? God's holiness is not just a trait to be admired, but God draws us into his holiness by forgiving our sin and showing us grace. He created us in his image so we can be holy, like he is holy. Wow!! Think about that today: You are holy as God is holy. What is your response to that? Shalom!

TODAY'S READINGS

Psalm 99 | Leviticus 9:1-11, 22-24 | 1 Peter 4:1-6

Tuesday | MAY 26

Above all, love each other deeply, because love covers over a multitude of sins. | 1 Peter 4:8

A Multitude of Sins

This is a great verse to remember whenever you're confused. You know, those times when you just aren't sure what to do next? Maybe you've helped someone in the past and it didn't work out well for you. And now the opportunity comes up to help them again and you're torn.

Remember Peter's words: "Above all, love each other deeply." Peter knew that we would struggle in our self-centeredness and sin, so it's like he is saying, "Look, you are going to say and do things that you will later regret. So, be in the continuous process of loving each other deeply."

It makes perfect sense to me. I tend to bulldoze over people in the process of trying to expand the Kingdom of God. I don't mean to be aggressive, but old habits die hard. I have noticed people who know me well are more inclined to give me a pass than people who haven't had the opportunity to know me well. I think that's because the people I know well feel loved by me. So, my love for them covers an occasional mishap. Love really does cover a multitude of sins. Where in your life can a loving attitude cover over hurts and sins? Where can you love more, even if it's difficult? Shalom!

TODAY'S READINGS
Psalm 99 | Numbers 16:41-50 | 1 Peter 4:7-11

Wednesday | MAY 27

Whoever believes in the Son has eternal life, but whoever rejects the Son will not see life, for God's wrath remains on them. | John 3:36

The Best Way

This verse flies in the face of the theology that says all religions lead to God. I don't think we need to be critical of the other world religions. But it's a little like leaving Cincinnati for the first time and asking directions to Florida.

If you said to me, "First, head to New York City and then when you get there turn right, and you will be right on track," I'd reply, "I suppose you could eventually get to Florida from Cincinnati by going through New York City but it's not the best route. Just pick up 75 South out of Cincinnati and you're good to go all the way to Florida."

So, when people ask me about Muslims and Buddhists and other world religions, I say they may eventually find their way to the God of Abraham and Isaac and Jacob, but somehow, eventually, they will need to go through Jesus Christ to get to him. Scripture is clear that Jesus is the way to the Father.

It's not up to me to decide the eternal destination for all the people on earth. However, just like taking 75 is the best way to get to Florida from Cincinnati, following Jesus is the best way to the sovereign God of the universe. So, we are to embrace and love people of different faiths as we pray and show them the best road to travel. Is there anything about today's study that makes you uncomfortable, and if so, why? What will you say to the one who hasn't found the direct path to God yet? Shalom!

TODAY'S READINGS
Psalm 99 | 1 Kings 8:54-65 | John 3:31-36

Thursday | MAY 28

We wait in hope for the Lord; he is our help and our shield. | Psalm 33:20

Our Hope

I needed this encouragement today. Actually, a lot of days I need it.

Have you ever been in a crisis and had someone ask you in frustration, "What are you doing about it?" Here's a great answer for the people of God: "I am just waiting in hope for the Lord."

Notice how the psalmist doesn't say there will be no crisis. However, he declares it is God who will deliver us from the crisis. He is our help and our shield. That may mean we'll have to endure the crisis for a season. Or even that we'll have to wait for life eternal to receive our ultimate delivery.

All the apostles except John were martyred for their faith. God delivered them by taking them home and giving them a front row seat to his glory. So, regardless of our circumstance, here is where we make our stand. We wait in hope for the Lord; he is our help and our shield. Think, what does it mean to you to wait in hope for God? Is it an active waiting? Shalom!

TODAY'S READINGS
Psalm 33:12-22 | Exodus 19:1-9 | Acts 2:1-11

Friday | MAY 29

For those who are led by the Spirit of God are the children of God. | Romans 8:14

God's Kids

I love this verse because it places the emphasis on God doing the work of leading while we simply submit to his leadership.

According to Paul, everyone who has willingly submitted his or her will to God and is attempting to follow it are the children of God. So, you see, we don't need to be perfect to be one of God's kids.

We simply need to be willing to follow the Spirit's leading in our lives, one step at a time. And the primary way the Spirit will lead us is through his inspired word. His leading in our lives is accomplished by our willingness to diligently search the Scriptures, hear the word of God proclaimed in public worship, and commit to a time of silent solitude each day.

If we faithfully do these disciplines and if we submit to his leading however he may speak to us, then according to Paul we are the children of God. We are given a seat at the family table with the family of God. What is the Lord leading you to do today? Shalom!

TODAY'S READINGS
Psalm 33:12-22 | Exodus 19:16-25 | Romans 8:14-17

Saturday | MAY 30

Blessed are those who mourn, for they will be comforted | Matthew 5:4

Mourning to Dancing

Grief is a tricky thing. This verse says those who are mourning are blessed and comforted. Are you mourning today?

When you lose someone close to you, you don't get over it like people want you to…especially if that loved one was a child. It has been my privilege to work with a great group of moms who share one painful common lot in life. They have all had to bear the grief of saying goodbye in this life to one of their precious children.

One of the lessons I've learned from them is that mothers who mourn the loss of a child are not left with emotional scars. A better way to describe it might be an open wound. It's a wound that never really heals up in this life. But in some incredible way that pain appears to connect these grieving mothers even more to the next life—to the child waiting there in their Savior's arms.

I leave you today with one of the lady's wise words: "Before my little boy went to be with Jesus, I thought about heaven. But now that I know he's there, heaven is way more real to me. I think more about heaven and what it will be like now because someone so close to me is there. So, I long more for heaven and I find myself drawing closer to Jesus because, quite frankly, I can't imagine how I could have gotten through this grief journey without him. And the more I serve him the more certain I am that he truly will wipe away every tear. He is my strength, my hope, my comfort, and my love."

Think about this beautiful verse and cling to it every day until we see Jesus face to face.

"Blessed are those who mourn, for they shall be comforted." Are you mourning someone or something today? Will you draw closer to Jesus today and allow him to comfort you? Shalom!

TODAY'S READINGS
Psalm 33:12-22 | Exodus 20:1-21 | Matthew 5:1-12

Sunday | MAY 31

May my meditation be pleasing to him, as I rejoice in the Lord. | Psalm 104:34

Pleasing God

This verse not only confirms our responsibility to meditate, but it encourages us to meditate in a way that's pleasing to God.

Notice how the meditation brings about rejoicing. This seems strange to me. We tend to think of meditation as silent and somewhat somber. This passage implies meditation leads to rejoicing. The psalm writers do have an uncanny ability for even their most despondent psalms leading to rejoicing.

So, what does this have to do with our own meditation? Well, when we sit in silence and solitude and think correctly about God, we are in a great place. The more we think correctly about God, the more we're aware of his glory and his love for us, which will endure forever. Rejoicing will be a natural response to the realization we're being loved perfectly by a God who chooses to do nothing else. How can you include meditation in your daily rhythm today? Give yourself at least ten minutes to focus on God's glorious attributes and see what happens. Shalom!

TODAY'S READINGS
Psalm 104:24-35 | Acts 2:12-21 | John 20:19-23

Monday | JUNE 1

> I consider that our present sufferings are not worth comparing with the glory that will be revealed in us. | Romans 8:18

A Future Glory

Paul was no stranger to suffering. He wrote to the church at Corinth that about three times he had been nearly clubbed to death by the Romans. Once, he was stoned and left for dead. Three different times while out on the sea he was shipwrecked. Another time, he had to tread water on the open sea all day and night. And that's just a glimpse of what he endured.

He was hated and slandered by the leaders of the church he loved. He lived his whole Christian life in turmoil. Oh yeah, by the way, then they cut off his head! Yet, he said all that is nothing compared to the glory we'll experience when we come face to face with the risen Lord.

Hey, we share in that promise! In just a little while, one way or another, we will be united with Christ. Regardless of our present suffering, we know Jesus is preparing a life for us we cannot even imagine—so glorious, words cannot accurately describe it. So, drive on, Christian! Compared with what Paul went through, how does this give you a new perspective on your suffering today? Shalom!

TODAY'S READINGS
Psalm 104:24-35 | Joel 2:18-29 | Romans 8:18-24

Tuesday | JUNE 2

In the same way, the Spirit helps us in our weakness. We do not know what we ought to pray for, but the Spirit himself intercedes for us through wordless groans. | Romans 8:26

Say What?

This is a great encouragement for us when we don't know how to pray.

I love the fact that whenever I'm frightened or confused, God the Holy Spirit takes over and prays for me. I guess I can say when I'm in that state of distress that I can sit quietly knowing he is saying my prayers for me, perfectly.

Isn't that a wonderful truth? Plus, it takes away my excuse for not praying just because I'm not certain how to pray. All I have to do is to be faithful to show up, and if he needs to, he will pray for me. What could be better than that? Are you finding anything hard to pray for today? Set yourself quietly before the Lord and allow him to intercede for you. This is our gift! Shalom!

TODAY'S READINGS
Psalm 104:24-35 | Ezekiel 39:7-8, 21-29 | Romans 8:26-27

Wednesday | JUNE 3

> ...Up to that time the Spirit had not been given, since Jesus had not yet been glorified. | John 7:39b

A Privileged Position

How privileged we are to have the Holy Spirit reside in us permanently!

Did you notice in our Old Testament reading that the Holy Spirit came on the elders of Israel and they prophesied—but did not do it again? This was typical of the Holy Spirit's work before the glorification of Jesus Christ. Men and women would receive the Holy Spirit for a season to do the work of the Lord.

But he did not reside in the hearts of all God's people all the time as he does today. This places us in a privileged position on this side of the Resurrection. When the Holy Spirit descended on the apostles at Pentecost, everything changed for the people of God.

Now, at the moment of our conversion, each of us receives the Holy Spirit. And it's not just for a season; it is forever. So, let's go out and live today, and every day, inspired and empowered by the Holy Spirit. With him guiding us and enabling us to do his good and perfect pleasing will, what can stop us from leading victorious lives?

Today, think about how the Holy Spirit worked differently before and after the work of Christ. How do you see him working in your life? Shalom!

TODAY'S READINGS
Psalm 104:24-35 | Numbers 11:24-30 | John 7:37-39

Thursday | JUNE 4

Brace yourself like a man; I will question you, and you shall answer me. | Job 38:3

Brace Yourself

This is one of the most illuminating verses in all of Scripture when it comes to human suffering.

God allowed Job to experience the most horrendous ordeal imaginable. Satan attacked the righteous Job, who had done absolutely nothing wrong. As a matter of fact, God held Job up to Satan as an example of the most outstanding man alive. So, to get Job to curse God, Satan bankrupted him. Next, he killed all his children. Then he covered Job's body with painful boils. The only thing Job had left was his wife and his friends. His wife unfortunately encouraged Job to curse God and die. His friends, well, they spent the next 30-some chapters falsely accusing Job of being evil and blaming him for his predicament. The Bible says Job endured all this unimaginable suffering and subsequent betrayal from his wife and close friends. And it says that in all this, Job did not sin.

Finally, in Chapter 38, the scene opens with Job finally getting his much-desired audience with God. One would think, *Good, now God will vindicate his trusted servant. Now Job will finally get an answer to his question, why?* But instead God says, "Brace yourself like a man. I will question you and you will answer me!"

Then God launches into this powerful response that glorifies God but never answers Job's question. It's a wonderful example that teaches us that some of our questions will not be answered this side of heaven. The end. Do you have questions of God today? How does the story of Job perhaps reshape your question? Shalom!

TODAY'S READINGS
Psalm 8 | Job 38:1-11 | 2 Timothy 1:8-12

Friday | JUNE 5

When I consider your heavens, the work of your fingers, the moon and the stars, which you have set in place, what is mankind that you are mindful of them, human beings that you care for them? Lord, our Lord, how majestic is your name in all the earth! | Psalm 8:3,4,9

O Lord, Our Lord

By Pastor Lynn Breeden

What a beautiful song of praise to our great God. Who is this God we serve? I look around this morning at all the beauty he created and I'm in awe of how much he must love us to have created all this beauty for us to enjoy. There are so many natural wonders in this world; how can we look at them without praising him and giving all honor and glory to his name?

I'm not sure how anyone can look at all he has created and not believe in this one true God. As I sit here in my sunroom and see how the lake looks like diamonds dancing on the water, the lush green of the trees, the flowers as they bud in the spring, and remember the colors of the leaves in the fall and the snow in the winter, how can we not praise his name for all of these blessings?

This world was created carefully and intentionally by a most gracious God. We have to say like the author of the psalm, "When I consider your heavens, the work of your fingers, the moon and the stars, which you have set in place, what is mankind that you are mindful of them, human beings that you care for them?" What an amazing God we serve. "O Lord, our Lord, how majestic is your name in all the earth!" What do you see when you look at creation? What details can you marvel at today? How do you feel about the One who made this for you? Shalom!

TODAY'S READINGS

Psalm 8 | Job 38:12-21 | 2 Timothy 1:12-14

Saturday | JUNE 6

"If you love me, keep my commands... | John 14:15

The Secret of Obedience

I wonder if the disciples were thinking, *If we could keep your commands, we wouldn't so desperately need you.*

So Jesus, knowing he is about to be crucified and leave them, comforts them with the fact that Holy Spirit will be coming alongside of them to enable them to keep his commands.

This is so very true for me today. Apart from God in my heart to intercede and to do for me what I can't do for myself, my goose is cooked. I tried for years being good without the Holy Spirit's help and all I accomplished was failure and disappointment. But when I surrendered my will to his will and began to try living for his glory, he came alongside me and empowered me to keep the commands of Christ.

So, what Jesus is revealing to them/us is that if we allow the advocate (the Holy Spirit) to come alongside us, we will receive his blessing as he walks with us every step of the way and enables us to live a life that's pleasing to God. Are you holding onto any areas that you are reluctant to surrender to God's will? Think about why you might be withholding and allow God to have his way in that area for you today. Shalom!

TODAY'S READINGS
Psalm 8 | Job 38:22-38 | John 14:15-17

Sunday | JUNE 7

> Then Jesus came to them and said, "All authority in heaven and on earth has been given to me. | Matthew 28:18

All Authority

When we put this event in its proper context, it is nothing short of amazing.

Think about the fact Jesus has recently been arrested by the Jews and handed over to the Roman authorities. He was tried and convicted, berated and tortured, stripped of all his rights, and executed as a common criminal.

In the meantime, the disciples had gone into hiding to save their own skin. After his resurrection, Jesus found them cowering in fear. Then, on this glorious day, Jesus encourages them to not only come out of hiding, but he expects them to take the world by storm. And guess what? That's exactly what they did.

This ragtag group of mostly uneducated commoners, led by the Spirit of God and inspired by a risen Savior, put their hand to the plow and never looked back. Wow! This is so amazing and encouraging and inspiring for me.

This encounter has everything to do with our grand opportunity to reach our community for the glory of God. Empowered by the authority of the risen Christ, what can stop us now? How will you allow this truth of Christ and the power we share in his resurrection move you to serve today? Shalom!

TODAY'S READINGS

Psalm 8 | Genesis 1:1-2:4a | Matthew 28:16-20 | 2 Corinthians 13:11-13

Monday | JUNE 8

"Do you hunt the prey for the lioness and satisfy the hunger of the lions | Job 38:39

Wait and Listen

The Lord isn't letting up on poor old Job, is he? God is really doing a good job of making his point. By now in this conversation, he has left absolutely no doubt who's in charge, and why.

I can't help but wonder what was going through Job's mind as God was pouring out this seemingly endless declaration. I wonder if, through all this, the thought crossed his mind, *Hey, I have lost everything in my life that matters. And through it all, I never sinned. Doesn't that count for something?* But Job just waited in silence.

There's a great lesson for us in this. Regardless of what life has laid at our feet, despite our mental and emotional anguish, sometimes the wise thing to do is simply wait silently on the Lord and listen to his marvelous word for us. We may be surprised. We may be confused. But the only way through our tragedy is by gaining the Lord's perspective.

If we patiently, diligently, and silently pursue his will for our lives, he'll come to us with a word of truth. So, if you're struggling today with the question why, listen for the voice of the Lord. Wait in silence, your path to freedom. What do you hear him saying to you? Shalom!

TODAY'S READINGS
Psalm 29 | Job 38:39-39:12 | 1 Corinthians 12:1-3

Tuesday | JUNE 9

The Lord gives strength to his people; the Lord blesses his people with peace. | Psalm 29:11

Peace for the Journey

We need to feel peace in our lives. But that isn't always easy. Many times we find ourselves in a hard season with seemingly endless struggles. Sometimes it lasts long. It's difficult to live in constant turmoil, pain and stress without being able to find peace and strength.

When God is not in your life, you try to draw strength from things that aren't real. This isn't a new concept. Even in Scripture we see people worshiping and praying to dead animals, idols and much more. Today, people read horoscopes and go to fortune tellers or rely on a saint in heaven to find strength in the tough times.

Honestly, this can be nothing more than modern day idol worship. If our source of help is anything other than God, it's not a real source and it becomes idolatry. It will not bring peace; it will steal that peace from you. God wants to help us because of his love for us that we know deep down we don't deserve. Sure, many of us worry over tomorrow, but God says not to worry but to pray instead and claim his promises from a God who cannot lie.

God will help you through the tough situations in life one step at a time. If you're watching, you can see the blessings and the promises in the struggles. The touch of his love is an amazing feeling. As I walk through these next few weeks, I'll be relying on his strength and promises of peace during grief and uncertainty. He's a faithful God and has never let me down. Be blessed with me today by one of my favorite verses in Isaiah, "Don't be afraid, for I am with you. Do not be dismayed, for I am your God. I will strengthen you. I will help you. I will uphold you with my victorious right hand." Meditate on that promise today until the peace of God girds you and lifts you up. His promises are true! Shalom!

TODAY'S READINGS
Psalm 29 | Job 39:13-25 | 1 Corinthians 12:4-13

Wednesday | JUNE 10

"Will the one who contends with the Almighty correct him?
Let him who accuses God answer him!" | Job 40:2

Never Mind

For 38 chapters, all Job wanted was to present his case before God.

It reminds me of a courtroom setting with God as the judge and Job as the defendant. But Job is so consumed by the righteousness and power and glory of God that when it's Job's turn to testify on his own behalf, he simply says, "God is so wonderful." Job will not testify in his own defense.

Now, remember Job is innocent. The Bible says in all this calamity and crisis, Job did not sin. So, what he thought he needed was to present his case to God. But what he really needed was to simply spend a moment in God's presence.

There's a marvelous message here for us if we don't hurry too quickly past it. The message is that we are merely actors in this drama of life. And God is the director. We are to play our parts under his divine direction. We are to faithfully serve him even when we're plagued with the question why. So today, let's once again resolve ourselves to the fact that some questions will not get answered in this life. Let's live in his specific blessing for each of us as we rededicate ourselves to serving him without reservation. What can you stop asking why about today, and simply be in awe of him? Shalom!

TODAY'S READINGS
Psalm 29 | Job 39:26-40 | John 14:25-26

Thursday | JUNE 11

Because he turned his ear to me, I will call on him as long as I live. | Psalm 116:2

He Heard Me

Although it seems like just yesterday to me, the years are starting to add up since I cried out to the Lord as a lonely, broken alcoholic. It had seized control of my life. I had tried everything on earth to quit with absolutely no success.

I was hospitalized twice with alcohol-related issues. My life was slipping away. I had a multitude of physical problems and was literally dying a slow, agonizing death. But the Lord wasn't through with me yet. He was determined to do for me what I could not do for myself.

Alcohol had been the one area in my life I had tried to keep from God. After all, I'm a pastor. I'm not supposed to be an addict. I joined Alcoholics Anonymous and was told to attend 90 meetings in 90 days. It was over those three months I relented and gave my life—all of my life, including my alcoholism—to God. I surrendered that part of my life as I called on him for mercy. He heard my cry and he rescued me from the depths of hell. I love the Lord. I will call upon him as long as I live. He's so good to me. What has God rescued you from? What impossible thing can you seek his help for today? Shalom!

TODAY'S READINGS
Psalm 116:1-2, 12-19 | Genesis 21:1-7 | Hebrews 3:1-6

Friday | JUNE 12

> The Pharisees and all the Jews do not eat unless they give their hands a ceremonial washing, holding to the tradition of the elders. | Mark 7:3

Man-Made Traditions

If we read Mark's words closely, we'll notice the people, in keeping with their hand-washing, were not observing the Law Moses received from God. They were keeping the traditions of men.

A couple hundred years before Christ came, the Pharisees began building a fence around the Law of Moses. They were suffering the result of their disobedience and were living in Babylonian exile. They knew from the teachings of the earlier prophets and from their first-hand experience they had really angered God. And he had poured out his wrath on them.

So, they decided they'd do everything in their power to keep from breaking the Law. They added hundreds of additional rules and regulations to the already perfect and complete Law.

What did Jesus think about their ceremonial washing? Remember his first recorded miracle when he turned water into wine? Where did he get the water? You guessed it—those ceremonial washing jars that were held in such high esteem by the Pharisees. Jesus took their stuffy old man-made tradition and made something celebratory and joyful out of it. So, it makes me wonder if we're clinging to any man-made traditions and missing his blessing for our lives in the process? Can you think of any traditions you're holding onto that may be getting in the way of freedom and joy in Christ? Shalom!

TODAY'S READINGS
Psalm 116:1-2, 12-19 | Genesis 24:10-52 | Mark 7:1-13

Saturday | JUNE 13

What shall I return to the Lord for all his goodness to me? | Psalm 116:12

Payback

What a great question! It's perhaps one we should ask each morning.

Most of us who live in this country have experienced a life beyond our ancestors' finest hopes. It's so easy to forget God's goodness to us as we focus on that one challenge he has allowed us to experience, that thorn in our side. Many of us do not carry our burdens well and can't help but verbalize it.

Have you ever wondered how you're doing in this area? Simply keep track of your conversations for a few days. Are they building up the body of Christ or are they negative or hurtful?

The Bible says, "Out of the overflow of the heart, the mouth speaks." So, our words are a true indication as to what is really going on in our hearts. For far too many of us, we must answer the question, "What shall I return to the Lord for all of his goodness to me?" And when we answer it, we must confess we often return complaints, bitterness and negativity. Let's do a little soul-searching today and resolve to return to the Lord praise and blessing and joyful worship. How will you return God's goodness back to him today? Shalom!

TODAY'S READINGS
Psalm 116:1-2, 12-19 | Genesis 24:1-9 | Acts 7:35-43

Sunday | JUNE 14

> When he saw the crowds, he had compassion on them, because they were harassed and helpless, like sheep without a shepherd. | Matthew 9:36

The Lost Shepherds

This is a stinging indictment on the Jewish leadership. These folks Jesus saw were good church-going people. They had men who were appointed to shepherd them. But the shepherds weren't doing their jobs. The sheep were, spiritually speaking, left to fend for themselves.

Have you ever noticed in the Gospels, Jesus' anger and frustration is never leveled at the crowds but only at the Jewish leadership? At some point in his ministry he realized he wouldn't be able to use the Jewish leadership to expand the Kingdom of God.

So, he sent out his disciples, a group of men with no formal training but who would prove to have the right attitude. This ragtag group of Jesus followers, empowered by the Holy Spirit, would be unleashed upon civilization where they would lead a movement that has changed the world.

The great lessons for us from this are two-fold. First, to be close followers of Jesus, we are to spend time in silent solitude with him every day. Second, when he sends us out, we humbly accept the leading of the Holy Spirit and go wherever he sends us. Where is Jesus sending you today? Shalom!

TODAY'S READINGS

Psalm 116:1-2, 12-19 | Genesis 18:1-15, 21:1-7
Matthew 9:35-10:23 | Romans 5:1-8

Monday | JUNE 15

Those who sow with tears will reap with songs of joy | Psalm 126:5

Divine Farming

It may not seem so at first glance, but this is a psalm of joy. After they had sown with tears, God restored the fortunes of Zion and their response was joy and laughter. Then we come to verse 5. So, what does this verse mean? "Those who sow with tears will reap with songs of joy." I was intrigued with this and remembered the words of my dear pastor friend Lynn, who had lost her young son to cancer:

"When life first fell apart after the loss of my little boy, honestly there were days I didn't think I could get out of bed. And there were days when I stayed there long past what I should have. But there were also days, thanks to the grace of God, that I could only do the next thing. Like a load of laundry, cook meals, clean, take care of my two boys, etc. And, when I say by the grace of God, I truly mean that. Sometimes I had to be pushed. Pushed to get outside and just live. Most of the time there were tears, lots and lots of tears. And sometimes, I just went through the motions of life. My boys struggled too. They struggled through so much, school, friends, when they got sick they were afraid they would die too. It was a hard time for us all. But we all just kept putting one foot in front of the other.

Now I see my family all together and there is great joy. We celebrate life and birthdays and celebrate graduations from high school and college. I prayed that life would somehow find a new normal again, many years ago, and now I can see it has happened.

I believe that is a huge accomplishment for my family. Don't get me wrong; I still grieve every day. But, today I'm thankful. I'm thankful for this life God has given me. I'm thankful for the hard things that have happened. I have to say, honestly, I wish they hadn't happened but even so, I would not change an instant of how God has used this to shape my life, how he has pursued me, and how, by his grace, I have to trust that this psalm is truth, that when the despair threatens to overcome me, and I feel I'm drowning in it, God will maintain his hold on my life and shouts of joy will continue to come again." Where have you sown in tears and found the joy of the Lord? Are you going through sorrow right now? How can you let God in to your sorrow today? Shalom!

TODAY'S READINGS
Psalm 126 | Genesis 23:1-19 | 1 Thessalonians 3:1-5

Tuesday | JUNE 16

> May the Lord direct your hearts into God's love and
> Christ's perseverance. | 2 Thessalonians 3:5

Love, Listen and Lead

I recently had to say goodbye to a fellow pastor and a dear friend. God was calling her to another church to serve him there. This is a good prayer to bless her with, as she follows God's leading to the next chapter of her life.

I don't know of anyone who has done a better job demonstrating God's love. And she has been relentless in three particular ways. Whenever I am asked, "Who is going to do her ministry?" I always say that we are. Actually, what she does is really quite simple.

It is extremely hard, but it isn't complicated. She has focused on three disciplines as she has ministered to this community for the last 10 years. First, she is always loving. Second, she takes the time to listen. And finally, she leads everyone in their next step toward Christ.

1. Love. 2. Listen. 3. Lead.

See, it's not complicated. We can all do that for each other and for the hurting people in our community. We each just need to step up and do our part. She's been called away from us, but I'm convinced her impact will last for decades. So, we will send her off with our blessing and we will honor her service here by following the Lord's direction on our hearts and receiving his blessing today as we persevere in Christ's love by loving and listening and leading each other in our next step toward Christ. How is the Lord directing your heart today? Let his love lead you today. Shalom!

TODAY'S READINGS
Psalm 126 | Genesis 25:7-11 | 2 Thessalonians 2:13-3:5

Wednesday | JUNE 17

> One of those days Jesus went out to a mountainside to pray,
> and spent the night praying to God. | Luke 6:12

Alone Time

Why did Jesus need to go off by himself in silent solitude to receive God's will for his life? I mean, after all, couldn't the Father make an exception for his only Son?

Jesus said he and the Father were one. Well, I'm now convinced they were one because of Christ's willingness to go off by himself and listen to the still, small voice of God. In other words, Jesus was so closely connected to God not only because he came from the Father—his connection was made complete because he was also the perfect man.

This has a tremendous effect on us if we let it. We've been given the same access to the Father as Jesus of Nazareth. But, like him, we have to be willing to discipline ourselves, in silent solitude, to hear the Father's still, small voice. What an incredible opportunity for us. The blessing is there, if and only if we are willing to come to him. Today, come to the Father in silence and be blessed by the still, small voice of God. What is he saying to you today? Shalom!

TODAY'S READINGS
Psalm 126 | Nehemiah 9:1-8 | Luke 6:12-19

Thursday | JUNE 18

> But there is a place where someone has testified: "What is mankind that you are mindful of them, a son of man that you care for him? | Hebrews 2:6

Thinking of You

When God is mindful of you, he sees everything in your life. No one cares more for you than him. No man, no woman, not even you.

That's why you can trust God with your life. He loves you perfectly and is always thinking about what's best for you. Whatever concerns you concerns God. Whatever you're worried about or afraid of, whatever keeps you up at night—he cares about all of that. What does it mean that God is mindful of you?

I think it means he is focused on and is paying attention to everything that's going on in your world. Remember the verse in Matthew that says not even a sparrow can fall to the ground without God noticing? He has numbered every hair on your head. He might even have a name for each strand! This's how closely God pays attention to you.

That's why it's worth going in the way of God rather than your own way. God knows the plan for your life and it is good. Today think about God's compassionate and intimate care for the details of my life. What is concerning you that you can unburden to him as he already is on it? Shalom!

TODAY'S READINGS
Psalm 86:1-10 | Exodus 12:43-49 | Hebrews 2:5-9

Friday | JUNE 19

> Then someone came and said, "Look! The men you put in jail are standing in the temple courts teaching the people." | Acts 5:25

Legacy Leaders

I can picture the Sanhedrin calling a meeting.

This was the Jewish Supreme Court, which was comprised of 70 of the most revered of all Jewish men in the world. They were the power brokers. They were the ones responsible for the death of Jesus.

Just a few days before this, the disciples had been holed up in a room cowering in fear of these men. So, here the Sanhedrin is in session, when someone—probably an assistant to one of these men—notices out the window the men they're searching for are not in hiding.

There they are in plain sight, teaching the people that this Jesus, who the Sanhedrin had crucified, is both Savior and Lord. There—that is our legacy.

When people ask me what I'm going to do next, I tell them I'm going to preach Jesus Christ and him crucified. It's our blessing and our legacy. How can you live out our legacy today? To whom will you teach of Jesus the risen Christ? Shalom!

TODAY'S READINGS

Psalm 86:1-10 | Genesis 35:1-4 | Acts 5:17-26

Saturday | JUNE 20

For you are great and do marvelous deeds; you alone are God. | Psalm 86:10

Just God

These are encouraging words when we're struggling in our helplessness. You know, those times when we're way overmatched and can't see the light at the end of the tunnel?

The psalmist is beside himself in grief and fear. I think of young David, whose life literally hung in the balance, as he desperately tried to evade evil King Saul. This prayer could have come from his pen in those dark days.

So, this prayer becomes our prayer when we are feeling hopeless. It deals beautifully with the two questions we can't help but wonder when we're crying out to God for his help. 1) Is he willing? 2) Is he able?

The former is answered once and for all by Jesus on the cross. God came near and gave himself up for us out of his great love. Yes, he is willing. The latter is confirmed wonderfully by the psalmist. He said, "There is none like you. No deeds compare with yours. You are sovereign. So, all nations will worship you. You are great. You do marvelous deeds. You alone are God." Yes, God is able to do for us immeasurably more than we could ever ask or hope for. Are you struggling with any hopelessness today? How can these truths about God help you in your time of need? He is more than willing and able. Shalom!

TODAY'S READINGS
Psalm 86:1-10 | Ezekiel 29:3-7 | Luke 11:53-12:3

Sunday | JUNE 21

...because anyone who has died has been set free from sin. | Romans 6:7

Death's Freedom

Paul talks about three distinct parts that sin plays in our lives.

First, he speaks of the PENALTY of sin. Which, according to Paul, is separation from God, in this life and in the one to come. Anyone who believes in their heart and confesses with their mouth that Jesus Christ is Lord is free from the PENALTY of sin.

Second, what he's talking about here is being set free from the POWER of sin. Those who have surrendered their lives to Jesus Christ are no longer in bondage to the POWER of sin. We now have been given, by the power of the Holy Spirit, the ability to not sin.

And finally, later in this wonderful letter to the church at Rome, Paul reveals to us the glorious existence of being free from the PRESENCE of sin. Unfortunately, we will not fully experience this final freedom until we are ushered into the presence of God.

So, what Paul is focusing on here in Chapter 6 is debunking any false teaching that has crept into the church regarding a casual attitude toward sin. He's exhorting us to keep taking our next step toward Christ. He wants us to experience the blessing of God today as we root out anything in our lives that would cause us or others harm. What sin in your life have you not claimed freedom from? Choose today to receive God's freedom. Shalom!

TODAY'S READINGS
Psalm 86:1-10 | Genesis 21:8-21 | Matthew 10:24-39 | Romans 6:1-11

Monday | JUNE 22

Teach me your way, Lord, that I may rely on your faithfulness; give me an undivided heart, that I may fear your name. | Psalm 86:11

An Undivided Heart

This could be an earnest prayer for us as well as a reality check on our worldview. It is the Lord's will that we give priority over every other influence.

This passage reveals that the psalmist has tied these two disciplines together. We must be passionately consumed every day in our pursuit of divine direction for our next step. That means more than hurriedly rushing through our devotions with minimal thought on how God's word is trying to shape our lives. We must sit with the words in silent solitude and let them sink in.

The more we allow his divine direction for our lives, the more we can expect to have an undivided heart. This undivided heart is so crucial to our spiritual direction because we will begin to see all of life through the lens of God's triumphant truth. This undivided heart clears away the mental clutter on every issue in our lives.

We'll notice we are now looking differently at our family and friends, our relations at work, and everything else that comes up. There is so much the Lord desires to teach us, if we will just show up and listen to his still, small voice. I'm amazed the Savior of the world would desire a few minutes with us this morning. Can you recognize where your divided heart comes from? What can you do today to bring your attention to the Lord for his direction in your life? Shalom!

TODAY'S READINGS
Psalm 86:11-17 | Genesis 16:1-15 | Revelation 2:1-7

Tuesday | JUNE 23

> Whoever has ears, let them hear what the Spirit says to the churches. The one who is victorious will not be hurt at all by the second death. | Revelation 2:11

Second Death

These were comforting words by John from the Holy Spirit. He's writing to churches under great affliction.

By the close of the first century and the writing of John's revelation, the church was experiencing widespread persecution. John had suffered the passing of all the other apostles by means of execution. So, his words of comfort could not mean that the Lord would prevent them from suffering.

He knew they would suffer and that many would die. The word of encouragement John received from the Holy Spirit drew their attention to the next life and the second death that would hold no claim on them. He said to be faithful, even to the point of death, because he knew their victory would not be fully realized until the life to come.

Now although we are not experiencing the suffering of the church in Smyrna, it serves us well to pause for a moment and review our own lives from an eternal perspective. We are just passing through here. The world is not our home. We will remain faithful, even to the point of death. And we will cry out with the apostle Paul, "For me, to live is Christ and to die is gain." Today, take comfort in the fact that the One you've given your life to has overcome suffering and death for you. Shalom!

TODAY'S READINGS
Psalm 86:11-17 | Genesis 25:12-18 | Revelation 2:8-11

Wednesday | JUNE 24

> You will be hated by everyone because of me, but the one who stands firm to the end will be saved. | Matthew 10:22

The Most Hated

This is quite the pep talk from Jesus!

He gives his closest disciples their marching orders and says, "Oh yeah, by the way, everyone is going to hate you because of your relationship with me." And we see in the Book of Acts that Jesus wasn't kidding.

Because of their faithfulness to Jesus, church tradition says that all the apostles, except John, were hated so badly they were executed. John was spared but lived out his years confined to a penal colony in Patmos. This is our heritage. This is our legacy. We can count on the world, and yes, perhaps even some of the religious establishment, to hate us because of our consistent pursuit of Christ. And so, what is the next step for us?

Well, I believe it is two-fold. Number one, we should not be surprised when we're hated for the cause of Christ. And number two, we should be careful that when we suffer, we suffer for doing good and not evil.

Let's pray today: Lord Jesus, may I be intentional about taking my next step with you. Forgive me for wanting everyone to love me so I can feel better about myself. Help me grasp and understand the gravity of your call on my life. Thank you for the opportunity to serve you. Come quickly, Lord. Amen. Shalom!

TODAY'S READINGS
Psalm 86:11-17 | Jeremiah 42:18-22 | Matthew 10:5-23

Thursday | JUNE 25

Who is a God like you, who pardons sin and forgives the transgression of the remnant of his inheritance? You do not stay angry forever but delight to show mercy. | Micah 7:18

Mercy's Delight

Do you accept God's forgiveness or waste time feeling guilty?

So many of us struggle with guilt. God's love is hard for us to accept, because in this world we have to pay for everything we receive. God is not like people. I am so thankful for that!!

We need to learn that whether we FEEL forgiven or not, we ARE forgiven. Feelings of guilt are just that—feelings. If you understand God's word, then no matter how you feel, you are forgiven. I wonder if we spoke Scriptures of forgiveness every day, how long would it take for us to believe in God's forgiveness?

One of my favorite verses about forgiveness is from 1 John 1:9. It says if we confess our sin, God is faithful to forgive us. That is a verse we need to hang onto. Maybe every time you confess your sin to God and still feel guilty, quote that verse to yourself. There is power in our hiding these verses in our hearts and speaking them aloud when we're struggling.

Praying these Scriptures renews our minds to think right and puts the evil one in his place. Someone has said that "whenever Satan reminds me of my past, I remind him of his future." What next step in God's forgiveness can you take today? Will you see yourself as forgiven today? Receive it. Shalom!

TODAY'S READINGS
Psalm 13 | Micah 7:18-20 | Galatians 5:2-6

Friday | JUNE 26

"A little yeast works through the whole batch of dough." | Galatians 5:9

False Doctrine

Some things never change.

The Galatians were being led astray by people who claimed the name of Christ. If you would ask them, they would tell you they were the "real" followers of Jesus. But Paul knew it wasn't enough to take parts of the gospel and disregard the rest of it. That's why it is so beneficial to the church to have these letters to help us to refute false doctrine.

Now, we are not troubled with so-called Christians who tempt us to disregard the grace of God so we'll reattach ourselves to the Law. But we do need to be on our guard and be ever vigilant to reject any false teaching. Remember, the enemy is subtle and he's the father of lies. He will send his agents as wolves in sheep's clothing.

They'll look like Christians and they'll sound like Christians. But after careful scrutiny we'll see they're promoting a false gospel. So, let's be disciplined about who we listen to and who we follow and who we allow to shape our worldview. Let's cling to the writings of the apostles and let's hold all that is said by others up to the light of Scripture. Can you think of any recent teachings you should reexamine in light of the gospel? Shalom!

TODAY'S READINGS
Psalm 13 | 2 Chronicles 20:5-12 | Galatians 5:7-12

Saturday | JUNE 27

But I trust in your unfailing love; my heart rejoices in your salvation | Psalm 13:5

Inside My Head

This is a great verse to memorize, especially if you're like me and the psalmist and have trouble wrestling with your thoughts. It can be a scary, depressing thing to be inside my head!

Can you identify with the statement here? "…day after day I have sorrow in my heart." I know I sure can. For me, there are days when I'm not even sure why. I love how the psalmist concluded that in spite of those negative thoughts that haunt him, he chose to focus instead on God's unfailing love and to rejoice in the fact that he's part of God's salvation.

This transitional process, where his thoughts progress from his seemingly hopeless state to trusting in God's unfailing love, makes him break out into a song of praise. Many of us today may not be where we want to be in life, but we can rejoice because God did not leave us where we used to be. The Lord is our Rock and our Salvation. Are you wrestling with any thoughts today? Purpose in your heart today to fix your thoughts on his unfailing love for you. See where his love takes you. Shalom!

TODAY'S READINGS
Psalm 13 | Genesis 26:23-25 | Luke 17:1-4

Sunday | JUNE 28

> So Abraham called that place The Lord Will Provide. And to this day it is said, "On the mountain of the Lord it will be provided." | Genesis 22:14

The Lord Will Provide

This is one of the most fascinating stories in all of Scripture.

Did you notice how when Abraham was asked by Isaac, "Where is the lamb for the burnt offering?" Abraham responded that the Lord would provide. This is a great testimony to his faith.

God called Abraham, this one solitary man out of all the men on earth, to be the father of his people. Ever since that calling, slowly but surely, God taught Abraham he would indeed provide for him. First, it was a place to live and prosper. Next, it was the miracle of having a son at the ripe old age of 100. Now, God was asking Abraham to sacrifice his only son.

The most incredible fact is that Abraham was willing to do it, believing, if nothing else, God would offer back his son from the dead. Abraham wasn't sure how this would play out. The one fact he had confidence in was the wonderful universal fact we see now for all of God's people: "The Lord will provide."

Whatever you're struggling with today, cling to the faith of our spiritual father and know the Lord will provide. Today, what are you trusting God for? Even if you can't see the way ahead, rely on him fully to be the provider he is—what you need at the right time. Shalom!

TODAY'S READINGS
Psalm 13 | Genesis 22:1-14 | Matthew 6:12-23 | Romans 6:12-23

Monday | JUNE 29

...and to make it your ambition to lead a quiet life: You should mind your own business and work with your hands, just as we told you... | 1 Thessalonians 4:11

Shhhhh

This is a good reminder for me.

I need to make it my ambition today to lead a quiet life. Where words are many, sin is not absent. I feel much of what's said most days is simply not necessary.

I like to use the "T.E.N." talking strategy: "1) Is it True? 2) Is it Encouraging? 3) Is it Necessary?" I ask myself, "Out of the seven billion people on earth, am I the one person chosen by God to share what is on my mind?" It may be true and it may even be encouraging but the final test is always, "Is it necessary?"

This is why Paul makes the interesting transition from what we say to a simple command to mind our own business. I'm sensitive about this in the church because I see it as the number one reason churches do not grow. We all have a tendency, if we're not careful, to let the enemy convince us we need to force our opinion into other ministries.

I need to remind myself God has called individuals in his church to administer the finances and to oversee the building and grounds and to shepherd our children and our teens and do other duties to lead his church forward. It is my job to cast the vision for the advancement of the church and to preach the gospel of Jesus Christ. It is not my calling to force everyone involved to perform up to my expectation. So, today, I will endeavor to simply be quiet and mind my own business and to do the work God has given me to do. Think, is there something you need to back away from, to keep quiet about, to take your hands off, and apply your work to God's tasks for you? Shalom!

TODAY'S READINGS
Psalm 47 | Genesis 22:15-18 | 1 Thessalonians 4:9-12

Tuesday | JUNE 30

> You, dear children, are from God and have overcome them, because the one who is in you is greater than the one who is in the world. | 1 John 4:4

Spiritual Stretching

What a great God we serve! I'm reminded in this verse that whatever you're facing in life, God has already given you the faith you need for it. It may not look like it, and you may not feel like you have what it takes to overcome, but faith in God isn't based on our circumstances or how we feel.

The enemy would sure like you to believe you don't have a chance in life, or that you're too weak, too poor, too whatever. But God has a different view of you. God sees you through eyes of love. He sees not what you've experienced, not what others see or say about you, but what he says about you and has already invested in you. The way God sees you leads you to a life of overwhelming victory. Yay, God!

But it takes faith. You can't just hear me tell you God loves you that much; you have to believe it. It takes faith to move forward and overcome the challenges you're facing. Faith doesn't do you any good if you don't release it. We release it through our words, actions, and most important, our prayers. It is up to you!

The truth is, the One in you is greater and HE loves you dearly. So, let's stretch our faith today and try to see ourselves as God sees us. It doesn't matter what the enemy wants you to see or how things might look. Our faith overcomes through the One who lives in us! How can you stretch your faith today? What lie about yourself can you reject that may be hindering you? What promise of God can you focus on today? Shalom!

TODAY'S READINGS
Psalm 47 | 1 Kings 18:36-39 | 1 John 4:1-6

Wednesday | JULY 1

For God is the King of all the earth; sing to him a psalm of praise. | Psalm 47:7

God's in Charge

I couldn't sleep last night from worry and stress. But these words fell on me this morning like rain on a parched and weary land. God is king of all the earth. My fate rests in his hands—his kind and gentle and loving hands.

This doesn't mean everything in my life will come up roses. But it does mean nothing will happen to me outside of his sovereign control. When it comes right down to it, when I am worried it means I'm either thinking God does not care about me or he isn't capable of protecting me.

It may be these ideas are in my subconscious, but that doesn't stop them from controlling my thoughts and attitude and actions. The passage I'm preparing for my Romans sermon series this week asks this question of me or anyone who's struggling with worry or stress: "If God is for us, who can be against us? If God is on our side, how can we be denied? In all these things we are more than conquerors through Jesus Christ our Lord. Nothing can separate us from the love of God." Let's sing that psalm of praise! What are you worrying about today that you can trust into the hands of God who loves you and is more than able? Shalom!

TODAY'S READINGS
Psalm 47 | Isaiah 51:1-3 | Matthew 11:20-24

Thursday | JULY 2

I do not understand what I do. For what I want to do I do not do, but what I hate I do... | Romans 7:15

Journey On

I can relate to this verse. It's incredibly significant when we pause for a moment and remember who wrote it.

The apostle Paul as much as any other saint is to be followed and admired. He was responsible for taking the gospel of Jesus Christ to the world of the Gentiles. The majority of your New Testament was written by him. Yet, in spite of his elevated position, here we have this great pillar of the faith saying, "I do not understand what I do. For what I want to do I do not do, but what I hate I do."

We're left to wonder, if Paul can't get it right what hope is there for us? This is why I love talking about taking our "next step." Paul was always in the process of working out his salvation with fear and trembling. While it's true Paul was further along his faith journey than any of us, what's crucially important to realize is that even Paul was pursuing taking his "next step."

This tells me that no matter how far we have traveled in pursuit of Christ, there is, indeed, a next step for each of us to take. So, journey on, precious believers. Be immersed in God's blessing for you in your pursuit of Jesus Christ, the One who died for us and who is calling us to pursue him for the glory of God. How will you follow Paul's lead today? No matter where you are in your faith journey, how can you humble yourself and take your next step? Shalom!

TODAY'S READINGS
Psalm 45:10-17 | Genesis 25:19-27 | Romans 7:1-6

Friday | JULY 3

> For the good I want to do, I do not do, but I practice the very evil that I do not want." | Romans 7:19

Tripped Up

Of all the verses in the entire Bible, this describes me best. Even after three decades of trying to get it right, I fail repeatedly. And that's just in the sin of which I'm aware. It seems like whenever I achieve a small victory in one area of my life, the Lord just reveals to me another door I must pass through to arrive at a new, more difficult challenge.

I'm beginning to realize why Paul described himself as the chief of all sinners. The further we're willing to journey down this path of faith, the more it seems we have so much further to go and more to learn than we ever realized. The obvious temptation is to just throw our hands in the air and declare, "There's no use!"

That's why I find great comfort in the "next step" concept of spiritual growth. Regardless of where I find myself along this journey of faith, I know God has a next step for me to take today. So, I'll focus on that step and leave the rest of the long road home in the safe and all-wise hands of our powerful and loving God. Today, work on celebrating where you are in Christ and, pressing ahead, taking one next step no matter how small toward Christ. Shalom!

TODAY'S READINGS
Psalm 45:10-17 | Genesis 27:1-17 | Romans 7:7-20

Saturday | JULY 4

> Then he turned to his disciples and said privately, "Blessed are the eyes that see what you see. | Luke 10:23

20-20 Vision

I believe Jesus was talking about something far more important than physical sight. The multitudes had seen Jesus with their eyes, but they did not perceive who he truly was.

No, Jesus is talking here about seeing and understanding that which God had obscured from the smart and learned but had revealed to little children and his closest followers. So, this is great news for us because even though we did not get to see Jesus with our own eyes, we can know him with our hearts.

It is to our great advantage we have these Gospel writings, as day after day they're transforming us for our good and God's glory. We have the opportunity on this day and every day to ask Jesus to open our eyes so we can experience his sacred truths. I can think of absolutely nothing we could do with our time, talent and treasure that could be more of a blessing than truly seeing Jesus and helping to reveal him to our community. So, I pray for his blessing that as individuals and as the collective body our Lord Jesus Christ will continue to reveal to us his glory and truth.

How has Jesus revealed himself to you? Remember, and stand on the revelations, from glory to glory. Shalom!

TODAY'S READINGS
Psalm 45:10-17 | Genesis 27:18-29 | Luke 10:21-24

Sunday | JULY 5

For my yoke is very easy and my burden is light." | Matthew 11:30

Hitched Up

This verse has always troubled me. These words from Jesus fell upon men and women who would live out their lives in some of the most difficult times imaginable. I think it's evident from other passages Jesus had some foreknowledge of the fate awaiting his followers.

So, if he was saying to them, "Come on, let's go! It's going to be a piece of cake!" he was intentionally deceiving them. And if that is true then I have wasted my life trying to get to know and serve him.

Maybe it would serve us well to look at this verse from the perspective of my grandparents' generation, who made their living working their farms with a team of horses. According to my grandpa and uncle, a good team of horses was a tremendous blessing and highly cherished. They did not negate the fact the ground was hard and difficult to prepare for the growing season, but a good hitched team made life so much easier.

What if Jesus is calling all his followers—past, present and future—to a difficult task? And he does so with the complete knowledge that the best and only way for us to accomplish the difficult task at hand is to attach ourselves to the One who is both gentle and humble at heart. That means that the blessing for us is to put our hand to the plow, yoked with the One who promises to be the perfect pulling partner. I am blessed to be yoked with my Lord. What tasks lay before you that you can get your strength from the Lord to accomplish? Shalom!

TODAY'S READINGS
Psalm 45:10-17 | Genesis 24:34-38, 42-49, 58-67 | Matthew 11:16-19, 25-30

Monday | JULY 6

> For since the creation of the world God's invisible qualities—his eternal power and divine nature—have been clearly seen, being understood from what has been made, so that people are without excuse. | Romans 1:20

God's Invisible Qualities

What I believe Paul is saying here is that every man, woman and child who has ever lived has had this internal sense of our living God.

Paul makes the argument that the results of creation and the nature that surrounds us bear witness to the fact there is a God and he must be amazing for having made all this. Think about it—we've all stood in the midst of one of God's glorious handiworks and without even thinking about it, utttered, "How can anyone witness this and then deny there's a God?"

When we said that, we weren't necessarily thinking theologically. We weren't looking for some divine proof. No, God just revealed his invisible qualities—his eternal power and his divine nature. This is why I find it helpful to start with nature when I'm speaking to someone considering taking their first step toward God. Without even realizing it, God has already gone with them on their first step by incredibly declaring his glory by what his hands have made. Think, what is your favorite aspect of God's creation? Shalom!

TODAY'S READINGS

Song of Solomon 2:8-13 | Genesis 27:30-46 | Romans 1:18-25

Tuesday | JULY 7

> My beloved spoke and said to me, "Arise, my darling, my beautiful one, come with me. | Song of Solomon 2:10

My Beautiful One

In the Song of Solomon, we see a poem about the love between two people. Many believe it's a metaphor for God's love. So, let's think about God's love today.

Some folks are a bit uncomfortable with this book of the Bible because of its passionate, romantic language. How does this book connect us to God's love? What I know is God longs to be intimate with us—intimate in the sense of becoming one or knowing each other completely.

But, being that intimate is kinda scary for us. We know all too well the scars we carry from people we've been intimate with who've hurt us deeply. I think we're okay just being friends with God. We love to sing "What a friend we have in Jesus." Friendship is good. Everyone needs a friend. We don't even mind getting up early and spending time with God. I love the phrase in a popular hymn, "And he walks with me and he talks with me and he tells me I am his own."

However, the intimacy in the Song of Solomon is a whole other level of intimacy. What I want you to know today is this: God is head over heels in love with you! God *does* want an intimate relationship with you. And there's nothing you can do to change God's mind. It is kinda scary and wonderful all at the same time. Today as you read these verses, will you consider letting God come closer to you than you ever have? Receive his safe love for you today. Shalom!

TODAY'S READINGS

Song of Solomon 2:8-13 | Genesis 29:1-14 | Romans 3:1-8

Wednesday | JULY 8

I have set you an example that you should do as I have done for you. | John 13:15

Carbon Copies

Most of the time the hero in our favorite stories goes out in a blaze of glory. But here we see our hero, Jesus Christ, humbly washing the feet of his followers.

No one could blame him if he was self-absorbed in his impending arrest and execution. Did you notice in the opening verse John writes, "Having loved his own who were in the world, he loved them to the end?"

I guess that's what a Christian hero looks like—one who is compelled to self-sacrificing service to those God has put in their life. This is a great lesson in vision casting for the church. We're always trying to seek the Lord's will and determine what our next step with him should be. And here we have a wonderful clue to point us in the right direction.

We should exhibit a supernatural focus in loving those around us. Our love for them should be extravagant and self-sacrificing. You know, the significant point in Jesus' foot-washing lesson was that each of his disciples had the choice to humbly wash the feet of their friends. They all refused. They didn't say no but their inaction revealed the condition of their hearts. Let that never be said of us. Who will you focus your love on today? How can you use Jesus' story as a model of servanthood to your brothers and sisters? Shalom!

TODAY'S READINGS
Song of Solomon 2:8-13 | Genesis 29:31-35 | John 13:1-17

Thursday | JULY 9

Your word is a lamp for my feet, a light on my path. | Psalm 119:105

Into the Light

There's a ton of power in this short verse. Many times in my life I've struggled to discern the right way to go. There have been times I made the wrong decision. And yet, when I look back on those bad decisions they have turned out for good.

Romans tells me according to God's purpose, all things work out for my good. Jeremiah 29 says God knows the plans he has for me and they're all for my good. Psalm 139 says my life and days were laid out for me before I was even born. When I put it all together, it's a beautiful picture of God's plan for my life. He's already made the way, prepared the work, and has a plan for my life. I only need to walk where the Lord is leading.

Even when I make the wrong choice, I have the promise that though I fall, the Lord upholds me with his hand. And so I know when we seek God through his word, we discover truth that lights our way. Sometimes we get to see the big picture; however, most of the time we only get to see our next step.

Through all our life, God is shining his light on our next step. We may not know where that step will lead, but we can trust he knows. God has already prepared our way. Even in impossible situations, his word promises to show us the way and that he is our light. Is there any darkness on your path today? Will you talk to God and let his light illuminate the way forward for you? Shalom!

TODAY'S READINGS
Psalm 119:105-112 | Exodus 3:1-6 | Romans 2:12-16

Friday | JULY 10

"And thus, I aspired to preach the gospel, not where Christ was already named, so that I would not build on another's foundation | Romans 15:20

Another's Foundation

My greatest joy is leading those outside the family of faith into a saving relationship with Jesus Christ. I'm aware of the statistics that say most of the current growth in American churches today is from membership transference. And it's also a fact, for most Christians, the longer they're in the church the fewer friends they have outside the body of Christ.

Like the great apostle, I prefer to write on blank slates. I write my sermons and communicate keeping in mind those who are taking their first step. I try to never assume those listening to me have a memory of Bible stories. It's so tempting to try and impress church people with things I'm learning, but if I'm faithful to my call, my focus on these new folks will remain intact.

I know everyone doesn't share my passion, nor should they. But for me, there's no greater joy than introducing someone to Christ and helping others take up the cause. We call this part of our Next Step ministry "First Steps." It's where I find my greatest blessing. Today, will you ask God to show you someone who may be considering their first step with Christ? How can you be sensitive to those who are hearing about God for the first time? Shalom!

TODAY'S READINGS

Psalm 119:105-112 | Deuteronomy 32:1-10 | Romans 15:14-21

Saturday | JULY 11

The one who looks at me is seeing the one who sent me. | John 12:45

Knowing God

Jesus wanted all who would listen to know that absolutely everything they ever desired to know about the God of their fathers, they could learn from being with him. The person of Jesus Christ reveals all the Father has decided to disclose about himself in this life.

So, for us, if we truly desire to know God's will, the best way to figure that out is to passionately study the life of Christ. That's why you receive a Gospel lesson 365 days a year. If you are ever wondering how God feels about a certain subject, all you must do is simply read about the life of Christ. The story of his life and teachings are preserved for us as a window into the heart of the Father.

Jesus was so connected to the Father he always said and did what the Father desired. Therefore, let's be committed to studying and knowing the life and teachings of Jesus Christ. He will lead us to our own life of victory and peace. All we have to do is commit ourselves to showing up every day and pray for a clear mind and a willing heart to receive God's glorious direction. It is the greatest blessing of our lives today. How do you see the Father in the story of Christ in today's reading? Come face to face with God in his word. Shalom!

TODAY'S READINGS

Psalm 119:105-112 | Isaiah 2:1-4 | John 12:44-50

Sunday | JULY 12

Therefore, there is now no condemnation for those who are in Christ Jesus | Romans 8:1

Absolutely Everyone

Isn't this what many of us have been looking for most of our lives? Guilt about our past can haunt us. It can be almost crippling at times. But Paul says through the amazing work of Christ on the cross, our slates are wiped clean.

What an amazing truth! Our past cannot be held against us. This changes everything. What more could we ask for? This is probably the most difficult Christian concept for me to embrace. Oh sure, I understand it in my mind, but in my heart the message seems to get lost. I'm not sure if it's because guilt played such a prominent role in my early religious experience or if there's just something down deep inside me that secretly likes to feel guilty.

I remember receiving counsel from a Christian woman who really had a handle on this subject. She asked me, "How do you teach this?" I launched into a passionate explanation of how God removes our past sins as far as the east is from the west and then remembers them no more. She then asked if this teaching was for everyone who claimed the name of Christ and had repented of their sins. I said, "Absolutely everyone!" Then she said, "Well, aren't you special that this truth applies to everyone but you."

I remember being a little offended but realized through her wise counsel that continuing to beat myself up over events in my past does not honor God. It is, in fact, arrogant to think that this verse applies to the entire Universal Church, but not for me. So, like Paul said, "Forgetting what is behind us, let's press on toward the goal to win the prize for which God has called us through Christ Jesus our Lord. Today, if you've ever struggled thinking God's promises were for you, take time to repent of it and then agree with God that you are one of his saints, wholly loved and forgiven. Shalom!

TODAY'S READINGS
Psalm 119:105-112 | Genesis 25:19-34 | Matthew 13:1-9, 18-23 | Romans 8:1-11

Monday | JULY 13

I cry to you, Lord; I say, "You are my refuge… | Psalm 142:5

No Fear

God is our refuge, our help and our strength. He is the One who deals with the struggles around us. What that means is that we don't have anything to fear, no matter what life throws at us.

I was thinking about a time when a group of Jesus' followers feared for their lives in a storm. One day, they were out in a boat in the middle of a lake when Jesus stood up and calmed the wind and the sea. They asked, "Who is this? Even the wind and the waves obey him!" The God of Jacob was their refuge that day.

Our faith is being subjected to the storms of life daily. Where do we find refuge, safety and security? This psalmist says, "I cry to you, Lord; you are my refuge…" The God who created us and our world has everything under control. No matter what our circumstances, no matter how bad it is, or how afraid we are, our God is unchanging, and he is our refuge and our strength. Today, will you remember to take refuge in God? Remember that he saved us once but he rescues us daily when we ask. It delights him! Shalom!

TODAY'S READINGS

Psalm 142 | Micah 1:1-5 | 1 Thessalonians 4:1-8

Tuesday | JULY 14

and do not give the devil a foothold. | Ephesians 4:27

On Guard

This verse illustrates Paul affirming with Jesus that there's a powerful enemy who exists. We know from our studies he is powerful and he desires to destroy us and, apart from God, we are no match for him.

So, what is Paul's solution? He seems to be advocating we don't open the door even a crack for him, because if we do he'll come crashing in with full force. Paul wants us to be mindful in absolutely everything we say and do. For me, this requires a great deal of diligence. It means I'll be thoughtful to carry out my Christian responsibilities in every interaction. I will prayerfully consider my day and pray for the discipline to honor God in words and deeds.

It also means I'll be on guard every day, watching for the devil's schemes. It means when I'm wrong, I'll promptly admit it. I'll ask for forgiveness and make my amends. I'll keep a loving attitude toward everyone. I'll take every thought captive, making sure they align with Christ. And finally, it means I'll maintain a vital and disciplined life that keeps me constantly involved in prayer, worship, Bible study, meditation and weekly communion.

Let's look at our day today and ask our Lord, Where does the devil desire to trip me up? And then let us endeavor to see to it we do whatever is necessary to prevent the enemy from having his way with us. Remember the Bible says our blessing today is that "greater is he who is in you than he who is in the world." Check your attitude today. Where are you vulnerable? What area do you need to gird up with God to thwart the enemy from getting a foothold? Shalom!

TODAY'S READINGS
Psalm 142 | Jeremiah 49:7-11 | Ephesians 4:17-5:2

Wednesday | JULY 15

I cry aloud to the Lord; I lift up my voice to the Lord for mercy. | Psalm 142:1

Our Heart's Cry

God's mercies are new every morning. And, oddly enough, every day also has its own share of new troubles. What I love about this is tomorrow's mercies are for tomorrow's troubles.

It makes the verse about not being anxious about tomorrow because tomorrow will take care of itself make more sense. We tend to want to take on tomorrow's troubles today, don't we? I also love that the character of God is shown in this verse.

God is always there when we cry out to him. He forgives, he loves, he pours his mercy onto us in so many beautiful ways. His mercy is new each day. Just enough to cover our sin, our pain and our hurt. What an amazing God! He meets us right where we are every day. We can trust that and live in his blessing today. What will you lift up to him today? Will you meet him where he is for the mercy you need right now? Shalom!

TODAY'S READINGS
Psalm 142 | Obadiah 1:5-21 | Matthew 13:10-17

Thursday | JULY 16

> Search me, God, and know my heart; test me and know my anxious thoughts. | Psalm 139:23

A Heart Exam

Some days when I read our lesson from the Psalms, I can't help but think it's been written specifically for me.

This is one of those days. I needed a heart exam today. I'm tired and frustrated and feel like I'm run ragged. But I have meetings today and people in the hospital to visit and these people are expecting me to bring a word from God. So, I need God to test me and to point out my anxiety, a process that usually leads me to be frustrated and crabby.

I've been called by God to be set apart to bless the people of my community with the love of Christ. I cannot do that if I'm feeling sorry for myself. And guess what? You've received the same calling on your life if you're a follower of Jesus Christ.

So, no matter which side of the bed we got up on, or regardless of how we've acted so far today, let's begin again with a fresh start. Let's ask God to show us where our attitudes and inner thoughts have fallen short. And then, by God's grace and the love of our Savior, Jesus Christ, let's go out and declare the glory of God! Ask God to search your heart today and see if there is any way unpleasing, and ask him to set you on the path of peace again. Shalom!

TODAY'S READINGS
Psalm 139:1-12, 23-24 | Isaiah 44:1-5 | Hebrews 2:1-9

Friday | JULY 17

And so after waiting patiently, Abraham received what was promised. | Hebrews 6:15

Not So Fast

Waiting seems to be a consistent theme in the lives of God's people. Abraham waited for a son, David waited for the throne, Moses waited for the Promised Land, the people of Israel and Judah waited to return from exile, everyone waited for the coming Messiah, and of course, all of creation awaits the Lord's return.

It looks like waiting is an intricate part of Kingdom life for all who follow him. The promise we're all waiting for is the one issued by Jesus shortly before his arrest and subsequent death and resurrection. His promise? He went to prepare a place for us and some day he will come back to get us so we can spend eternity with him.

So, we are a people who are waiting for Christ's return. We demonstrate our faith in his promise by the way we faithfully live out our lives while we wait. Which means we hold on loosely to the things of this world while we consistently endeavor to take our next step with him. We wait patiently like our father Abraham, but we are busy in the process. God has laid before each of us his blessing through the wonderful works of service he leads us to pursue as we wait for his wonderful return. In what situations is waiting patiently difficult for you? What does active waiting look like for you? Shalom!

TODAY'S READINGS
Psalm 139:1-12, 23-24 | Ezekiel 39:21-29 | Hebrews 6:13-20

Saturday | JULY 18

> ...and the Israelites went through the sea on dry ground, with a wall of water on their right and on their left. | Exodus 14:22

Just Showing Off

Now God is just showing off, am I right? Not only did he part the sea, but even the ground they walked on was dry! Not even a little mud.

Most scholars believe there was at least a million Israelites who made their way through the parted water that day. That must have been a majestic sight to behold. The world's largest standing army was in hot pursuit of a ragtag bunch of unarmed and untrained slaves. There was no reason on earth for the Israelites to have any hope for their safety. But what they were about to learn was their hope would not come from anything on earth but the Lord their God. He and he alone could deliver them from certain death.

They were no match for the Egyptian army, but that army was no match for the God of the Israelites' ancestors. The battle belonged to the Lord. He would fight for them. And just to leave no doubt this miracle was by his hand, they walked through the sea on dry ground.

A lesson for us to learn here is we should always go where the Lord leads us. Even when it seems like impossible odds. We need not fear. The battle belongs to the Lord. We simply need to put one foot in front of the other, always taking our next step toward him. And with confidence, we move forward on dry ground as he displays his wonderful glory. Is there something impossible looming in front of you? Against all odds, will you move forward today with God by faith? He's big enough. Shalom!

TODAY'S READINGS
Psalm 139:1-12, 23-24 | Exodus 14:9-25 | Matthew 7:15-20

Sunday | JULY 19

When Jacob awoke from his sleep, he thought, "Surely the Lord is in this place, and I was not aware of it." | Genesis 28:16

Hanging On The Steps

God has never spoken to me in a dream like this, but I've had encounters with him where it was evident he had shown up in a big way. Sometimes it's been during a public worship service. At other times it was in private conversations with someone about God. And there have been times when I've been by myself and the experience was so incredible I knew the Lord had been in that place.

I know the Bible promises the Lord will never leave us; however, there are certain times when his presence is just more obvious to me. I thank the Lord for his Holy Spirit who engages us, and prompts us, and prods us, and promises us, much in the same way he did for Jacob.

May we be ever mindful of his glorious presence and may we wait on him with holy expectation. He knows exactly what needs to be done and he always does it with perfect timing. I can't help but wonder how many opportunities I've missed simply because I was not aware of his holy presence. I pray you will feel his blessing and today's worship experience will take you to the very gates of heaven. When was a time God showed up for you? Meditate on how that felt, the emotions you had. Remember and give thanks today. Shalom!

TODAY'S READINGS

Psalm 139:1-12, 23-24 | Genesis 28:10-19 | Matthew 13:24-30, 36-43
Romans 8:12-25

Monday | JULY 20

> For you created my inmost being; you knit me together in my mother's womb... | Psalm 139:13

No Oops

God's got this. He's not caught off guard by anything we're going through. He never panics. He has prepared all our days. He's not like us in that you'll never hear him say, "Well, in retrospect I would have done that differently." Or, "If I knew then what I know now, I never would have allowed that to happen."

He knows everything. He knew you would be in the situation you're in right now. All he desires from you is that you diligently seek his will for your circumstance and have the integrity to actually do his will.

Let's not waste a moment on worry. He's all knowing and all powerful. He has the capacity and the desire to bring whatever situation we are in to a godly conclusion, for his glory and our ultimate good. "God is working all things together for the good of those who love him and have been called according to his purposes." He's been in the process of doing this for you since the beginning of time.

He not only was working things out for your good in your mother's womb, but he was preparing for your arrival since before he said, "Let there be light." So, if you're diligently searching for his will and if you're passionately following his leading in your life, then despite how things may appear, you're right where he wants you. Is there a circumstance in your life where you're struggling to trust God? Today lay it before him and remember, he knew you'd be here. Invite him in. Shalom!

TODAY'S READINGS

Psalm 139:13-18 | Genesis 32:3-21 | Revelation 14:12-20

Tuesday | JULY 21

> How precious to me are your thoughts, God!
> How vast is the sum of them! | Psalm 139:17

Precious Thoughts

God's mind is so incredible I cannot even fathom his greatness. Think about it. For years now, or even decades, we've been in passionate pursuit of the mind of God. We struggle to know him more intimately.

Every day we read his word and he reveals to us some of his thoughts. Even though the Bible is just one book, we're convinced by now we'll never understand all he has revealed to us in Scripture. And that includes revealing his thoughts to us through his incredible natural world.

So, I was thinking this morning that he has revealed to us seemingly more than anyone could grasp, and yet how much more is there in that great mind of his that he has chosen in his infinite wisdom to keep concealed? Is it possible we may only be exposed to the tip of the iceberg regarding the mind of God?

This is why I believe the psalmist is saying, "Were I to count them, they would outnumber the grains of sand…" Therefore, go ahead, dear brother; dive in deeply, precious sister, and plumb the depths of his vast knowledge. There is plenty more where all this comes from. "How vast is the sum of them!" Indeed! Today, purposefully imagine in our mind's eye what God is able to do in your situation. This God so vast—what is he really capable of? Shalom!

TODAY'S READINGS

Psalm 139:13-18 | Genesis 33:1-17 | Galatians 4:21-5:1

Wednesday | JULY 22

In his name the nations will put their hope... | Matthew 12:21

Hope for the Nations

Some translations of this verse say nations and others say Gentiles and others say islands.

There weren't many nations who heard the actual words of Christ. As an adult he never traveled very many miles from where he was born. His greatest trip came as a small toddler when his father Joseph took him and his mother Mary to Egypt to escape the evil King Herod. Other than that, as far as we know, his travels were limited between Jerusalem and Galilee.

I can only assume, then, the nations didn't begin to put their hope in him until Paul and some of the other apostles took the greatest story ever told on the road. And now, for the past 2,000 years, great orators have proclaimed the Good News, as well as plain old people like you and me who go about our business day after day. All the while we have this driving urge to spread hope to the people of our community.

No one will ever write a book about us, but every time we find a hurting person and help them take their next step toward Jesus Christ, we are spreading hope. We're spreading the exact same hope Jesus proclaimed to the large crowd following him that day. We share in the blessed challenge of bringing hope to the nations. And that, my friend, is all the reason I need to get up in the morning. What can you do to spread hope today? Shalom!

TODAY'S READINGS
Psalm 139:13-18 | Genesis 35:16-29 | Matthew 12:15-21

Thursday | JULY 23

Look to the Lord and his strength; seek his face always. | Psalm 105:4

Strong and Gentle

This verse requires some closer observation. "Look to the Lord and his strength" is something most of us can get on board with. It's a great source of comfort to think rightly about God's strength and his ability and willingness to provide for our needs. We cry out triumphantly with the apostle Paul that "…if God is for us, who can be against us? If God is on our side, how can we be denied?" We truly are more than conquerors with Jesus Christ as our Lord!

But it's the second part of the verse that caught my eye. I would think after drawing attention to the Lord's strength the psalmist would direct us to the Lord's mighty hand. This would be the natural progression, because in Scripture God's hand often is the way his strength is described.

Here we are to focus on his face instead. When we think about God's face, we are drawn to his attributes of love, like gentleness and kindness and compassion and mercy. This verse then becomes a wonderful reminder for anyone who will pause for a moment and think about it, that our Lord is both infinitely strong and incredibly gentle. Strength and gentleness. This is exactly what we need and deep down inside have been longing for.

So, take heart, dear child of God, the Lord our God is powerful enough to fight all your battles and gentle enough to hold you close through the toughest times. What does it mean to seek his face? How will you look to the Lord today? Shalom!

TODAY'S READINGS
Psalm 105:1-11, 45 | Genesis 29:1-8 | 1 Corinthians 4:14-20

Friday | JULY 24

> He remembers his covenant forever, the promise he made,
> for a thousand generations... | Psalm 105:8

Promise Keeper

Have you ever had someone you love break a promise? When that happens it really hurts, especially if it's someone you really love and trust. It's easy to wonder if you can ever trust them again.

Can the relationship be repaired? Anyone can make a promise, but let's be honest—how many of us have actually kept every promise we've ever made in our lifetime? A promise only has real value if it holds hands with commitment, faithfulness and perseverance. Broken promises hurt. They have the potential to sever relationships, bring heartache, and wound deeply.

In this tough world we live in, struggles and heartache are inevitable, and they can leave us wondering, who can we trust? Is there anyone out there who actually keeps a promise? The answer is a very resounding YES and we find proof in our verse today.

God makes promises and he loves us enough to keep his promises. God is worthy of our trust. We can count on him. He has already kept his greatest promise by sending his Son Jesus to die on our behalf so we can have eternal life through him. God will do what he says he will do. Have you ever broken a promise? Think about how it felt, and consider the kind of promises that God keeps to us today. Shalom!

TODAY'S READINGS
Psalm 105:1-11, 45 | Genesis 29:9-14. | Acts 7:44-53

Saturday | JULY 25

> Then God remembered Rachel; he listened to her and enabled her to conceive. | Genesis 30:22

Hurry Up

Think about all the dysfunction Rachel could truly have saved her family if she had just waited patiently for the Lord's perfect timing!

I can really empathize with Rachel. I sometimes grow impatient waiting on God. To be brutally honest, he is at times simply too slow for my liking. I know that sounds harsh and maybe I should not say it out loud, but I tend to be like Rachel and grow frustrated waiting on God.

Ah, but in the end, it is obvious God had planned on giving Rachel a child. She was just too impatient to wait on God's timing. So, this story reminds me God's timing is always perfect. He is never too late or too early. He will provide for us exactly what we need, exactly when we need it. We are simply to wait with quiet confidence on the Lord's perfect timing.

Think what an incredible blessing Rachel could have been for everyone around her. She could have responded to her lot in life with quiet confidence and said, "The Lord gives and the Lord takes away. I will wait patiently on the Lord's perfect timing."

What area in your life is God slow in responding to? Today is a great opportunity for you to draw attention to the glory of God as you wait patiently on the blessing of his perfect timing. Shalom!

TODAY'S READINGS

Psalm 105:1-11, 45 | Genesis 29:31-30:24 | Matthew 12:38-42

Sunday | JULY 26

> And we know that in all things God works for the good of those who love him, who have been called according to his purpose. | Romans 8:28

In All Things

The grammar in this verse has caused a great deal of debate over the years. It is not clear in the original language if it should be translated, "All things worked together for good" or "God works all things for the good."

It may seem like a minor difference, but it's really quite significant if I understand it correctly. For some Christians, the discrepancy led to the interpretation that God is promising all things that happen are ultimately good, in spite of how it feels. But try telling someone who is burying their baby that it's a good thing. This interpretation ultimately leads to people desperately looking for the proverbial silver lining.

Whereas in the other interpretation, it is recognized that bad things happen to people. And that even the most faithful Christian will experience loss and can suffer greatly. But amid our pain and suffering, we take solace in the fact we know God is in the middle of our suffering, working for our ultimate good. My study and experience have led me to believe the latter is the correct interpretation. When you think on this Scripture today, what interpretation do you agree with and why? Shalom!

TODAY'S READINGS

Psalm 105:1-11, 45 | Genesis 29:15-28 | Matthew 13:31-33, 44-52
Romans 8:26-39

Monday | JULY 27

"Who among you is wise and understanding? Let him show it by his good behavior, his deeds in the gentleness of wisdom." | James 3:13

Gentle Wisdom

I was just thinking about the saying that "violence is a tool of the ignorant."

I lived through the turbulent '60s as a child. Perhaps at no other time in my life did I feel angst and concern like I do today about the prevalence of violence in action and speech. My nightly TV is absorbed in unthinkable acts of violence as well as hateful speech.

What a wonderful opportunity for the church to glow like a shining city on a hill. If there was ever a time in our collective history that godly wisdom was needed, it's now. I'm very apolitical, so my passion is neither to advocate for nor be critical of either national party. My passion is to lead our flock in the discipline of passionately pursuing the Father's will for our little American experiment.

I believe James is advocating that as Christ's followers we have the task of manifesting the solution to our current crisis with "the gentleness of wisdom." That means the proof of true godly wisdom cannot be found in the most powerful voice, nor in any attempts to wrestle that power away through violent actions and rhetoric. No, God's wisdom will be revealed only through the church's commitment to our gentle response.

So, let's not give in to the enemy's ploy to incite us to violence on either the left or the right. The church, by God's perfect design, is "the light of the world." May we experience the blessing of his transcendent peace today through our commitment to his "gentle wisdom." Today, think how you might bring a strong, gentle and godly wisdom to your sphere of influence where there is only strife. Shalom!

TODAY'S READINGS
Psalm 65:8-13 | Genesis 30:25-36 | James 3:13-18

Tuesday | JULY 28

> "…and after you have done everything, to stand.
> Stand firm then…" | Ephesians 6:13b-14a

One More Turn

This passage always gets me fired up. I love to read verses 13 and 14 together. It's like Paul is saying, "You keep standing until you have stood as long as you possibly can. Then after you have endured to the point where it seems impossible to continue standing, you stand some more!"

I remember when I was a first-year apprentice pipefitter and we were running 3-inch and 4-inch threaded pipe. The wrenches we used were 48 inches long. So as I began to tighten my first joint, I turned to the journeyman I was working with and asked him, "How tight do I need to get it?"

He smiled and said, "Son, you get it as tight as you possibly can and then take it one more turn." That's what Paul is saying to us today. We go as long as we can, as hard as we can, to faithfully serve our Lord. And then when it feels like we can't go any longer and we feel like giving up, that's when we commit ourselves to keep on taking our next step.

Remember that Paul is not calling us here to be fabulous or famous or even successful. Our call is to simply stand firm and be faithful. May God richly bless you today as you take it one more round. What would this look like in your life, to keep standing even after you've fought the long, hard battle? How does this verse help you today? Shalom!

TODAY'S READINGS
Psalm 65:8-13 | Genesis 30:37-43 | Ephesians 6:10-18

Wednesday | JULY 29

Again he said, "What shall we say the kingdom of God is like, or what parable shall we use to describe it? It is like a mustard seed, which is the smallest of all seeds on earth. Yet when planted, it grows and becomes the largest of all garden plants, with such big branches that the birds can perch in its shade." With many similar parables Jesus spoke the word to them, as much as they could understand. | Mark 4:30-33

A Mustard Seed of Faith

I was just thinking about the parables Jesus told. I love how he used familiar things to help his listeners understand what he wanted them to know.

In this parable, he's helping them appreciate what heaven is like. He said it's like a tiny mustard seed. When the seed is scattered it grows into a plant that's the largest in the garden. How this growth happens for us is complex. It starts with one person of faith–and it grows and spreads.

It starts with someone just like you and me who may not possess greatness but believes in the sacrifice Jesus made for our sins, and the forgiveness and freedom this belief causes in our lives. We influence our families and friends by the peace and joy we display in our own lives. It changes the atmosphere of our homes and where we work. Impatience, criticism and selfishness begin to melt away. Friends, neighbors and co-workers start to notice. And before you know it, this small mustard seed of belief and faith has turned into a large plant and we've spread the joy of Jesus to so many.

It doesn't take much because God does all the work. We don't even have to understand how it works; we just need to surrender our lives to him. How will you use your mustard seed of faith today? Just one small step is all it takes. Shalom!

TODAY'S READINGS
Psalm 65:8-13 | Genesis 46:2-37:12 | Mark 4:30-34

Thursday | JULY 30

"I can do all things through him who gives me strength. | Philippians 4:13

His Strength

This is a well-known and often-quoted verse. It's usually used standing alone, apart from its context. Paul, of course, is speaking here about being content in want or plenty. He's learned the hard way he can endure the most difficult experiences empowered by the strength of God. Notice how Paul doesn't claim any special ability or trait of his own. No, it is God's strength that enables him to endure during tough times.

This verse gave me pause today, because there is a lesson here for me to learn and to embrace. Paul said he had learned the secret, so this means to me, this way of thinking wasn't as simple as "pulling yourself up by your bootstraps" or "when the going gets tough, the tough get going," or "no pain, no gain." No, what the old apostle means here is something supernatural. It's a strength only God provides. It's a power no one can develop on their own or learn through positive thinking.

It is, plain and simple, a free gift from a God who gives graciously without reserve, and it is given only to those who are in passionate pursuit of him. Let's follow Paul's lead and be blessed by God today as we once again take our next step toward the One who will be with us in plenty and in want. What do you need his supernatural strength to do today? Shalom!

TODAY'S READINGS
Psalm 17:1-7,15 | Isaiah 14:1-2 | Philippians 4:10-15

Friday | JULY 31

In other words, it is not the children by physical descent who are God's children, but it is the children of the promise who are Abraham's offspring." | Romans 9:8

Children of The Promise

We are "Abraham's offspring," the "children of the promise." Think about that. Quite simply, it's the most important fact about your life. When God called Abraham, this single solitary figure from obscurity, to be the father of his people, he entered into an eternal relationship with a select group of people, of which you are included.

This makes me want to dance in the bright sunlight this morning. I thank God for graciously including me in the promise. My heart is full of joy.

As we navigate through the joys and struggles of this life, we're reminded to closely observe our spiritual relatives who have gone before us. We diligently look at Scripture and the children of the promise, on whose shoulders we stand. When we do, their struggles become our struggles, and we share in their victories as well. And now the children of the promise who proceeded you are cheering you on, step by step.

So, take heart Christian; you are not alone. Someday, hopefully soon, we will join all our spiritual siblings and together we will glory in the presence of our heavenly Father. Meditate today on what this means to be God's child and the promises that go along with this inheritance. Shalom!

TODAY'S READINGS

Psalm 17:1-7,15 | Isaiah 41:8-10 | Romans 9:6-13

Saturday | AUGUST 1

"Ask and it will be given to you; seek and you will find; knock and the door will be opened to you." | Matthew 7:7

Knock, Knock

How I love the idea of knocking on God's door! Our Jesus desires that we long for him and him only. But it makes me think how it can be hard to knock when we're sad or hurting. It requires admitting we need him.

Sometimes we don't even know what we're asking for, let alone know how to knock. Our heavenly Father will only do what's best for us. Maybe you've been hurt or disappointed by your earthly father. And maybe that has clouded your vision for your heavenly Father. But, you need to know the truth is this: your heavenly Father cannot love you any more than he does right now.

He knows every hurt you have ever felt. He understands you completely. Go ahead, give the door a knock and fall into his loving arms. He is ready to embrace you and love you perfectly. Today, enter in to the secret place with him and tell him all your cares and let him minister to you. Shalom!

TODAY'S READINGS

Psalm 17:1-7,15 | Genesis 31:1-21 | Matthew 7:7-11

Sunday | AUGUST 2

"For I could wish that I myself were cursed and cut off from Christ for the sake of my people, those of my own race." | Romans 9:3

Sell Out

Paul had once said, "For me to live is Christ and to die is gain." Now here in his epic letter to the church in Rome, he shares that he would sacrifice his very soul if it could bring about the salvation of his fellow Israelites. His testimony reaffirms his statement that he had "…become all things to all men that I might win some."

For Paul, like Christ, everything was about helping people take their next step with Jesus in the Kingdom of God. They weren't playing at church. They didn't wake up one morning and think about paying tribute to God. They were obsessed with the advancement of God's Kingdom.

I remember a woman telling me, after coming to church for a couple of years, that she used to think it was important for Jesus to be a part of her life, but now she had learned that Jesus *is* her life.

So, let us ask the Lord to do absolutely anything in our hearts necessary for us to be completely sold out to God. May our lives be consumed with the task, each and every day, of helping everyone take their next step toward Jesus Christ. And finally, let us not even consider the cost to us for accomplishing this amazing mission as we trust in God's blessing for the salvation to come. Will you lay out your heart to God today to let him do whatever it takes to be all in for Jesus? Shalom!

TODAY'S READINGS
Genesis 32:22-31 | Matthew 14:13-21 | Romans 9:1-5

Monday | AUGUST 3

> "I am obligated both to the Greeks and the non-Greeks, both to the wise and the simple." | Romans 1:14

Our Debt

This verse reminds me of a pastor I served with in a previous church.

My passion for ministry has always focused on the poor and the hurting and the disenfranchised. I continue to see them as my mission field, ripe for the harvest. But one day this pastor friend pulled me aside and said, "You know that rich people need Jesus too, right?"

Evidently I'd been so laser-focused on one group of people, I had begun to disregard another. I believe one of the things Paul is driving at here is that he knew everyone needs Jesus. So, this is a good reminder for me to try always to be "all things to all men so that I might win some," as Paul is famous for saying.

Know that Jesus isn't always going to bring us people who are like us, or even people who like us. But we have the wonderful blessing and awe-filled responsibility to help every man, woman, and child we encounter to take their next step toward Christ. Everyone, without exception, needs Jesus. Who might you be overlooking in your sphere of influence because they don't look like they need help? How can you better see people from God's point of view? Shalom!

TODAY'S READINGS
Psalm 17:1-7,15 | Genesis 31:22-42 | Romans 1:8-15

Tuesday | AUGUST 4

> They devoted themselves to the apostles' teaching and to fellowship,
> to the breaking of bread and to prayer. | Acts 2:42

Clingy Christians

This is a marvelous verse any time we are unsure of our "next step."

Digging deeper, this word translated "devoted" also can mean "to tenaciously cling to." I love this interpretation because it emphasizes an uncompromising laser-focus on their lifeline, committing themselves to these four disciplines in the Lord.

First, these early believers literally had the sound of the apostles' voices washing over them. Nowadays, we have the teaching known as the New Testament. Second, they "tenaciously clung" to each other, fellowshipping daily as folks from each neighborhood would share their evening meal together. Third, they were absolutely committed to the remembrance of the Lord through the Eucharist. And finally, they prayed without ceasing.

So, if you're struggling with your next step, first ask yourself, Am I tenaciously clinging to these four pillars of the faith? If the answer is no, them immediately seek godly counsel to make sure your next step is taking you closer to the risen Savior. Shalom!

TODAY'S READINGS
Psalm 17:1-7,15 | Genesis 32:3-21 | Acts 2:37-47

Wednesday | AUGUST 5

> "How many loaves do you have?" Jesus asked. "Seven," they replied, "and a few small fish." | Matthew 15:34

Multiplication Theory

Isn't it interesting that the first thing Jesus asked them was to use what they already had? On the surface, it's easy to wonder why he would concern himself with that paltry amount of food when he needed a massive amount of bread and fish. But if we allow ourselves to go deeper for a moment, it's obvious Jesus intended the disciples to first use everything they had, regardless of the amount.

Why? Why not just provide all the bread and fish in this wonderful miracle? That would have been a couple of semi-loads of food. It's obvious Jesus didn't need the meager amount they had to begin this great feast. Matthew doesn't make clear to us why Jesus asked for what they had on hand. We're left to speculate.

I believe it's significant there are not two separate groupings of food here. We never see the seven loaves and the two fish in one pile alongside the semi-loads of supplies Jesus prayed for in another pile next to it. No, we start only with the seven loaves and two fish Jesus prayed over. And it was upon that meager beginning offered to Jesus that he just kept building. I can't help but think, if we will just show up with whatever God has graciously given us, if we offer it wholly and completely to Jesus, then he'll take our meager offering and do with it immeasurably more than we could ever ask or hope for.

The disciples put limits on what Jesus could do with the little that they had. Will we? What can you bring to Jesus today, no matter how meager? And watch what he will do with it! Shalom!

TODAY'S READINGS
Psalm 17:1-7,15 | Isaiah 43:1-7 | Matthew 15:32-39

Thursday | AUGUST 6

Now the Berean Jews were of more noble character than those in Thessalonica, for they received the message with great eagerness and examined the Scriptures every day to see if what Paul said was true. | Acts 17:11

Noble Character

I've always been fascinated by this verse and by the Bereans. Here they are held in high esteem because they refused to simply accept Paul's unique teaching without first holding it up to the light of the Hebrew Scriptures.

This verse can be a great encouragement to examine closely everything we're being taught. Let's not assume that just because a pastor said it, or it was spoken by someone who had his or her own TV show, or it was on the internet, we should accept it as truth. Let's be of more noble character and let's examine the Scriptures to see if what is being taught is consistent with the teachings of the people of God.

It is our honor and our distinct responsibility to be good students of the word of God. Wherever we find ourselves on our journey of faith we can and should take our next step each day to know and love his word all the more. How can you go a little deeper today in your study of God's word? Where is God leading you to plumb the depths of his word? Shalom!

TODAY'S READINGS
Psalm 105:1-6, 16-22, 45 | Genesis 35:22-29 | Acts 17:10-15

Friday | AUGUST 7

For he vigorously refuted his Jewish opponents in public debate, proving from the Scriptures that Jesus was the Messiah. | Acts 18:28

Proof of The Promise

Here again we see how much emphasis Luke, the author of Acts, placed on the connection between Jesus the Messiah and the consistent theme of the Old Testament.

From the opening pages of Genesis, we see God pointing to the arrival of his Son, Jesus Christ. No person in all human history has been more accurately and extensively predicted. The message of the Hebrew Scriptures prepared the world for the coming of the Savior. And now, for those of us who live on this side of the cross, we have the opportunity and awesome responsibility of joining our brother Apollos to show anyone who is willing to listen.

Jesus Christ is the One who Scripture promised. Think about this: He is the gift humanity waited for generation upon generation. So, let's not get so wrapped up in our daily tasks that we neglect to take time to appreciate the glorious truth we live in. Jesus Christ is God with us. Today, what next step can you take to present the Gospel to a waiting world? Shalom!

TODAY'S READINGS
Psalm 105:1-6, 16-22, 45 | Genesis 36:1-8 | Acts 18:24-28

Saturday | AUGUST 8

A wicked and adulterous generation looks for a sign, but none will be given it except the sign of Jonah." Jesus then left them and went away. | Matthew 16:4

The Main Thing

I was just thinking about what Jesus knew and when he knew it.

We're told through Scripture that as a boy Jesus grew in stature and wisdom. But when was he aware of his looming crucifixion? He certainly knew of it here in this dialogue with the religious leaders. It seems he grew short and almost dismissive with them by this point in his ministry.

It must have been unbelievably mentally oppressive for him to carry this burden hour by hour as that fateful day grew closer. Yet through it all he continued to stay on task and follow perfectly the will of his Father. Nothing, absolutely nothing, could sway his focus from the Father's will.

What are we to do with these amazing truths? Well, we can redouble our efforts to stay on our God-designed spiritual path. Let's give ourselves wholly and completely to knowing and doing the will of God. Let's follow Jesus' example and not let the trials and tribulations we encounter prevent us from pursuing our goal. He is our prime and perfect example. Let's draw strength from his life and passion from his death and unending joy from his glorious Resurrection. Today, purpose in your heart to know your Father's will and draw strength from his example to obey, no matter what circumstances you face. Shalom!

TODAY'S READINGS
Psalm 105:1-6, 16-22, 45 | Genesis 37:5-11 | Matthew 16:1-4

Sunday | AUGUST 9

> But Jesus immediately said to them: "Take courage! It is I.
> Don't be afraid." | Matthew 14:27

Storm Prep

"Don't be afraid" is a reoccurring command from Jesus to his first disciples. It was like he kept saying, "There's a great lesson for you to learn here, but you'll never learn it if you're overcome with fear."

Peter would have never mastered the courage to walk on the stormy sea and the disciples would have never witnessed that great event if they had their heads buried, cowering in fear. No, Jesus calmed them enough to teach them a lesson that would embolden them for the rest of their lives. These are the men who would spend much of the remainder of their lives in the midst of the storm. Most of the time Jesus chose not to calm the storm raging around them; rather, he chose simply to comfort them with his powerful presence.

What does this have to do with us? Well, we seem to spend a great deal of our time in prayer asking God to calm the storm. Maybe we should be asking him to calm our fears and remind us of Christ's presence in the storm. Then we fix our eyes on Jesus, the author and perfecter of our faith. We need to train ourselves to not be afraid in the midst of the storm so we can glorify God, for the furthering of his Kingdom and for our greater good. What storm is raging in your life today? How can you shift your attention to the Calmer of the storm? Shalom!

TODAY'S READINGS
Psalm 105:1-6, 16-22, 45 | Genesis 37:1-4, 12-18 | Matthew 14:22-33
Romans 10:5-15

Monday | AUGUST 10

The Lord is my strength and my shield; my heart trusts in him, and he helps me. My heart leaps for joy, and with my song I praise him. | Psalm 28:7

Cardiac Care

Funny how one minute I can be calm and happy and the next minute someone walks into my office upset with me about something, and my heart skips from its happy place and lands right in a place of stress. Other days I'm feeling great joy and a friend calls upset and sad over a marriage that's crumbling, and my heart is afraid for her future.

Then, I'm feeling settled and I hear of a friend with brain tumors who dies a couple months later. Sometimes receiving news like this can leave our hearts in tatters. A tattered heart can overtake our emotions and leave us struggling to carry out all we're called to do each day. Try as we might, it's so hard to focus. Our minds wander and our hearts are afraid. Is there a remedy for our tattered hearts? Or are we destined to live on this teetertotter of emotions swinging back and forth, from happy to sad, which threaten to undermine our peace?

Today's verse holds the answer for us: "The Lord is my strength and my shield; my heart trusts in him, and he helps me. My heart leaps for joy, and with my song I praise him." When it feels like our hearts can't take any more, we need to surrender them to God. He is our strength. He is our shield. He brings harmony and balance. What are you worried about today? Will you step into the presence of your savior and allow him to steady you? Shalom!

TODAY'S READINGS
Psalm 28 | Genesis 37:29-36 | 2 Peter 2:4-10

Tuesday | AUGUST 11

> the Lord was with him; he showed him kindness and granted him favor in the eyes of the prison warden. | Genesis 39:21

Persistent Presence

How many of us, after having been sold into slavery by our brothers, would feel like the Lord was with us? What a great story and life lesson for all of us! Joseph was on a rollercoaster ride. His lot in life went from spoiled rich kid to tragedy to hope and back again to tragedy.

Yet in all he did, whatever he put his hand to, the Bible says the Lord was with Joseph. He could have withdrawn and sulked when he was placed in prison. He could have given up and served out the rest of his days as an angry, bitter man. But evidently, he kept getting up every morning and putting his hand to whatever God put before him.

God was with him—every moment of every day, in good times and bad. God never left Joseph's side, from that horrible day when he was beaten and abandoned by his brothers until he eventually became the leader of the most powerful nation on earth.

What does this have to do with us? I believe God will have us know, he is with each of us as well. We are just like Joseph in his eyes. We should get up every day and faithfully put our hand to the task before us. Then we can stand back and see what God will do for his glory and our good. What has God tasked you with today? How can you pull strength from Joseph's diligence? Shalom!

TODAY'S READINGS

Psalm 28 | Genesis 39:1-23 | Romans 9:14-29

Wednesday | AUGUST 12

Suddenly a furious storm came up on the lake, so that the waves swept over the boat. But Jesus was sleeping. | Matthew 8:2

Uncommon Peace

I wonder if Jesus was sleeping because he was dog-tired. I mean, he really did keep a packed schedule. I could see how he could have worked himself to the point of pure and utter exhaustion. Or was he sleeping because he simply didn't fear the situations that would scare the daylights out of most people.

The Sea of Galilee was known for its sudden hurricane-like storms caused by violent winds. These storms were certainly capable of sinking a small boat like the one they were in. At least four of the men with Jesus were seasoned fishermen who were used to being out on the unpredictable sea. Yet they were frightened for their life. And through it all Jesus was sound asleep.

When they woke him, he scolded them for their lack of faith. Did he mean they shouldn't have been frightened because no harm would come to them? I don't think so, because it wouldn't be much further in the future when all of them, except John, would die for their faith.

No, I think Jesus meant for them not to be afraid when they faced death. He knew even death couldn't separate them from the love of God. And so it is with you, precious child of God. Examine how strong your faith is today. Are you at peace with such things? Shalom!

TODAY'S READINGS
Psalm 28 | Genesis 40:1-23 | Matthew 8:23-27

Thursday | AUGUST 13

How good and pleasant it is when God's people live together in unity! | Psalm 133:1

Perfect Harmony

This appears fairly straightforward. God wants all his children to be in unity.

Perhaps the best way to describe unity is to think of musical harmony. It is an interesting and, yes, even at times fascinating experience to play an instrument in a large band or orchestra. When it's done well, it's a very pleasing sound. But the curious thing is, for the sound to come together to make beautiful music, some of the instruments are quite often playing different notes. When you hear each part played separately you can't even tell they belong together. But when the conductor raises his baton and the band begins to play in unity, together they produce a beautiful sound.

Hey, that's the way it is in our lives as fellow Christians. Are we all playing the same note? No, but if we are living together in godly harmony, then we are music to the ears of our Great Conductor. So, let's remember that today as we strive to glorify God in this great Christian experience we call life. Nothing could be more pleasant to the ears of God than to hear our lives being played out together in perfect harmony. Where or with whom in your life do you need to work on harmony? Shalom!

TODAY'S READINGS
Psalm 133 | Genesis 41:14-36 | Revelation 15:1-4

Friday | AUGUST 14

…They stoned Paul and dragged him outside the city, thinking he was dead. But after the disciples had gathered around him, he got up and went back into the city… | Acts 14:19b-20a

By Divine Design

I thank God for the apostle Paul and for the example he set for us. Absolutely nothing, outside of the will of God, would prevent him from helping others to take their next step toward Christ. Paul gave his life to advance the Kingdom of God.

God has called each of us to service for the Kingdom as well. Paul served God beyond anything he could ever have imagined possible. The truth is we were all put here on earth to serve. We weren't just created to take up space—God designed us to make a difference.

I love the verses in Psalm 139 that describe how God knew us before we were even in our mother's womb. He created us for a purpose. Most think this is just for pastors or priests or missionaries, but God says every member of his family is designed for ministry. Once you have chosen to live for God and honor him with your life, he uses you for his Kingdom. Do you know what God is calling you to? Ask him for a clear vision today and purpose to go in that direction. Shalom!

TODAY'S READINGS
Psalm 133 | Genesis 41:37-57 | Acts 14:19-28

Saturday | AUGUST 15

> When Jacob learned that there was grain in Egypt, he said to his sons, "Why do you just keep looking at each other?" | Genesis 42:1-28

Do Something

My dear dad, who I love and has now passed, used to tell his sons when something needed to be done, "Do something even if it's wrong!"

Jacob knew the Lord would not have them just sit around and starve to death. Why would they purposely choose to allow their families to perish when the answer was right there in front of their noses? So it is with us. I've noticed oftentimes when we're struggling to know the will of God in our lives, he has given us an obvious answer. So obvious, in fact, that we just need to embrace it and step out in faith and simply do. As we say in AA, "What is the next right responsible thing?"

Try it the next time you have a decision to make. Ask yourself, "Is there a next right thing here that needs to be done?" Then put your hand and heart to the task of doing it. Stop waiting for the answer God has already provided you. Do something. God has promised to go with you every step of the way. What is your next right responsible thing to do? Don't delay—go do it! Shalom!

TODAY'S READINGS
Psalm 133 | Genesis 42:1-28 | Matthew 14:34-36

Sunday | AUGUST 16

Then the disciples came to him and asked, "Do you know that the Pharisees were offended when they heard this?" | Matthew 15:12

Christ's Comfort

Jesus came to comfort the afflicted and to afflict the comfortable. He would not do well in most American churches today.

It's so easy to focus our ministries on the middle class because if they come and participate, they may contribute substantially of their time, talents and treasures. I'm convinced most of our churches are busy tallying up the wrong stuff. As long as church attendance continues to rise, they assume they're doing God's best and so they celebrate it. They're careful not to offend the "church people," both their own and the folks who come from other churches. And much of what they teach is behavior modification.

People are obsessed with knowing and living out the church rules with detailed precision. That's how the religious leadership was in Jesus' day. They faithfully kept the letter of their laws and they condemned those who didn't. Jesus was not gentle and patient with these revered church leaders. He called them "blind guides." Nothing could have been more offensive. And because they hated Jesus for his message, they killed the One who comforted the afflicted but afflicted the comfortable. Think about it. Won't you? Is there something in Jesus' message that offends your heart? What truth might he want you to see? Shalom!

TODAY'S READINGS
Psalm 133 | Genesis 45:1-15 | Matthew 15:10-28 | Romans 11:1-2, 29-32

Monday | AUGUST 17

Out of the depths I cry to you, Lord; | Psalm 130:1

Cry Out

Sometimes we have no answers. All we can do is cry out to Jesus and ask for help!

We don't know what he knows. We can't see to the end. It can feel like everything is lost, and so in desperation we cry out to God and ask for help. But, I'm wondering, why does it take desperation to cry out to him and ask for help?

Why aren't we starting each day by crying out to him, asking him to help us realize he's in our world, our homes, our lives, our hearts? The picture of Jesus standing at the door of our hearts and knocking wasn't written to the lost, but to the saved who had taken their walk with God for granted. So, let's not wait till desperation sets in to cry out to him. Today, whether you're happy or sad or struggling or at peace, begin to cry out to him and invite his help. Shalom!

TODAY'S READINGS

Psalm 130 | Genesis 43:1-34 | Acts 15:1-21

Tuesday | AUGUST 18

But with you there is forgiveness, so that we can, with reverence, serve you. | Psalm 130:4

Beautiful Forgiveness

Allow these words of a fellow servant of Christ to wash over you today. Forgiveness might be the most beautiful word in Scripture. I love it because it cancels out the word sin. The word forgiveness describes everything about God, his wisdom, his power, his holiness, his justice, his goodness, and of course his truth.

It shines light into darkness. Forgiveness is the thread that connects everything in Scripture. How many Bible stories are there where forgiveness is the theme? Joseph, torn from family and friends, cast into slavery, accused of a crime he didn't commit. And then, God stepped in in a mighty way.

Reconciliation brought Joseph and his brothers back together—repentance on their part, forgiveness on Joseph's. And the dying thief on the cross as he said, "Remember me," and Jesus' response of forgiveness.

No wonder we love this word! It releases us of our sin and God's grace covers us. There was a cost for this word and the cost was death—Jesus' death on a cross. We have been set free. Yay, God!! Today can you trust the Lord to forgive you? Is there anything you've held back from him in self-pity or condemnation? Allow his forgiveness in today. Shalom!

TODAY'S READINGS
Psalm 130 | Genesis 44:1-34 | Romans 11:13-29

Wednesday | AUGUST 19

A man with leprosy came and knelt before him and said, "Lord, if you are willing, you can make me clean." Jesus reached out his hand and touched the man. "I am willing," he said. "Be clean!" Immediately he was cleansed of his leprosy. | Matthew 8:2-3

He Is Willing

Jesus has just finished his sermon on the Mount. He's coming down the mountain and a leper reaches out to him for help. The man says, "If you are willing, you can make me clean." He clearly trusts Jesus can do this. But he doesn't presume Jesus *will* do it. So, after he offers this humble expression of need and trust, Jesus responds, "I am willing, be clean."

It's interesting this man is a leper, which means he was a social outcast. Lepers were typically the kind of people you'd avoid at all costs. Jesus didn't care about that. He cared about his heart and his faith.

That should cause us to think about the value we place on our owned troubled lives and others as well. I love this lesson for us in finding the hurting and helping them. Who does this message make you think of in your life today? Or perhaps you are the leper in the story and you need to know, Jesus is willing. Just ask. Shalom!

TODAY'S READINGS
Psalm 130 | Genesis 45:16-28 | Matthew 8:1-13

Thursday | AUGUST 20

…if the Lord had not been on our side when people attacked us… | Psalm 124:2

Our Help

For King David, his God was not just one of many possible solutions. No, God was the *only* solution. It served David and the ancient people of Israel well to remember as they returned to Jerusalem for worship that their fate rested solely in the hands of the sovereign God of the universe. A God who had intervened on their behalf in the past. The one true God, who refused to let his people go down in defeat.

The great news for us in the church today is we serve and are protected by this same all-powerful God. Sometimes in this busy, chaotic world it can seem as though we've been set adrift on a sea of uncertainty.

That's why this psalm is so important. We should keep it fresh on our tongues. I read it every day during my noon prayers. It reinvigorates me as it reminds me God's people have often been under attack. But he is a good and faithful God. Just when it seems everything is hopeless, don't be surprised when he intervenes. Sometimes, I think he waits until all other avenues of rescue have proved unsuccessful. Then he comes to save the day!

So, don't give up, pilgrim. The God we serve specializes in miracles. Be blessed today by the fact there is no obstacle too great for him to outmaneuver. "Our help is in the name of the Lord, the maker of heaven and earth." Are you feeling under attack either in life's circumstances or emotionally? Today turn your ear toward him who is at your side to deliver you from all your sorrows. Shalom!

TODAY'S READINGS

Psalm 124 | Genesis 49:1-33 | 1 Corinthians 6:1-11

Friday | AUGUST 21

But, "Let the one who boasts boast in the Lord." | 2 Corinthians 10:17

Don't Brag

This is a good rule for me to live by. When I pause to think about it, my accomplishments aren't that great anyway. I think all my boasting is just a desperate attempt to cover up some of my insecurities. And I don't think Paul is condoning the current practice of so many in ministry who brag on and on about how well they've performed and then tack on a "to God be the glory" at the end.

I think Paul is mindful of how, when Jesus was confronted, he did not run through a very impressive and exhaustive list of supernatural works he had done. No, the Bible says he simply entrusted himself to the One who judges justly (the Father) and refused to boast about his deeds.

If Paul and Jesus saw no need to boast, then I'm thinking this is a pretty good route to follow. The truth is, it comes natural for me to be quick to take the credit, even if in secret, and to be very slow to take the blame. I believe I'm ready and willing to take my next step in this area.

Please pray for me. Pray I'll be mindful of the temptation to boast in the victories. And pray God will continue to humble my heart so I can be at peace knowing I've entrusted myself to the One who judges justly. Can you think of anything you are insecure or arrogant about today? Can you sacrifice that confession to the Lord and receive his grace and give him the glory? Shalom!

TODAY'S READINGS
Psalm 124 | Genesis 49:29-50:14 | 2 Corinthians 10:12-18

Saturday | AUGUST 22

You intended to harm me, but God intended it for good to accomplish what is now being done, the saving of many lives. | Genesis 50:20

Good and Evil

This ties in nicely with Paul's letter to the Romans. Especially when Paul said God was working all things together for the good of those who love him and have been called to his purpose.

Joseph's brothers had evil intent in their hearts when they callously sold him to the Ishmaelites. And all that evil lies squarely at their collective feet. God had no hand in it. God does not partner with evil. But once the dirty deed was done, the God of Joseph's fathers began to put into play a complex series of events to enable this Hebrew slave to become one of the most powerful men on earth. And Joseph used this God-given power to bring glory to God and good to God's people.

Now, the interesting thing about all this is that Joseph had to wait decades to see God's plan unfold. All those years he must have struggled with abandonment issues and seething resentment and incredible hurt for what his brothers had done to him. However, Joseph kept his eyes to the Lord and doing his will. Whether he found himself as a servant or a prisoner or the ruler of Egypt, there was always a choice for him to make, a step to take toward God. And Joseph was faithful to do it.

So it is with each of us. We've all experienced evil at the hands of others. What do you say that today we simply trust what they meant for evil, God is using for good. And then we search the will of God for our lives and take a step toward him for God's glory and our blessing. What situations where you faced evil in your life can you rise above today to see God's hand leading you to victory? Shalom!

TODAY'S READINGS

Psalm 124 | Genesis 50:15-26 | Matthew 16:5-12

Sunday | AUGUST 23

Pharaoh's daughter said to her, "Take this baby and nurse him for me, and I will pay you." So the woman took the baby and nursed him. | Exodus 2:9

Tragic Blessing

I rarely know what God is up to, but I always know whatever it is, it's good and gracious and great.

This is a great example of God's goodness and greatness, graciously working behind the scenes. It's a tragic and horrible time for the people of God. Many of us know their story, but let's slow down and notice the details as if we were hearing them for the first time. Every family who received a baby boy from God was seeing their precious child drowned at birth. It's estimated there were over a million Israelite slaves who Moses would lead to the Promised Land.

We're talking about thousands of babies being killed. Yet out of this tragedy, God decides to intervene and save one little boy. When he does, he not only places the boy to be raised in the home of the very man who was responsible for the slaughtering of the innocent, but God also saw to it Moses' own mother would be hired to nurse her baby boy.

That's right, Pharaoh's daughter would actually pay her to do so. Moses would be raised in the finest household in the land, educated like no other. He would have been taught the skills of leadership. These would prove to serve him well 80 years later, as he would lead the people of God in war against the very palace where he was raised. Talk about someone working behind the scenes in a great and glorious way for the good of God and his people! It may appear to you God is not active in your situation today. Don't sell him short. You can trust he is working behind the scene, in ways that for now remain unseen.

Today, trust that God is working in your life, transforming you even in situations that appear to be unchanging. Agree with him and thank him! Shalom!

TODAY'S READINGS
Psalm 124 | Exodus 1:8–2:10 | Matthew 16:13-20 | Romans 12:1-8

Monday | AUGUST 24

Lord, our Lord, how majestic is your name in all the earth!
You have set your glory in the heavens. | Psalm 8:1

Glory Sighting

No doubt David, the author of this psalm, had the same feelings of awe and "smallness" when he looked up at the heavens. He spent decades evading the evil King Saul, hiding in the dark shadows of different caves in the wilderness.

There is something incredible about looking at the night sky from on top of the mountains. When I go skiing in the Rockies, I'm amazed at how bright the stars appear away from all the light pollution from civilization. David experienced that each night as he sat beside the fire and considered his ongoing crisis. He must have felt how small he was compared to King Saul's elite fighting force who were always just one step behind him. Perhaps his mind drifted to how small and insignificant he was compared to the vast universe displayed in all its brilliance before him.

But, from God's perspective, David embraced the truth that we are much more than specks in the vast universe. Psalm 8 is a hymn of praise to God for his marvelous works of creating and his amazing plans for every one of us. So, take a moment today and be blessed by the glory of God's handiwork. Praise him and thank him and stand in awe of him today as you marvel in his majesty and his great love for you! Shalom!

TODAY'S READINGS
Psalm 8 | Exodus 1:1-7 | Romans 2:1-11

Tuesday | AUGUST 25

Who has known the mind of the Lord? Or who has been his counselor?" | Romans 11:34

Who Knows the Mind of God?

Have you ever secretly questioned the actions of God? Here, Paul is quick to remind us God acts differently than we do because he thinks in ways our feeble minds can't grasp or fathom. When someone acts in ways we don't understand, it's common to ask, "What on earth were you thinking?" We somehow hope if we could get into their minds or understand their thought processes, it could shed light on their actions.

One could make the argument Paul knew the risen Christ better than anyone, having been schooled by him in a supernatural way. But even after all that intense interaction and education, Paul can say the mind of the Lord is so vast and complex, we all fall short in our understanding. The Lord doesn't think like us. His ways are not our ways. Of course, some of his actions seem strange or out of place to us because we're not processing with the same type of mind.

But if we pause for a moment and think clearly, we'll not be disappointed by his actions. Think about it. We are counting on the Lord to transcend time and space and rescue us from this sin-filled world and somehow transform us into the glorious existence of "eternal life." How is he going to pull that off? The truth is, after the greatest minds in history have worked on this for 2,000 years, they've all fallen short in their answers. Why?

Because we're working with limited mental capacity and the Lord is not. So, I rejoice and revel in the fact that I serve a Savior who is too deep and complex for me to fully understand. And that's the kind of God I'm looking for to come usher us all into eternity. Come quickly, Lord Jesus! We are waiting for you, Lord! Today when you think about the all-knowing mind of God, let the mystery of his impossible greatness give you joy and peace. Shalom!

TODAY'S READINGS
Psalm 8 | Exodus 2:11-15 | Romans 11:33-36

Wednesday | AUGUST 26

> When the disciples saw this, they were indignant.
> "Why this waste?" they asked. | Matthew 26:8

Unholy Indignation

The disciples' response to the woman who poured the jar of perfume over him was a slap in the face to Jesus.

His mind was busy trying to come to grips with his impending arrest and crucifixion. The perfume she used was usually placed on the dead. She was preparing him for his execution. He was wrestling with the overwhelming mental oppression of taking on the sins of the world. His selfless act would have the most meaningful impact in human history. And what made things even worse was he had consistently and clearly explained to these so-called friends of his what was about to take place.

They should have made Jesus and his tragedy the focus of everything they were doing. But they didn't. In fact, this encounter demonstrates their lack of connection and concern for his upcoming torture and death. So, what do his closest friends in the world say when someone honors him like this? They coldly blurt out, "What a waste."

Wow! Talk about being betrayed by your only friends! How lonely Jesus must have felt. And yet he managed to treat each of them with relentless love and grace.

How about us today? This is a wonderful, albeit tragic, snapshot for us when we feel abandoned or betrayed by so-called friends. We can take it to Jesus because he knows perfectly well what it feels like. We can commit ourselves amid our anger and sadness to follow the lead of our blessed Savior and not sin. Unfortunately, enduring the betrayal of false friends is part of our journey with Christ. Yes, it hurts and yes, it isn't fair, but there is One who understands. He promises to be closer than a brother and it is in him and him alone we place our trust and receive our blessing today. How will you rise above the actions of so-called friends today? Have you been hurt or saddened by someone's neglect or betrayal? Will you do the good thing and choose to honor Jesus? Shalom!

TODAY'S READINGS
Psalm 8 | Exodus 2:15-22 | Matthew 26:6-13

Thursday | AUGUST 27

> and walk in the way of love, just as Christ loved us and gave himself up for us as a fragrant offering and sacrifice to God. | Ephesians 5:2

Christ's Way

Paul doesn't leave us any wiggle room here. Jesus Christ is to be our example. Paul draws specific attention to Christ's self-emptying sacrifice on the cross. It's not just his general attitude of selflessness we are to model. That would require a lifetime of effort.

No, it is the fact he sacrificed himself for the good of those he loved. Now, Paul is advocating to the church in Ephesus, and to us, that we are to adopt this same attitude. This brings some clarity to how we are to interact with others. We are plain and simply called to put our own feelings and desires on the back burner so we can be of the best possible service to everyone who God brings into our sphere of influence.

Think about this, won't you? We spoke yesterday of how Christ's so-called friends had deserted him. Not one had his back. But he willingly, without hesitation, allowed himself to be treated like a vile criminal so he could be the best possible good for the very people who had betrayed and abandoned him, and even for those who hated him.

So, where does that leave us today? For me it calls for an attitude readjustment. Big time! May God have patience with me as I struggle to take my next step with him. In what way does this verse make you feel uncomfortable? Are you able to fully walk in the way of love as Christ did? Shalom!

TODAY'S READINGS
Psalm 105:1-6, 23-26, 45 | Exodus 2:23-24 | Ephesians 5:1-6

Friday | AUGUST 28

He sent Moses his servant, and Aaron, whom he had chosen, that they might keep his precepts and observe his laws. Praise the Lord. | Psalm 105:26,4

Love's Law

The way this psalm is laid out here in the lectionary, you get the feeling God's purpose for the Children of the Promise was two-fold. First, it was to relieve their suffering, and second, it was to enable them to observe God's precepts and obey God's laws.

Now, during this time in the life of God's people, they didn't have a written document conveying the laws and precepts of God. Once on the road to the Promised Land, God would take Moses up on a mountain and give to his servant his holy word. Moses then would take the word of God to the people of God. Then, because they refused to obey his word, they would be given a 40-year timeout to wander the desert and learn the precepts and laws of God.

What does this ancient story have to do with us today? For one, it speaks of God's commitment to work corporately with the people of God. Whatever happened to them, they were all in it together. There was no talk of individuals "taking God as their personal savior."

I'm always encouraged when the Bible reveals we should think of ourselves as a faith community. We see God's passion to teach his people to know and obey his word. This inspires me to continue to dig deeply each day into the precious law of love. Let's be about knowing and serving our King, a little bit more today than yesterday, as we purposefully and passionately take our next step toward our Lord and Savior, Jesus Christ. How important is to you to walk in faith alongside a community of believers? Think about ways you can invite others into your journey and enter into theirs. Shalom!

TODAY'S READINGS
Psalm 105:1-6, 23-26, 45 | Exodus 3:16-22 | 2 Thessalonians 2:7-12

Saturday | AUGUST 29

> He touched her hand and the fever left her, and she got up
> and began to wait on him. | Matthew 8:15

Jesus Heals

When Jesus heals someone in the Gospel accounts, they're always healed instantly, completely and permanently. I think of this when I see a so-called healing service on television. Sometimes they'll bring a person up on the stage in a wheelchair. The men will pray over them and the person gets up out of their wheelchair and limps off. Whenever I see that kind of healing, I can't help but to contrast it with the biblical accounts of Christ's healings.

The reason Matthew made special note of Peter's mother-in-law getting up to wait on Jesus was so we could see, when Jesus healed someone it was instant and complete and permanent. There was no need for her to lie down and rest. She didn't need to catch her breath. She was healed. I just love this about our Savior.

What are we to do with this truth about Jesus today? We can take comfort in the fact we serve a God who is not playing around. There is no form of sickness or evil that is any match for him. This means, no matter what happens in our lifetime, if we are faithfully participating in taking our next step toward him then we are on the right side of history. The world may not all know it now, but someday soon everyone will bend their knee to our Great Physician, to the glory of God. Let it be said of us that we came early to the party! How can you apply your faith in Jesus' power to heal today? Shalom!

TODAY'S READINGS
Psalm 105:1-6, 23-26, 45 | Exodus 4:1-9 | Matthew 8:14-17

Sunday | AUGUST 30

> Then Jesus said to his disciples, "Whoever wants to be my disciple must deny themselves and take up their cross and follow me. | Matthew 16:24

The Walking Dead

Jesus was talking about "dead men walking." This would have been a clear word picture for all the disciples. Any man who was seen carrying a cross was on his way to his own execution. Rome used this tactic to publicize a criminal's admission of guilt. The convicted man was saying by his public embarrassment that he was indeed guilty of the capital offense for which he had been convicted. And everyone who saw him knew he was on his way to be executed.

Wow! What a vivid scene for the Lord to conjure up in the minds of his disciples when he told them to take up their cross. Jesus was not looking for "self-made men." He was calling all who would follow him to let go of their own agenda and turn to, and then willingly submit to, the Lord's plan for their lives. There was no wiggle room for the Lord's first disciples. And I would submit to you today that when it comes to his followers, he still looks for the same sacrifice.

The Lord isn't looking for folks to sit on some type of divine advisory board. He's quite simply looking for dead folks walking—men and women who will willingly die to their own agenda to faithfully live out his glorious plan for their lives. What does it mean to you to "take up your cross" for Jesus? How can you die a little bit more today? Shalom!

TODAY'S READINGS

Psalm 105:1-6, 23-26, 45 | Exodus 3:1-15 | Matthew 16:21-28
Romans 16:21-27

Monday | AUGUST 31

O God, do not remain silent; do not turn a deaf ear, do not stand aloof, O God. | Psalm 83:1

Yo, God!

I was encouraged with the wise words of Pastor Lynn about this verse:

When God says his ways are not our ways, he really means it. Sometimes we have these amazing encounters where God breaks into our lives with power and answers prayers and wins our trust. We truly feel the Holy Spirit working in and around our family and our churches and our lives during these times.

And then…. there are the times where chaos and drama seem never-ending and our lives are shattered and dark. We go through months… seasons… years when things are happening we don't understand, and we feel so distant from God. We cry out to him in our confused anguish and he is silent… He seems absent…

My best friend's brother is an atheist and I can almost hear him saying, "The reason God seems silent is because he *is* absent. No one is home at that address. Duh…!"

In the silent suffering seasons, we can be tempted to believe the lie. Silence is how we perceive it. It's how it feels, but it isn't the whole story. There are many accounts in Scripture of those who felt God was absent, like David and Job. When we feel forsaken by God, we're not abandoned. We're simply called to trust in the promise more than the perception. You are not alone. God is with you! And he is speaking all the time in this wonderful text called Scripture. When you feel alone, pull out your Bible and read. What has God been silent about with you? Can you talk to him about it again and allow his presence to give you peace? Shalom!

TODAY'S READINGS
Psalm 83:1-4 13-18 | Exodus 4:10-31 | Revelation 3:1-6

Tuesday | SEPTEMBER 1

I am coming quickly; hold fast what you have, so that no one will take your crown. | Revelation 3:11

Hold Fast

As I approach my 62nd birthday and wrestle with the prospect of Social Security, I can't help but contemplate that I'm running the last part of my race here in this world. As I do, it's only natural that John's revelation becomes more relevant. Christ is indeed coming quickly for me.

Whether it will be the rapturing of his church or my inevitable final step in this life, the sand in the hour glass is running out. I'm surprised this truth doesn't make me want to coast to the end. On the contrary, I've never been more excited about proclaiming Jesus Christ and him crucified.

I don't feel desperate about the fleeting hourglass, but I'm more determined to finish strong. My finish line rests securely in the hands of God and I intend to be found sprinting my hardest and straining for the prize that's the blessing for all of us who are committed to holding fast to the key to eternal life. Take stock of where you are in your race…are you running excitedly toward the finish, limping weakly along, or just waiting for it all to be over? How can you get back in the race with a zeal that befits a son or daughter of the King? Shalom!

TODAY'S READINGS
Psalm 83:1-4 13-18 | Exodus 5:1-6:13 | Revelation 3:7-13

Wednesday | SEPTEMBER 2

Whoever is not with me is against me, and whoever does not gather with me scatters. | Matthew 12:30

Pick One

Jesus doesn't leave any wiggle room here for marginal Christianity. In the Book of Revelation, he said he was upset with a church that was neither hot nor cold. He would rather have them be one or the other but not lukewarm. Because they were neither, he said, "I spit you up!"

And this is a *tempered* translation. Jesus never desired a church to be sitting on the fence. I wonder what most self-professed Christians in the United States would say if they asked, "Are you gathering with Christ or are you scattering against him?" And then for those who claimed to be gatherers, to respond next to the question, "What are you doing specifically that is gathering people to Christ?"

I'm afraid most of us would have a difficult time pointing specifically to those we've helped gather. But we certainly don't want to be considered scatterers. The problem is, Jesus hasn't left open the option of anything other than gathering with him or scattering against him. That gives us something to meditate on today. What side are you on right now? Where will you be found faithful? Shalom!

TODAY'S READINGS
Psalm 83:1-4 13-18 | Exodus 7:14-25 | Matthew 12:22-32

Thursday | SEPTEMBER 3

For the Lord takes delight in his people; he crowns the humble with victory | Psalm 149:4

Humbly Submit

I was just thinking how "the Lord takes delight in his people, he crowns the humble with victory." Let's ponder this verse for a few minutes. God's people are often the lowliest and most humble on this earth. Look at the disciples; from the world's perspective, they were not great leaders of their day—just a ragtag collection of blue-collar fishermen for the most part.

Yet, look how those disciples changed the world because God put a new song in their hearts. Humility was at the core of their joy in serving I believe. Sometimes we are so prideful. But, I believe the opposite of pride is trust in God. Pride begs us to believe it all depends on us. Trusting in God requires us to place our dependence on him. And the path that leads us away from pride and into a place of truly trusting God is always paved with humility.

God may be using humbling circumstances in your life today to get you to a place of deep and unshakeable trust in him. If God sees big things ahead for you, and I believe he does, then he has to remove all hints of pride. Pride has the potential to take away all God has called you to. Let this day be full of joy and praise to our God who is in control. Will you choose the path of humility today? What can you submit to him today in complete trust? Shalom!

TODAY'S READINGS
Psalm 149 | Exodus 9:1-7 | 2 Corinthians 12:11-21

Friday | SEPTEMBER 4

And Isaiah boldly says, "I was found by those who did not seek me; I revealed myself to those who did not ask for me." | Romans 10:20

Banquet Beggars

Paul is quoting here from the prophet Isaiah, who was unwittingly predicting the Kingdom of God being open to Gentiles. Paul not only got to be a witness to this glorious unveiling, but he was actually commissioned by God to be at the leading edge of what has now become a 2,000-year-old miracle.

It would serve us well to think of ourselves as being grafted into the Kingdom of God. We are beggars at the banquet. God reached down into utter darkness and plucked us out and into the beautiful light. What did we do to earn this wonderful calling? Nothing! Nada! Zippo! God in his amazing grace made a way for us to share in his generous inheritance. That way is through the work of his Son.

What should our attitudes be as beggars at the banquet? We should be obsessed with sharing the Good News to anyone who will listen. And we should be living our lives in such a way the people of our community are compelled to know what makes us so different from everyone else around us.

So, let us live today as beggars at the banquet. Let us go out among our friends and relatives and associates and neighbors and do our small part in attracting folks to our Lord and Savior, Jesus Christ. Think back on where you were when God found you and brought you into his family. How can you use that glorious grace to bring others to the banquet table? Shalom!

TODAY'S READINGS
Psalm 149 | Exodus 10:21-29 | Romans 10

Saturday | SEPTEMBER 5

"You snakes! You brood of vipers! How will you escape being condemned to hell? ... | Matthew 23:33

You Snakes

Jesus reserved his harshest judgment for the religious leaders. Held in such high esteem, these men were respected and revered by all of Israel. Yet, whenever Jesus encounters them, he is angry almost beyond description.

Jesus wasn't fooled by their religious actions. He didn't seem to care they all had a better education than he did. He knew they were responsible for leading the lost sheep of Israel astray. I think by this time in his ministry, he was aware they would be largely responsible for opposing his apostles.

It seems like nothing frustrated Jesus more than those he called "blind guides." And yet, when we see him coming face to face with prostitutes and adulterers and tax collectors, he is patient and kind and eager to forgive. I've always been struck by how patient Jesus was with the very people the church largely rejects today. He was indignant with those who were held in high regard. It makes you wonder what he would do if he were here today. Who would he be patient and kind with and who would his anger burn against? And if we think we know the answer to that, how should we be living our lives differently? Think about it, won't you? Do you have any snake-like religiosity you want to get rid of? Shalom!

TODAY'S READINGS

Psalm 149 | Exodus 11:1-10 | Matthew 23:29-36

Sunday | SEPTEMBER 6

Let no debt remain outstanding, except the continuing debt to love one another, for whoever loves others has fulfilled the law. | Romans 13:8

Whoever Loves

I like the way Paul clears away any mental clutter that might linger from previous passages in his letter to the Romans. For eleven chapters Paul laid out in specific detail the doctrine of the Christian faith. For many scholars, it is believed to be the greatest Christian document ever crafted. A person could spend their entire life digging deeply into Paul's seemingly endless well of theology.

Then in Chapter 12 he launches into the application of that theology. And just in case he's lost anyone by this point in the letter, you can always pause for a moment here in Chapter 13 and realize Paul has simply been advocating a life of love. He wants us to get up every morning driven by the Spirit of God to repay our constant debt of love.

For Paul, the key to remember when we're frightened or unsure of what our next step should be is simply to "do the next right, loving thing." It's usually not difficult to figure out. We can proceed, confident we're going forth under the blessing of the Holy Spirit and the power of God Almighty. So, whatever you may be struggling with today, simply pray to God and ask him to reveal to you what is the next right, loving thing for you to do. He'll be faithful to show you the way. And you can be confident you're working for his glory and your ultimate good. Will you ask him today what your next right, loving thing is, and listen for his direction? Shalom!

TODAY'S READINGS
Psalm 149 | Exodus 12:1-14 | Matthew 18:15-20 | Romans 13:8-14

Monday | SEPTEMBER 7

Live such good lives among the pagans that, though they accuse you of doing wrong, they may see your good deeds and glorify God on the day he visits us. | 1 Peter 2:12

Glorify God

It's important oftentimes when we're reading Scripture to ask whether what we're reading is "prescriptive" or "descriptive." In other words, is it revealing something we should be doing, or is it simply describing an event in the lives of the people of God?

In this case, regarding Peter's words, I believe it is both. It describes his exhortation for the early church as well as prescribing how we should live our lives today. That means in everything we say and do, we are to humbly glorify God in our actions.

I'm a descendant of the Mennonites in Elkhart County, Indiana. They have, still today, a custom that bears out Peter's caution. They always put their poorest fruit on the top of the basket. When they display their fruit on the roadside or in the market, instead of taking the poorer pieces of fruit and hiding them in the bottom of the basket, they show their poorest fruit first so no one can accuse them of anything underhanded. It also reminds them to live out every detail of their lives openly, in a way that points folks to the glory of God.

So, let's pause for a moment today and ask ourselves if we have let the customs of our culture cause any slippage. Then let's recommit ourselves to living such good lives that everyone will take notice and it will glorify God because of your actions on the day he returns. What simple ways will you choose today to glorify God? Shalom!

TODAY'S READINGS
Psalm 121 | Exodus 12:14-28 | 1 Peter 2:11-17

Tuesday | SEPTEMBER 8

I lift up my eyes to the mountains—where does my help come from? | Psalm 121:1

Help, Please

There are storms hitting many of us today—and I don't just mean the weather. As I watch the news, anxious about loved ones who may be in the path of this destructive weather front, I'm aware not just of those struggling with grief, loss of belongings and homes, or electricity. It makes me wonder, are you in a storm? Maybe it's your health, finances, the death of a loved one, job loss, a difficult boss, an unsupportive family member, a wayward child or spouse. Are you exhausted by unanswered prayers? Are you scared, lonely, heartbroken or depressed?

Whatever you're facing today, our God is a mighty God. "When we lift our eyes to the mountains, where does our help come from? Our help comes from the Lord, the maker of heaven and earth." When I see these verses, I think of the Casting Crowns song, "Praise You in This Storm." This song is so powerful. It helps me feel a sense of security knowing we can praise him in our storms. He is God no matter where we are. Every tear we cry he holds in his hands. He never leaves our side. Even when our hearts are torn, we can praise him in the storm.

We may not always understand the cause of the storms, but they come into everyone's lives. No one is immune from them and when they hit, they are usually unexpected. They're scary but they point to a God who is greater than ourselves. And his amazing blessings are hidden in the storm. Can you praise God in your storm today? Remember his blessings for he is always good. Shalom!

TODAY'S READINGS
Psalm 121 | Exodus 12:29-42 | Romans 13:1-7

Wednesday | SEPTEMBER 9

My help comes from the Lord, the Maker of heaven and earth... | Psalm 121:2

Raw Hope

On a mission trip to Haiti, we worshipped every night with the people of Calvary Church in the town of Jacmel. It really was an amazing experience. They're a great joy to be around while they're worshiping God. Their unbridled enthusiasm reveals, among other things, they get this verse from the psalmist.

They're convinced their only hope comes from the Lord. The experience of generation after generation of Haitian people has been that life is hard and there is no one to help. The government is always corrupt and even despises the poor people of its own country. There is an 80 percent unemployment rate, so there's little hope of ever finding a job. The average annual salary is $500. So they get up every morning and pray for a chance to have something to feed their families.

The only relief comes from the food God sends them through his church. Every day, before the children eat, they gather together and give praise to God for helping them survive another day. It is a "raw" type of hope many of us here in America have never experienced. May God bless the church in Haiti. You may have a lot or a little today—maybe even nothing. Let your help come from the Lord today. With thanks and praise present your needs and receive his kindness. Shalom!

TODAY'S READINGS

Psalm 121 | Exodus 13:1-10 | Matthew 21:18-22

Thursday | SEPTEMBER 10

> For this is the message you heard from the beginning:
> We should love one another. | 1 John 3:11

Uncommon Compassion

Remember the song from the '60s, "All You Need is Love"?

The old apostle had a profoundly simple message for us today. In everything we say, in everything we write, and in everything we do today, let the love of Christ shine through. There is nothing more important than doing everything in self-sacrificing love.

I believe this is why John holds up the life and death of Christ as an example for us with regard to how we're to love today. Christ, John said, laid down his life for us. This means he willingly loved those who hated him—the very people who had him arrested and spat in his face and shouted their contempt at him as he went to Calvary. Yes, those very people. Christ prayed over them and asked the Father to forgive them because they didn't know what they were doing.

Jesus is our example. He is our role model and our goal. It is his footsteps we follow. So, let's go out today and love everyone with uncommon compassion. If we do, John says they will hate us for it. But, we never look more like Christ than when we love everyone, especially our enemies. All you need is love. Who will you show uncommon compassion to today. Shalom!

TODAY'S READINGS
Psalm 114 | Exodus 13:17-22 | 1 John 3:11-16

Friday | SEPTEMBER 11

The Lord will fight for you; you need only to be still. | Exodus 14:14

Freeze

I wonder how often in my life I've either been in dire distress with incredible anxiety over a situation, or I've lunged out ahead of God in utter fear, trying to win a battle on my own power.

In either case, I find this both a powerful and comforting verse.

There are times for the people of God when the proper response is neither fight nor flight. Sometimes the only God-honoring response is to freeze. I have to admit, I haven't yet mastered this discipline. I always have this voice in my ear from my childhood, shouting, "Do something, even if it's wrong!" That is my go-to response. "Here's the enemy—now let's go get 'em!"

However, the older I get, the more it's becoming clear that if I'm patient and I'm willing to wait on the Lord, he'll show up and fight the battle for me in ways I could have never conceived.

So, how about you today, pilgrim? Do you have an enemy in hot pursuit? Do you feel trapped by the forces of evil, bent on destroying you? Try to allow God the opportunity to fight in your place today. Stand down this time and see. "The Lord will fight for you, you need only to be still." Shalom!

TODAY'S READINGS

Psalm 114 | Exodus 14:1-18 | Acts 7:9-16

Saturday | SEPTEMBER 12

> For if you forgive other people when they sin against you, your heavenly Father will also forgive you. | Matthew 6:14

Forgiven

This is all the encouragement we need to be a forgiving people. Each of us have things that were said and done against us that for us have been so cruel they feel almost impossible to forgive. But here is our beautiful motivation. Jesus told us to forgive in the same way we want to be forgiven.

Now I know after speaking with countless brothers and sisters on this journey that this is a very touchy subject. Some of us are afraid to let go of the anger and pain we've held in our hearts for so long because, to a large degree, it has now become part of who we are. The resentment is so ingrained in our psyche, if we ever let it go we fear we might somehow lose a sense of who we are.

But here's the command for us, plain and simple. There's nothing missing here in the translation. We must forgive in the same way we want to be forgiven. So, for those of us holding a grudge we've refused to turn loose, let's take our next step in this area today. Let's humbly offer up our prayers to God and tell him today we are willing to allow him to begin to soften our hearts so someday we'll be able to forgive. We don't have to release the ones who've so deeply hurt us today. But we can AT LEAST be willing to begin the process. Try it, won't you? You'll be blessed doing it. Shalom!

TODAY'S READINGS
Psalm 114 | Exodus 15:19-21 | Matthew 6:7-15

Sunday | SEPTEMBER 13

So then, each of us will give an account of ourselves to God. | Romans 14:12

Ourselves

After studying this passage to prepare to teach it, I'm convinced Paul would have us emphasize the word "ourselves." He's reminding us we'll only give an account for ourselves and we will not give an account for anyone else.

Therefore we can be at peace with those in the church who embrace different beliefs. We will give an account for what we believe and also for how we treat those who disagree with us. We are not to demonize them. Often we are so incredibly insecure we demand everyone else believe exactly what we believe. But Paul reminds us each of us must decide in our heart what God is calling us to do. And then we will only be accountable for how we respond.

This passage has brought me some peace in the Lord. I have often been frustrated and confused by some Christian leaders who have interpreted some Scripture differently. Now, I've learned to simply entrust them to the "One who judges justly." And as my mom used to tell me, I will "mind my own P's and Q's." Is there anyone you've been unnecessarily critical of or too focused on? Try releasing them to God today and see how he wants to minister to you. Shalom!

TODAY'S READINGS
Psalm 114 | Exodus 14:19-31 | Matthew 14:1-12 | Romans 14:1-12

Monday | SEPTEMBER 14

…By faith… | Hebrews 11:23-29

Active Faith

Faith seems to be an overused word in Christian circles. It's easy to talk about but hard to practice.

Faith is the process of aligning your behavior, your decisions and ultimately your whole life with what God asks you to do, without knowing how it's going to work out in the end. I read this about faith not too long ago and loved it: "Faith is acting like it is so, even when it is not so, so that it might be so, simply because God said so." I loved that then and I still love it!!

Acting on the promises of God and not just talking about them is where faith comes alive. It's trusting God in the small things of life so when the big things come along, you're practiced at giving it to God and trusting him.

Maybe God is asking you to pay for a stranger's meal or mend fences with a friend. Or something bigger like moving from one state to another. We need to be committed to identify and follow the Lord's leading in our hearts. This is the key that will not only unlock the door to a whole new realm of being connected to the Father, but it will also protect us from the enemy when he attacks. Will it be easy? No. But over time we'll learn to trust God enough to move forward at his word. I can only imagine the adventures he will bless us with as we follow his leading. What can you have faith for today? How can you act on it? Shalom!

TODAY'S READINGS
Psalm 77 | Joshua 3:1-17 | Hebrews 11:23-29

Tuesday | SEPTEMBER 15

Therefore let us stop passing judgment on one another. Instead, make up your mind not to put any stumbling block or obstacle in the way of a brother or sister. | Romans 14:13

Stop Judging

We could use a good healthy dose of this in the American church today. How often do we find ourselves passing judgment on other believers?

In Paul's day I think it was mostly about food being sacrificed to false idols. In our day, we judge along political lines. We fall into the trap the elites have set for us. Their goal is to divide everyone. We're tempted to follow them instead of our true leader, Jesus Christ. He led the apostle Paul to encourage us to prayerfully obey God's leading in every situation.

As we learn to do that, it's natural to look around and wonder why everyone else isn't in step with us. I mean, after all, they claim to be Christians too. It can be frustrating when other "so called" Christians don't see things the way we do. Paul says when these differences come up, we are not to judge but simply go in the direction God is leading us and treat everyone with love and respect.

The division in our country is worse than any time since the 1960s. The Lord is counting on his people to be the great unifying force. If the church would stop passing judgment on each other, our nation could experience total healing. May it be said of us that we were faithful to be willing to reach out the right hand of fellowship for our good and God's glory. Today think of one way you could reach out in love to someone across the aisle—then go do it. Shalom!

TODAY'S READINGS
Psalm 77 | Nehemiah 9:9-15 | Romans 14:1 –15

Wednesday | SEPTEMBER 16

"Truly I tell you, if anyone says to this mountain, 'Go, throw yourself into the sea,' and does not doubt in their heart but believes that what they say will happen, it will be done for them. | Mark 11:23

Mountain Movers

Jesus knew his death was imminent. He was troubled by the horror awaiting him. Yet he was still about the business of giving his precious disciples everything they would need in his absence.

When he refers to "this mountain," he's in the shadow of the massive temple situated high above him, as tall as a fourteen-story building. So, I wonder if it's specifically the temple he's referring to here. He knew it was coming down. A task, by the way, that would have seemed impossible to the disciples. He also knew now from experience that when someone walks closely with his Heavenly Father, they would be so in tune with him that their desires would become the Father's desires. Jesus knew the temple would be destroyed because evil men had turned it into "a den of thieves and robbers."

Jesus could pray for and trust the mountain would be thrown into the sea because it would literally come true—the temple would come down. While many fine teachers would say this passage is about us "having faith to move a mountain," I'm convinced it's mostly about developing a relationship so in tune with our Heavenly Father that we always pray for his will to be done, as he reveals it to us—his good and perfect and pleasing will. How will you tune in to the Father's will today? Shalom!

TODAY'S READINGS

Psalm 77 | 2 Kings 2:1-18 | Mark 11:20-25

Thursday | SEPTEMBER 17

Glory in his holy name; let the hearts of those who seek the Lord rejoice. | Psalm 105:3

Let's Glory

I love to sing in worship on Sunday! I especially love the songs that declare God's glory. Our band does such a great job of escorting us into his presence. I like to close my eyes and imagine I'm in the throne room of God. When I do, everything else just seems to melt away.

There's something wonderfully transcendent about worship. It reminds me we serve a God who sits sovereign over everything we encounter. Ultimately it comforts me, because I know I'm just passing through here. Whatever tragedy and sadness and death I encounter is brought into divine perspective by our offerings of praise, thanksgiving and worship. Like the psalmist says, let's glory in his holy name. And let our hearts rejoice as we seek the Lord.

There's nothing we can do with our time more valuable than thinking rightly about God. And when we sing true, theologically sound songs, it helps guide us into right thinking. So, we will continue to join our spiritual ancestors as we "make a joyful noise unto the Lord." Today, allow your heart to rejoice and sing glory to our Father as you think on his beauty and majesty. Shalom!

TODAY'S READINGS

Psalm 105:1-6, 37-45 | Exodus 15:22-27 | 2 Corinthians 13:1-4

Friday | SEPTEMBER 18

Look to the Lord and his strength; seek his face always. | Psalm 105:4

Total Dependence

Society teaches us to depend on ourselves, to get a good education so we can secure a well-paying job so we won't be dependent on anyone else. When that plan fails, many of us turn to the government, expecting them to rescue us from our financial woes. We tend to admire the financially successful and don't respect those who struggle, especially when we feel they've made poor choices. As a culture in 21st century America, we tend to judge folks primarily based on their ability to make money.

However, the psalmist here seems to be delivering a different message of success—one of total reliance on the Lord's strength. Did you notice he didn't say to seek God's hand? It is in the habit of seeking his face we find our strength. In the final analysis, when our time here is finished, we will have succeeded or failed wholly by our willingness to humbly submit ourselves to the Lord and to follow his will for our lives.

Especially for those of us who are strong-willed and tend to be independent and self-sufficient, it takes an act of the will to lay that down and let God be in charge. It is good to draw our strength from the One who is all-powerful. Do you take pride in doing everything yourself? Do you think it's all up to you? Today, seek his face and hand him the reins, again. Shalom!

TODAY'S READINGS
Psalm 105:1-6, 37-45 | Exodus 16:1-21 | 2 Corinthians 13:5-10

Saturday | SEPTEMBER 19

> When the disciples heard this, they were greatly astonished and asked, "Who then can be saved?" | Matthew 19:25

Great Lie

The disciples, along with the rest of God's people, had become convinced the rich were rich because of God's blessing. Guess who taught them that convenient truth? You guessed it! It was the rich who said they'd been blessed because God loved them more. And of course, the natural conclusion was God did not love the poor.

So, when Peter and the boys heard Jesus say it was difficult, nearly impossible, for a rich man to see the Kingdom of God, they were stunned. This turned their entire worldview upside down. As far as we're concerned, we are a product of 2,000 years of church teaching emphasizing God's great concern for the poor and less fortunate. Even so, after Jesus' clear teaching and the doctrine of the church, we still tend to hold the rich and famous in high regard.

My television is full of news spotlighting the lives of the wealthy elite. This news wouldn't be there if people were not obsessed with knowing all the details about the rich and famous. So, let's be mindful of the fact Jesus did not place the rich in an enviable position, as we often do.

May God give us an eternal perspective for the day when his glory is revealed, and we will see that the ground is indeed level at the foot of the cross. Examine your thoughts today and see, are you idolizing the lives of the wealthy? Are you overlooking what's important? How can you get a godly perspective on the least of these today? Shalom!

TODAY'S READINGS
Psalm 105:1-6, 37-45 | Exodus 16:22-30 | Matthew 19:23-30

Sunday | SEPTEMBER 20

> For it has been granted to you on behalf of Christ not only to believe in him, but also to suffer for him... | Philippians 1:29

Divine Suffering

What would we think if a great Christian leader of our day sent us a letter affirming we had a divine appointment to suffer for Christ? Probably wouldn't go over too well.

We'd likely launch into an immediate prayer chain begging the Lord to remove our suffering. I don't take suffering very well. I've always believed if I'm suffering, even for the cause of Christ, something must be horribly wrong. Now, I know most of the bad things that have happened to me have been brought on by my own selfish actions. But what about those rare times when we seem to really be suffering for serving Christ? Could it be that on those occasions God has given us an opportunity and a privilege? When it does happen, perhaps we should be more willing to endure it rather than flee from it and see what God might want to teach us.

Maybe through suffering he is molding us into the image of his Son. I know we may never be asked to give up our lives for the sake of Christ like Paul and many of his followers. However, there are many ways we may suffer to a lesser degree. Let's be mindful amid whatever suffering we're called to endure that we do so for God's ultimate glory and out of the love we have for his Son who suffered in our place, so we can be faithful and blessed followers of him. Today can you see your suffering in a different way? Can you see where God may use it for his glory? Can you even thank him in it? Shalom!

TODAY'S READINGS

Psalm 105:1-6, 37-45 | Exodus 16:2-15 | Matthew 20:1-16 | Philippians 1:21-30

Monday | SEPTEMBER 21

Oh, how I love your law! I meditate on it all day long. | Psalm 119:97

Alone Time

Every verse in this psalm refers in some way to spending time in Scripture, and all we receive from God as we do. Why is having a regular time with God important?

We spend time with him to deepen and strengthen our relationship with the One who created us and longs to be with us. But because we're all different and because each of us has a unique relationship with God, no one devotional pattern will work for every one of us. And no one way works for anyone, all the time. I devoted a whole retreat to this topic.

I learned you need to experiment until you find the time of day, the content, and the amount of time that will help you feel connected with God. A basic pattern to follow is to start with quieting yourself. Try to find a way to just be still before God.

Maybe follow with a quick prayer asking God to open your heart to his message today. Read some Scripture, just like we have provided for you here from the Lectionary. The most important thing to remember as we try to grow closer to God is he is already reaching out to you. He desires for you to grow. When we keep showing up—even when we don't feel particularly holy or loving or eager to—be assured God will show up too. What new thing can you try today in your alone time with God? Trust he will meet you there. Shalom!

TODAY'S READINGS

Psalm 119:97-104 | Exodus 16:31-35 | Romans 16:1-16

Tuesday | SEPTEMBER 22

> The God of peace will soon crush Satan under your feet. The grace of our Lord Jesus be with you. | Romans 16:20

Satan Crushers

Someone once told me whenever Satan reminds me of my past, I remind him of his future. That stuck with me. I carry a lot of guilt about my past. There are so many things I regret and wish I could go back and do over again.

I always knew better, but I chose to ignore God's leading. I look forward to the day when Christ will return and the enemy will no longer hold sway. Even now, I'm still tempted to choose the wrong path. So, what do we do in the meantime?

Well, I loved our reading today from the Psalms. Paul is living a faithful life, taking his next step toward the God he loves, primarily because he's become obsessed with knowing and doing the word of God. He said, "I gain understanding from your precepts; therefore, I hate every wrong path." There. I would say this is our divine protection against the evil one.

We are to fill our heads with God's holy word. Remember the verse from our childhood? "Thy word have I hid in my heart, that I might not sin against thee." So, take heart, Christian. The God of peace will soon crush satan under your feet. In the meantime, we will meditate on God's glorious word all day long and be showered with his blessing. Are you giving the enemy power he doesn't have? Today meditate on your standing with God and how he is crushing your enemy in any area you have doubt. Shalom!

TODAY'S READINGS
Psalm 119:97-104 | Numbers 11:1-9 | Romans 16:17-20

Wednesday | SEPTEMBER 23

> And whoever humbles himself as this child, he is the greatest in the kingdom of heaven. | Matthew 18:5

Kid Stuff

The command of Christ here, to be like a little child, has more to do with the inherent vulnerability of all children in that culture. Children were not protected and held in high regard.

The Romans had no problem discarding newborn babies to the elements if she was a girl. Jews had a slightly better perspective. They saw each child as a potential person. Many of them would not survive diseases or live to see their fifth birthday. A father would not spend any time with his younger children; it was only when a boy was old enough to go to work and be a part of the culture that the father would begin to invest his time with him.

Young children were the most humble because there wasn't anyone to recognize their worth. We might say they were viewed as "nobodies." So, what could Jesus possibly mean here when he demands we all assume the humility of a little child? If my interpretation is correct, he is advocating we make a conscious decision to let go of everything we cling to that makes us feel important and begin to regard our own nothingness.

I know this flies in the face of everything we've learned in our American culture. But if we're willing to lay aside our preconceived notions, we will realize Scripture plainly teaches our path to spiritual wholeness is paved with our own willingness to place ourselves in humble submission to the lover of our soul. It is only there we will find our blessing today. Is it difficult for you to make yourself like a child? Today ask the Lord to show you what this means. Shalom!

TODAY'S READINGS
Psalm 119:97-104 | Numbers 11:18-23, 31-32 | Matthew 18:1-5: 1

Thursday | SEPTEMBER 24

> There is only one lawgiver and judge, the one who is able to save and destroy. But you—who are you to judge your neighbor? | James 4:12

Judge Not

Back in the '60s we used to ask, "Who died and made you God?" I think what James is driving at here is there is only one God and the last time I checked, you ain't him. This seems like a clear and straightforward command—simply DO NOT JUDGE. I don't know how it could be made any clearer.

When you look back at the life of Jesus, you can see where James learned this valuable lesson. When they brought the woman caught in adultery to him, Jesus told the men who were about to stone her that whoever was without sin should throw the first stone. One by one, they all slinked off. Then Jesus asked the woman, "Where are your accusers? Does no one condemn you?" She said they had all left. She stood in front of the Sovereign One, who had the right and the authority to judge and condemn her.

However, the most beautiful part of this story is when Jesus said, "I don't condemn you, so go and leave your life of sin." Wow! This is our example! There is only one Judge and you ain't him. So, keep your judgments to yourself until you can take your next step toward Christ and learn to simply stop judging altogether. Look how Jesus was qualified to judge the woman but did not. How can you apply that wonderful grace to others in your life you may be tempted to judge? Shalom!

TODAY'S READINGS
Psalm 78:1-4, 12-16 | Isaiah 48:17-21 | James 4:11-16

Friday | SEPTEMBER 25

We will not hide them from their descendants; we will tell the next generation the praiseworthy deeds of the Lord, his power, and the wonders he has done. | Psalm 78:4

Spiritual DNA

I love having the children with us at our church. They're one of my greatest joys. It's the most noble and noteworthy task to bring them up in the faith, for our teachers to share with them the stories of God.

These stories the psalmist is referring to are the stories of God's people. They are our stories, so it is our responsibility to teach them to the next generation. My hope and prayer is that each of them will embrace the great teaching of our faith. And that they will be infused with the love of Christ by being in our midst.

This is why we have them bring food to the altar during each worship service. I want them to live out, in real time, our caring for the poor. I want this kindness to be so ingrained it becomes part of their spiritual DNA.

Of course, we only get to spend time with the next generation for a couple hours every Sunday. So, the rest of the week it's all about you, as parents and grandparents, who are trying your best to raise your children up in the faith. My deepest prayer is that each of our congregations may be a system of great support and encouragement. What can you do today to help raise up the children, supporting, encouraging and teaching by example? Shalom!

TODAY'S READINGS
Psalm 78:1-4, 12-16 | Numbers 20:1-13 | Acts 13:32-41

Saturday | SEPTEMBER 26

> "By what authority are you doing these things?" they asked.
> "And who gave you authority to do this?" | Mark 11:28

Power/Control

Most of religion throughout human history has been concerned with power and control. The religious leaders of Jesus' day had both. They conspired with the power of Rome to take control over the rank and file of God's people. And tragically, like most religious folks of every generation, the people were subservient to these religious leaders. The people admired, respected and obeyed them.

When Jesus came along and began explaining the true nature of the Kingdom of God, he drew the ire of the religious elite. It wasn't so much that Jesus had a new perspective on following God that upset them; as he grew in popularity they realized they were losing their power and control over the people. It was of particular importance to them because they were making a good living off the backs of these poor folks. So, when they could not discredit Jesus in debate, and when they feared Jesus might be a threat to their power and control, they killed him.

However, Jesus had no problem speaking truth to power. He was only and always concerned about his Father's will. So, let's be mindful today of the authority we've been given to speak on God's behalf. It is crucial to attach ourselves to the mission of Christ and no one else. As Christians, our primary allegiance is to God and him alone, through the authority of the Scripture. Let's not fall into the age-old trap of trying to use religion to accumulate authority and power. Ours is to be a life of peace as we humbly live out our lives in direct obedience to the One who challenges us to simply take our next step toward him. In what ways have you been tempted to use your spiritual power and authority to control others? How can we lay that down today? Shalom!

TODAY'S READINGS

Psalm 78:1-4, 12-16 | Numbers 27:12-14 | Mark 11:27-33

Sunday | SEPTEMBER 27

> not looking to your own interests but each of you to
> the interests of the others. | Philippians 2:4

Job Descriptions

I originally learned this verse in another translation, and it was a slightly different interpretation. It said, "… not looking only to your interests." In other words, it seemed to be saying we should tend not only to our own needs but to the needs of others as well. Then when I came across this translation years ago, I thought, "Wait a minute, which is it. Are we supposed to look at OUR needs, in addition to others'?" I looked it up in the original Greek and it actually does not say anything at all about our own needs.

What I believe Paul is driving at here is we don't need to spend time worrying about ourselves. We need to be about the business of finding hurting people and helping them. It's not our job to be obsessed with getting more and more stuff for ourselves. You may be wondering, "Well, if I don't look out for me, who will?"

The answer is God will supply all your needs. It may not happen the way we planned it or think it should be, but we need to learn to embrace the fact God is in the full-time, 24-hour-a-day business of loving us perfectly. And he wants us to demonstrate the certainty of that love by the way we humbly serve those he has put in our path. So, don't look to your own interests today, but ask God to show you who he wants for you to humbly serve. Then he'll take care of you. Shalom!

TODAY'S READINGS
Psalm 78:1-4, 12-16 | Exodus 17:1-7 | Matthew 21:23-32 | Philippians 2:1-13

Monday | SEPTEMBER 28

As the deer pants for streams of water, so my soul pants for you, my God. | Psalm 42:1

Hot Pursuit

A deer instinctively knows if it doesn't find water it will not survive. Nothing can replace water for it; there's absolutely no substitute. The psalmist appears to be in a most sorrowful, desperate place in his life. He's beside himself with grief. It seems very difficult for him as he struggles to find the words to sufficiently express his despair.

We've all been in this tragic place where it seems there's no hope, no way out, no light at the end of the tunnel. But I believe, like the deer desperately searching for water, God would have us to adopt the same spiritually instinctive attitude for him. The truth is he is our only true source for peace.

I've learned there is no lasting peace apart from drinking from the flowing river of his marvelous grace. The big difference between the deer and me is the deer is not confused. It has set its sight on finding water. I have spent too much of my time desperately looking for relief in all the wrong places.

I'm like a deer thirsting to death on the riverbank, chewing on the bark of a tree instead of drinking the water. I pray God will instill in all our hearts today that he alone is the sole source for our emotional and spiritual survival. Let us drink deeply from his endless stream of grace and love as we passionately take our next step with our great Savior, Jesus Christ. What places have you searched for peace only to come up thirsty still? Will you satisfy your thirst today with the living water of Christ? Shalom!

TODAY'S READINGS
Psalm 42 | Exodus 18:13-27 | Philippians 1:15-21

Tuesday | SEPTEMBER 29

Why, my soul, are you downcast? Why so disturbed within me? Put your hope in God, for I will yet praise him, my Savior and my God. | Psalm 42:11

Ever Hopeful

The Bible doesn't ignore trouble. From the Garden in Genesis to the final battle in Revelation, trouble seems to find its way into the picture. Many of you have experienced trouble in your life as well.

When we're feeling troubles, we are downcast, scared, fearful, angry, desperate, and sometimes hopeless too. How often do we see our troubles as an object of hope? We have all experienced our souls being downcast. Anything that can go wrong does go wrong. Maybe you've lost your job, failed a friend, lost a loved one or your home, failed a test, etc. I know you've experienced any one of these things and so have I. But, our hope—the totality of our confidence, trust, and faith—is founded upon the Lord God Almighty.

We may struggle in the troubles of life, but we're connected to our Lord, Jesus Christ. And at the end of the storm there will be a rainbow and the sun will peek from behind the clouds and we will feel the warmth on our faces. Our hope is founded on a belief that the end of our trials, struggles and troubles of this world will come, and we'll live with the lover of our soul for eternity. And so, we praise him and are blessed by him as we put our hope in God. Today, put your hope in God again. In fact, put your troubles and struggles into his very hands and let his hope fill you again. Shalom!

TODAY'S READINGS
Psalm 42 | Exodus 18:1-12 | Philippians 1:3-14

Wednesday | SEPTEMBER 30

And he got up and went home. | Matthew 9:7

Get Up

I wonder how this played out, with the church leaders attacking Jesus and our Lord explaining to them the divine truth that he was indeed God in the flesh. The guy who was healed just got up from his mat and went home to get ready for a roller-skating party or something. It's like his exit is declaring, "Whatever—you guys can stay and argue about this, but I ain't got time for that; I need to go enjoy this new gift I just received."

Think about it—he would've been viewed as an outcast because not only was he a cripple, but the religious leaders taught everyone he was a cripple because the Lord didn't like him. And the reason the Lord didn't like him, they said, was because he was evil. With this healing, his life was now suddenly, fundamentally and permanently made right.

For some reason this got me to thinking about those of us who've also received some sort of divine healing from the gracious hands of Jesus. For me it was an addiction to alcohol; for you it may be something else. But what's true for most of us is Jesus reached down into the midst of our own crippled lives and said, "Your sins are forgiven."

Perhaps from shame and guilt or maybe the fear of the unknown, we still are lying around on our mats. Oh sure, we may get up and walk around a little here and there, but we never seem to get to the point where we leave the past in the past and live victoriously for Christ. How do you identify with the healed man today? Are you still lying on your mat or are you ready to get up and go enjoy your healing? Shalom!

TODAY'S READINGS
Psalm 42 | Exodus 19:9b-25 | Matthew 9:2-8

Thursday | OCTOBER 1

The law of the Lord is perfect, refreshing the soul. The statutes of the Lord are trustworthy, making wise the simple. | Psalm 19:7

Wise Guys

The psalmist is convinced God's word is both trustworthy and perfect. If this is true, and we concede it is, then we should be willing to sacrifice everything for the opportunity to know and understand it.

God has communicated to us perfectly through his word so we can know and love and serve him. All of life's questions are tucked away in this book. So, it becomes our main source of spiritual nourishment. If we find ourselves in need of wisdom—and I always do—our path to right living lies right here in our laps.

I love the fact the psalmist is perfectly clear that even the simple, like me, can find our God-given path. Now this doesn't mean whenever we struggle with a problem we can simply open up the Bible to any random page and find our answer. No, wisdom—true, life-changing wisdom—is given only to those who diligently search his whole word. Therefore at our church we are committed to working our way through God's word every three years. And just like growing children, day by day we are nourished and growing up in the faith. So, take heart, Christian. If you are constantly being nourished by this wonderful book, then you're right where God wants you. What answer do you need today from the Lord? How can you seek out him and his truth in the word today? Shalom!

TODAY'S READINGS
Psalm 19 | Exodus 23:1-9 | Colossians 2:16-23

Friday | OCTOBER 2

Do everything without grumbling or arguing, so that you may become blameless and pure, "children of God without fault in a warped and crooked generation." Then you will shine among them like stars in the sky, as you hold firmly to the word of life. | Philippians 2:14-16a

Right Fighter

I never noticed before, there is an incredible payoff here for us if we refrain from grumbling and arguing. Did you see, if we can learn to bring our tongues under control we will become blameless and pure? Hey, I would love to feel blameless and pure, wouldn't you?

I struggle with this because I've always been a "right fighter." That is, whenever I experience a perceived wrong, I feel compelled to speak up and make sure everyone involved knows the "right way" to think on the matter. The truth is, I'm constantly being exposed to situations and experiences I feel have to be made right. Some of my experiences in the AA community compel me to "fight for the right." Most everything I see on television news is "grumbling and arguing."

If I continue to be affected by all this grumbling and arguing, it only stands to reason I will get sucked into fighting for *my perception* of whatever is right. But I notice here, Paul doesn't say, "Don't be running your mouth unless you're sure you are right." The truth is, the world doesn't need me to put my moral two cents into every situation.

I'm trying to learn to embrace our principle of T.E.N. talking: Do not even open your mouth unless what you're about to say is True, Encouraging and Necessary. What can you apply T.E.N. talking to today? Can you practice humbly staying quiet and allowing others' opinions to have airspace without challenging them? Shalom!

TODAY'S READINGS
Psalm 19 | Exodus 23:14-19 | Philippians 2:14-18; 3:1-4

Saturday | OCTOBER 3

Thus, the people were divided because of Jesus. | John 7:43

Redeeming Grace

Jesus was a very controversial figure from the beginning of his ministry. When he spoke with such eloquence and power, his words inspired some and infuriated others. The poor rank and file loved him at first because his message concerning his Father's Kingdom was an invitation for everyone to come and participate. He spoke especially to the poor, who made up most of the population. They were predominantly uneducated and were treated like second-class citizens by the religious elite. But Jesus' kind words lifted them up and gave them hope.

It's obvious this wasn't working out well for the "powers that be." They preferred the status quo and were resistant to this new message from this uneducated rabbi from Galilee who had no apparent credentials. But Jesus did not concern himself with their rejection of him. He always spoke truth to power.

Fast-forward 2,000 years and his enduring message continues to give salve to the souls of the hurting and is a threat to the powerful who reject his message. The confrontation is evident in almost all walks of life in 21st century America. He's still the most polarizing figure of our day. God's name can be evoked in the public square with widespread acceptance, but if anyone brings up the name of Jesus Christ, the division is instant and stark.

So, for those of us today who claim his name, we have a choice to make. We can fall in line with the powerfully elite and allow his message of grace and redemption to be silenced. Or we can follow his lead and passionately look for hurting people and share the Good News with them. Today will you open your mouth and speak truth to whoever needs to hear it? Shalom!

TODAY'S READINGS
Psalm 19 | Exodus 23:10-13 | John 7:40-52

Sunday | OCTOBER 4

Brothers and sisters, I do not consider myself yet to have taken hold of it. But one thing I do: Forgetting what is behind and straining toward what is ahead, I press on toward the goal to win the prize for which God has called me... heavenward in Christ Jesus. | Philippians 3:13-14

Press On

I was just thinking about the phrase, "But one thing I do." Most people attempting to take their next step toward Jesus probably struggle with the poor choices they've made in the past. I know I surely do. I really do feel like Paul, who described himself as the "chief of sinners."

If it's true many if not most of us share in this guilt, we know it can be debilitating at times. We experience periods of remorse and blame that prevent us from pursuing the path Christ has graciously cleared for us. What are we to do when we find ourselves in this spiritual funk? Well, first, I see Paul is encouraging us to forget about the past and instead focus on the future. For those of us who consciously choose a future under Christ's leadership, there is indeed a great experience awaiting us.

It is one immersed in the love, forgiveness and grace of God. It is not promised to be easy, but it is glorious beyond anything we could ever hope for or imagine. But the catch is this incredible experience is reserved only for those who are willing to leave the past in the past and pursue instead the path of peace. Is there anywhere you are stuck in the past with shame, remorse, guilt or condemnation? Will you sit with the Lord today and put that in his care once more so you can reach for the prize he's called you to? Shalom!

TODAY'S READINGS
Psalm 19 | Exodus 20:1-20 | Matthew 21:33-46 | Philippians 3:4-14

Monday | OCTOBER 5

> Remember your word to your servant, for you have given me hope. My comfort in my suffering is this: your promise preserves my life. | Psalm 119:49-50

Suffering Hope

Even though our Scripture today is in Psalms, my thoughts stray to James. It's interesting how the Book of James begins and ends with the same idea: in all things good or bad, we can look to God in joy, even when there are trials and different types of suffering.

James looks at suffering so differently. He says it's good for you. I believe he understands suffering. He just sees it as an opportunity to count it as joy. We see it as a means to an end, but that eliminates any opportunity for growth or even hope. We put our hope in many things—life with our family and friends, job security, wealth, our favorite sports teams—anything that will make us healthy or feel happy and safe. But, everyone, and I do mean everyone, knows the feeling inside your gut when your favorite team loses. Or a friend you trust lets you down or a loved one betrays you. Or the money you thought was in the mail isn't. I could go on and on here…but I think you get what I mean.

Everything and everyone will let you down. BUT GOD WILL NOT!! In suffering God is always our strength, even when the world lets us down. He fulfills his promises. His wisdom has made a way for us to see his goodness in our suffering. Isn't that cool!?

Don't take your suffering for granted today. God is doing amazing, life-changing work through it in your life. And if you allow it, he will always bless you in the process. How are your difficulties in life bringing about God's blessings? Can you see what he's doing? It's always good! Shalom!

TODAY'S READINGS

Psalm 119:49-56 | Deuteronomy 5:1-21 | 1 Peter 2:4-10

Tuesday | OCTOBER 6

> All this is from God, who reconciled us to himself through Christ and gave us the ministry of reconciliation: that God was reconciling the world to himself in Christ, not counting people's sins against them. And he has committed to us the message of reconciliation. | 2 Corinthians 5:18-19

Divine Reconciliation

Much of my early experience in the church was influenced by men and women who believed God called them to reach others for Christ using shame, guilt and humiliation. I'm convinced now a great deal of focus in both the Catholic and Protestant churches over the last few hundred years has been about shame and guilt.

Different movements have chosen to focus on different activities they believed were particularly offensive to God. Therefore, their divine task from their mistaken perspective was to simply shame, guilt and humiliate people until they broke down and surrendered. But after years of studying the life of Christ and the teachings of his apostles, I've concluded our task is not to shame, guilt and humiliate.

In my experiences, most people are aware of their offenses—painfully aware. They're immersed, even drowning, in their guilt and don't need reminding. Thus, I decided early in my ministry to focus on reconciliation instead. Christ has commissioned me with the message of reconciliation. It's what motivates me to receive everyone regardless of where they are on their journey of faith and to simply help them take their next step toward Christ. Who do you know today that needs to hear Christ's loving message of reconciliation? Shalom!

TODAY'S READINGS

Psalm 119:49-56 | Deuteronomy 5:22–6:3 | 2 Corinthians 5:17-21

Wednesday | OCTOBER 7

You do not realize that it is better for you that one man die for the people than that the whole nation perish." | John 11:50

Heart Stuff

What these men meant for evil, God was about to use for the greatest good. It's hard to believe these deeply religious, highly educated elite leaders of the people of God could have been so wrong. The blood of God's Son ended up on their hands. Jesus consistently and sometimes quite forcefully warned them. He used their own Hebrew Scripture to explain it to them, and he did so perfectly.

My question is obviously, What happened? How could it be the very leaders of the people of God got it so horribly wrong? I have an unfinished and even a bit of an uncertain answer. I believe although they knew lots of stuff about God—after all, they were the academically elite men of their day—their knowledge about the history of God's people and God's interaction with those people was not enough to prepare them for the coming of the Messiah. I believe the information was in their brains but it never made that twelve-inch journey to their hearts.

They knew stuff about God, but they didn't know God. The challenge for us from the lesson of their tragic lives is to not only give to God our heads to be educated, but to willingly offer him our hearts to be transformed as well. Then and only then will we be able to discern his will for our lives—his good and perfect, pleasing will. Today, focus on going beyond your thoughts, beyond knowledge, and giving your heart to the Lord in relationship. Shalom!

TODAY'S READINGS
Psalm 119:49-56 | Deuteronomy 6:10-25 | John 11:45-57

Thursday | OCTOBER 8

Greet one another with a kiss of love. Peace to all of you who are in Christ. | 1 Peter 5:14

Holy Kiss

I listen to lots of old songs, especially on Saturday mornings with coffee. This verse makes me think of an old favorite song by Louis Armstrong, "What a Wonderful World." It says, "I see friends shaking hands, saying 'How do you do?' They're really saying, I love you." How true that is of this verse!

I think even a smile with a sparkle in your eye tells someone even before you say a word how glad you are to see them. Our greetings for each other are so important. It sets the tone for the conversation you will have with them. It could actually set the tone for their whole day.

The point here is to greet Christians in a way that displays even more intimacy and affection than how you would at work or someone in the grocery store. What we have with other Christians is a love that the business world will never know, that clubs would be impressed with, that neighbors don't have automatically just because they live side by side. The issue is more than a kiss. It is a love that says, I care deeply about you, my brother or sister. Today, if they know we are Christians by our love, we will live in the blessing of Jesus Christ. How will you greet your brother or sister in Christ when you see them today? How can you honor and love them? Shalom!

TODAY'S READINGS
Psalm 106:1-6, 19-23 | Exodus 24:1-8 | 1 Peter 5:1-5, 12-14

Friday | OCTOBER 9

Humble yourselves before the Lord, and he will lift you up. | James 4:10

Upside Down

Our spiritual progress is always and mostly only dependent upon humility. To put it another way, there will be no spiritual progress before us unless or until we willfully choose to be humble. According to James, we are responsible to choose and then to pursue a path of selflessness.

This is one part of our faith journey we must do on our own. Humility is such a foreign concept to most of us because we've been taught in our competitive culture to always look out for number one as we claw our way to the top. Humility is even regarded as a sign of weakness in some quarters. This means as true followers of Christ we must first be willing to embrace the concept of humbling ourselves.

For some of us, this would mean we need to make some serious personal adjustments. For me, I think I'm humble around people who are hurting and going through a difficult time. But whenever I'm challenged by someone who's assertive and powerful, I tend to puff up and fight back with all I have. Recently, I've been made aware this is a real lack of humility.

When Jesus and then later his apostles were confronted with the powerful men of Rome, they never stood up for themselves and fought back. Instead, in humility, they simply entrusted themselves to the One who judges justly. This is my next step. I want to learn to be humble in the face of power. Are there any situations where humility doesn't come naturally to you? Where you're tempted to puff up in pride? Let God show you these areas today and transform you. Shalom!

TODAY'S READINGS
Psalm 106:1-6, 19-23 | Exodus 24:9-11 | James 4:4-10

Saturday | OCTOBER 10

They forgot the God who saved them, who had done great things in Egypt... | Psalm 106:21

Our Story

It's easy and almost natural to look back on the lives of the ancient people of God with great disappointment. We ask, "How could they have so gloriously participated in their salvation and yet so quickly and easily forgotten the very one who had saved them?" But if we pause for a moment and meditate on our own experience with our Savior, we realize their story is our story.

We share with the ancient people of God a periodic divine amnesia. We too have experienced the salvation of the Lord. Each of us who claims the name of Christ has our own unique story about how God reached into this human experience and miraculously brought us into our own spiritual Promised Land. We once were on our way to sure and certain spiritual death until Jesus intervened and, as only he can, then placed us on this amazing journey of faith. It was indeed a miracle of mammoth proportion. Amid this salvation experience then, life happens. Calamity comes calling. Disease or divorce or death is laid at our feet.

Far too often we temporarily forget the God of our salvation. We begin to panic. Instead of reaching out and holding on to Jesus with all our strength, we seek comfort and solace from our old false gods. Suddenly, we find ourselves worshipping at the temples of drugs or alcohol or worry or despair. We forget the God of our salvation. We lose sight of the truth: our God is all over our circumstance. So, take heart, rescued one. Remember and receive today the blessing of the God of our salvation. He is a good and great God. He will never let us down. Today, remember times when God intervened on your behalf. He did it before and he will do it again, every day if you need it. Shalom!

TODAY'S READINGS
Psalm 106:1-6, 19-23 | Exodus 24:12-18 | Mark 2:18-22

Sunday | OCTOBER 11

Rejoice in the Lord always. I will say it again: Rejoice! | Philippians 4:4

Rejoice, Rejoice

I hadn't realized, the context of Paul's exhortation here is the fight between those two ladies. I guess I always thought Paul brought up the quarrel and then changed the subject to rejoicing. But what if he is offering this encouragement to rejoice as a means to stop or prevent quarreling? What if Paul is saying, "Instead of bickering with each other, make a gratitude list?"

We are encouraged to do this in recovery. My sponsor writes out about thirty things he is grateful for every morning. It is his way of rejoicing in the Lord. I am not as disciplined, but whenever I think of all the blessings in my life, and there are many, I can't help but feel some of the tension fade. As the tension fades, I suddenly feel myself letting go of whatever is frustrating me.

Let's just consider for a moment I'm on to something here. Why not give it a try? The next time we find ourselves in conflict with someone, let's rejoice in the Lord. Let's make a list of all our blessings. Then instead of being consumed by our anger and frustration, we can focus instead on our many blessings. How can you practice gratitude today? Shalom!

TODAY'S READINGS
Psalm 106:1-6, 19-23 | Exodus 32:1-14 | Matthew 22:1-14 | Philippians 4:1-9

Monday | OCTOBER 12

Now go, lead the people to the place I spoke of, and my angel will go before you. However, when the time comes for me to punish, I will punish them for their sin." | Exodus 32:34

It Just Happened

God's talking to Moses about the golden calf Aaron created for the people. We know creating that golden calf required some intense effort. Aaron oversaw the artistic creation of a false god, made for the purpose of idolatrous worship. The truth is there probably wasn't anything he could have done that was more deplorable than to replace with an inanimate object the God who had just miraculously rescued them.

When Moses confronts Aaron about it, Aaron tries to minimize his involvement. He basically says to Moses, "Well, I'm not sure how this happened. It was incredible. I actually had very little to do with it. I mean, sure, I did ask them to take off their jewelry. But, hey, it's not my fault the gold magically melted into this perfectly shaped calf. It just happened!"

This got me thinking how I minimize my own sin and try to deflect and distort my involvement. While I don't think I'm in danger of ever worshipping a golden calf, I do have my own idols I tend to turn to in times of crisis. The Israelites needed only to patiently wait on the Lord in their crisis; instead they pursued other options. Same with me—when I'm in crisis or frightened, I'm quick to try and work my way out of the situation. And if that doesn't work, my go-to plan is to raise enough money to buy my way out. But today in my spiritual journey I'm more likely to simply wait on God. Can you think of situations where you too easily fall into sin? How can you strengthen yourself in the Lord in those times? Shalom!

TODAY'S READINGS
Psalm 97 | Exodus 32:15-35 | Jude 1:17-25

Tuesday | OCTOBER 13

> But our citizenship is in heaven. And we eagerly await a savior from there, the Lord Jesus Christ... | Philippians 3:20

Heavenly Passports

I think of this verse every time I use my passport. I remember returning from Guatemala with my daughter's little baby who she had just adopted. It was a very harrowing time because the last week before the adoption was to be final and we would be allowed to bring home our precious bundle of joy, the Guatemalan government suspended all American adoptions. We were racing against the clock as we scurried to Guatemala. What I instantly realized there, to my great fear, was I had no rights in that foreign nation.

In the United States, wherever I go and whatever I do, I'm enshrouded in protection as guaranteed by our great Constitution and our Bill of Rights. But in Guatemala, they do not recognize any of our civil rights. Knowing the clock was ticking and we were literally adopting one of the very last babies from that country, we struggled through form after form of required paperwork. Finally, after what seemed like an eternity, we were given permission to bring our baby Lucia home. But I can remember, my greatest fear was clearing immigration in the United States. I knew once they stamped the paperwork "approved" for Lucia, we were on our way home. I was never so proud to get us all back on American soil and hear the agent declare to my grandbaby, "Welcome to America."

However, Paul says we have an even more glorious trip to make. And on that trip, we will be going home to stay. The day is rapidly approaching when we will be ushered through a divine customs process into a new Kingdom. It will be Jesus Christ himself who welcomes us home. I can't wait. Today, take a moment to embrace all the truth that your citizenship in heaven entails—not only for your arrival there, but now. Shalom!

TODAY'S READINGS
Psalm 97 | Exodus 33:1-6 | Philippians 3:13–4:1

Wednesday | OCTOBER 14

Then Jesus declared, "I am the bread of life. Whoever comes to me will never go hungry, and whoever believes in me will never be thirsty. | John 6:35

Life's Bread

By Lynn Breeden

Not that many years ago, most of the bread we ate was baked at home or in bakeries. Now, all we have to do is go to the store and we can have any type of bread we can dream of. Bread has always been a staple in our diets and supplies some of our daily nutrition as well.

The Bread of Life remains indispensable for good spiritual health. In fact, Jesus says it is a daily requirement for us. He says we don't live on bread alone…I just told the story of the "loaves and fish" to my "littles" at the preschool last week. Interestingly, over 5,000 people left that day to hear Jesus and forgot to take their lunch. As the day grew longer, Jesus noticed they were hungry and a young boy offered his lunch for Jesus to share. Jesus prayed over his bread and of course you know what happens next. In Jesus' hands, just a few loaves became thousands. All the work normally required to make a loaf of bread is bypassed, and yet this bread fed a multitude.

Isn't Jesus cool? After the meal, Jesus was leaving and many were following him. Sadly, he knew their hearts: "You are looking for me, not because you saw the signs I performed, but because you ate the loaves and had your fill." Not much different for us today, they wanted a quick fix for their hunger that day and so do we. Jesus wisely connects the bread that fed the crowds to the bread of heaven and says, "I am the bread of life. Whoever comes to me will never go hungry, and whoever believes in me will never be thirsty." Oh Jesus, fill me with only you today. How does Jesus feed you today? Will you seek the Bread of Life that truly satisfies? Shalom!

TODAY'S READINGS
Psalm 97 | 2 Kings 17:7-20 | John 6:25-35

Thursday | OCTOBER 15

The Lord would speak to Moses face to face, as one speaks to a friend. | Exodus 33:11

Intimate Interaction

This must have been an incredible experience for Moses. I can't help but be a little envious. I mean, if God would show up every day and speak audibly to me, it would be a lot easier to understand his will for my life.

I passionately pray to know his will for my life. Sometimes the answer is swift and obvious, but often it's slower and requires more patience on my part. When I read some of the testimonies of great Christian men and women I admire, I notice they, too, often struggle with discerning God's will for their lives. It can make a person wonder, *Why doesn't God do for me what he did for Moses?*

We could all use a little face-to-face time ourselves. But then I remind myself the Lord is perfect in all he says and does. He knew we would be searching for his will in our lives in the 21st century. He isn't caught off guard. He's not confused or wondering why Christ hasn't returned yet to rapture his church. No, he knew this would be the way we communicate with him—to read and meditate daily on his word and then to wait patiently for his Holy Spirit to guide us into our "next best step."

He knew it and because he willed it for our intimate interaction with him, it's the perfect way for him to communicate with us. We need not question the process. We simply are called to humbly submit to his good, perfect, and profitable interaction with us. Today, allow your faith to lead you into intimacy with God and trust he will speak to you in the way he has laid out for us. Shalom!

TODAY'S READINGS
Psalm 99 | Exodus 33:7-11 | 3 John 1:9-12

Friday | OCTOBER 16

> ...All of you, clothe yourselves with humility toward one another, because "God opposes the proud but shows favor to the humble. | 1 Peter 5:5b

Humble Outfits

Peter seems to be making a straightforward declaration. If we want God to shower us with his divine favor, then we must treat each other with humility.

The older I get and the further I travel on this amazing journey of faith, the more convinced I become that humility is the key to a life that honors God. Humility is not an attribute that is highly valued in our culture. Most of our heroes from screen and television are rarely humble. We admire men who are good at finding the bad guys and then destroying them. But have you ever noticed that the heroes of our faith found in the New Testament are never violent or even aggressive? They respond to every situation with great humility. And they maintain that humility even while they are being tortured and executed for their faith.

Peter, who penned this letter we are reading today, came to Jesus as a rough, aggressive brawler. But after watching Jesus live out his life and even his death, Peter learned humility was the key.

Eventually, they would come to Peter and arrest him for leading the Christian church. He was given the opportunity to renounce his faith and deny Jesus or be crucified as Christ was. Peter, according to the church tradition, did not fight back. So they decided they would crucify Peter's wife and force him to witness the horrible ordeal. Then surely he would turn his back on Jesus. But Peter just humbly repeated to his lovely dying bride, "Remember our Lord, remember our Lord." After she died that horrible death, Peter requested they crucify him upside down because he wasn't worthy of the same type of death as Jesus Christ. Will you put humility in the forefront of your mind today and allow Christ to come to the forefront of your interactions with others? Shalom!

TODAY'S READINGS
Psalm 99 | Exodus 31:1-11 | 1 Peter 5:1-5

Saturday | OCTOBER 17

The Israelites had done all the work just as the Lord had commanded Moses. | Exodus 39:42

Quiet Confidence

If we aren't careful, reading the description of the tabernacle's construction can become tedious. It reads like a spec book. But, look deeper—is there something important here for us?

God is communicating clearly to his people that he is a God of order and structure. We see in the tabernacle's construction, and then later in the elaborate design for his temple, how incredibly concerned he was with every detail. He is extremely organized in the way he would have his people worship him. From his very first acts in the creation account we see unquestionable evidence of his amazing, intricate design.

I enjoy watching the scientific community as they continue to unlock details of their various disciplines, only to discover that beneath this recent temple discovery there are even more layers of intricacy yet to be explored.

Yes, our God is a God of order. And the opposite of order is chaos. So, the more godly discipline I incorporate into my life, the more order there is and the less inner chaos I experience. It's possible to be in a very chaotic situation but to maintain our internal order if we will faithfully attach our lives to the same God who laid out the worship plans for his people thousands of years ago. If we maintain a structured and disciplined spiritual routine, it is possible to live our lives in quiet confidence. What godly discipline can you include in your life today? Shalom!

TODAY'S READINGS
Psalm 99 | Exodus 39:32-42 | Matthew 14:1-12

Sunday | OCTOBER 18

> If you are pleased with me, teach me your ways so I may know you and continue to find favor with you… | Exodus 33:13a

Finding Favor

This is a great prayer not only for Moses but for all God's people who earnestly desire to take their next step with him. He is truly the answer to all our questions and the solution to all our problems.

I find it interesting that at such a critical time in the journey of God's people, the leader found it necessary to ask for God's revelation. I assume God would have just forced himself on Moses to ensure his divine will was being carried out for his people. But evidently Moses had to ask. God didn't force his will upon Moses. And we can conclude from that, he will not force his will upon us.

So, if we too are to truly find favor with God we should ask him to teach us his ways so we may know him and find favor with him. Our primary means of knowing him is by interacting personally with him through prayer, Bible study, worship, meditation, and ministry. As we passionately pursue these disciplines, we'll consistently experience the revealing of God's character in our lives. What can you request of God today to draw you closer and to be found in favor? Shalom!

TODAY'S READINGS

Psalm 99 | Exodus 33:12-23 | Matthew 22:15-22 | 1 Thessalonians 1:1-10

Monday | OCTOBER 19

Because your love is better than life, my lips will glorify you... | Psalm 63:3

His Love

God's love is better than life. Do you believe that? God created us as an object of his love. He made us so he could love us and so we can love him. His love is the reason we're breathing. His love is what keeps us going on our good days and our bad days. We can feel his love when nothing else makes sense. And when we can't feel it, we can know it is still present.

The truth is, he loves us whether or not we think we deserve it. Nothing will make God stop loving us. His love is based on his character and not on anything we do or say or feel. How cool is that? This is why the last part of this verse says, "My lips will glorify you." He loves us and we glorify him. Can you have faith today to know his love for you? Will you praise him with your lips and rejoice in his love? Shalom!

TODAY'S READINGS

Psalm 63:1-8 | Exodus 40:34-38 | Revelation 18:1-10, 19-20

Tuesday | OCTOBER 20

(Now Moses was a very humble man, more humble than anyone else on the face of the earth.) ... | Numbers 12:3

Controlled Power

In Hebrew life, humility was described as "controlled power." It was used to define a wild stallion that had been trained to ride. The horse was still incredibly powerful, but that power had been brought under control. This is why humility is the perfect description for godly leaders on earth.

Moses was never meek and mild. As a young man, he saw an Egyptian picking on a fellow Hebrew, and Moses beat him to death and buried him in the sand. He spent the next 40 years in the harsh, rugged wilderness tending to his flocks. Then, when the timing was right, God chose Moses from a million other Hebrews to be his leader. He enabled Moses to preside over the defeat of the most powerful army on the planet. Moses was a man of immense authority. Yet, God's word describes him as the most humble man on the face of the earth.

"Controlled power" is a fascinating description of humility. Think, what needs to happen in your life for you to take your next step in this discipline of humility? Most of us have some control in our lives, whether it's at home with our kids or at work. How are you doing bringing that power under God's control? Humility is the key to a God-honoring life. Shalom!

TODAY'S READINGS

Psalm 63:1-8 | Numbers 12:1-9 | Revelation 18:21-24

Wednesday | OCTOBER 21

You, God, are my God, earnestly I seek you; I thirst for you, my whole being longs for you, in a dry and parched land where there is no water. | Psalm 63:1

Spiritual Thirst

Much of what has been taught in American churches over the past 300 years has focused on a type of "revival focused" theology. For these teachers, the path to salvation focused on a once-in-a-lifetime decision to be "saved." The gospel was often presented in a way fixated first on convincing someone they were a sinner who was headed to hell. But, if they would confess their sin and surrender their life to Christ, he would save them from hell and then when they died, they would go to heaven. The choice was either spend eternity in hell where there will be unbelievable, eternal torment or…Jesus.

Now, given the front end of this option, of course most folks would choose anything else! Hell would be the worst option! So, folks would choose Jesus over eternal torment. But as I grew older and patiently studied the Bible, determined to allow God to shape my theology, I discovered what he wanted from me wasn't just a once in a lifetime decision to pick him over eternal torment.

No, he wanted me to passionately pursue him in a lifelong relationship, one step at a time. It's truly like a thirsty man desperately pursuing water. I particularly was drawn to the psalmist's phrase here, "in a dry and parched land." This reminds me there is nothing in this world that will satisfy my spiritual thirst short of a consistent, ongoing, step-by-step pursuit of our glorious God. Are you just trying to get to heaven, or are you thirsty for Jesus? How will you pursue him today? Shalom!

TODAY'S READINGS
Psalm 63:1-8 | Number 13:1-2, 17-14:9 | Matthew 17:22-27

Thursday | OCTOBER 22

In the morning it springs up new, but by evening it is dry and withered. | Psalm 90:6

Don't Blink

As I look back now on 63 years of life, my first thought is, *Where did the time go?* It seems like just a few years ago I fell in love and got married. Last month we celebrated our 43rd anniversary. Yes, the psalmist really nailed it when he said our lives quickly fade away. Or like the wise words of the old man in the country song, "Don't blink." But for me, this passage has an inspiring effect.

It reminds me, yes, my life is quickly fading. As it does, I'm inspired by God's word and the encouragement of his people to simply get up every day and endeavor to know Jesus more intimately. I'm now convinced the closer I get in my relationship with him, the more productive I am in God's Kingdom. Now, and hopefully for the rest of my life, my focus is to finish strong.

As Paul said, "Forgetting what is behind me, I press on to the prize for which Christ Jesus is calling me heavenward." For me, the way to finish strong is to get up every morning and immerse myself in knowing and loving and serving Jesus Christ, my Lord and Savior. He is laying out a path for me to follow and I intend to be about the business of passionately pursuing him down that path. Are you letting life pass by without focusing on what's important? How will you prepare to finish strong in your journey toward Jesus today? Shalom!

TODAY'S READINGS
Psalm 90:1-6, 13-17 | Deuteronomy 32:1-14, 18 | Titus 2:7-8, 11-15

Friday | OCTOBER 23

Satisfy us in the morning with your unfailing love, that we may sing for joy and be glad all our days. | Psalm 90:14

Be Glad

By Lynn Breeden

What is the secret to having a good day? Maybe it's to wake up immersed in God's unfailing love. This should make us sing for joy and bring our hearts overflowing with love. Everything in our lives is built on the foundation of being thankful. Maybe, each night before we go to sleep, we can think about how much we are loved and all we are grateful for.

Last week, I woke up one day kind of grumpy. Most days I wake up pretty happy but it was one of those mornings when I didn't want to wake up, so I started going through the previous day, thinking, *I've got to exercise!* But then I shifted my thinking and my day started to change…I love having a body that CAN still work out. What a gift that is! Then I got in some reading on a book I've been wanting to get to. I love learning. I got to travel some place, even if it was just to work. People in other centuries never got to do that and they would have given anything to travel like I do. I got to read to children today. Many people don't ever get to see children every day like I do. Before it was all over I was thinking, *I got to live that day! Are you kidding me? And today I get another day?*

So I prayed, "Oh thank you, God! What an unbelievably good God you are to think of this world, and a life, and a body, and Jesus above all." Pretty soon I was just overwhelmed with gratitude and a feeling of God's unfailing love for me. Your blessing for today is the psalmist's prayer: "Satisfy me in the morning with your unfailing love, that I would sing for joy and be glad all of my days." What needs adjusting in your attitude today? How will you seek God's love for you? Shalom!

TODAY'S READINGS

Psalm 90:1-6, 13-17 | Deuteronomy 32:1-14, 18 | Titus 2:7-8, 11-15

Saturday | OCTOBER 24

If you believed Moses, you would believe me, for he wrote about me. | John 5:46

It's Me

Jesus makes a blockbuster statement here. Think about it. Here we have this blue-collar carpenter from a hole-in-the-wall town, Nazareth. He's boldly proclaiming to some of the most educated men in the Scriptures that much of what they've been studying their whole lives is really about him.

Jesus could have drawn their attention to the very opening pages of Genesis. He could have said to them, "You know when God confronted Adam and Eve and the serpent in the Garden? And he turned to the serpent and declared, 'You will strike at his heel, but he will crush your head'? Well, I am the head crusher. I was sent here by my Father to defeat the evil one."

I would say the consistent theme running like a scarlet thread from these opening words in your Bible to John's Revelation is the person of Jesus Christ, the Son of God. Jesus came to us from heaven in human form to reveal everything we will ever need to know about God in this lifetime. What he was revealing to the Jews of his day he continues to reveal to us today, and his message is quite clear: "Follow me." So, let's do that today. Let's receive the divine blessing of our God as we humbly submit to his leading, for his glory and our ultimate good. Today, meditate on the magnitude of the carpenter from Nazareth who came to you. Shalom!

TODAY'S READINGS
Psalm 90:1-6, 13-17 | Deuteronomy 32:44-47 | John 5:39-47

Sunday | OCTOBER 25

Relent, Lord! How long will it be? Have compassion on your servants. | Psalm 90:13

How Long

I can remember times in my life when I was waiting on the Lord and it seemed like he was taking forever. Why does he seem to be so slow to respond sometimes? Have you ever felt like the psalmist and me and wondered, "How long is this going to drag on? This is killing me!"

There is ample scriptural evidence, confirmed by our own experience, that the Lord is working on his timetable and certainly not ours. So, what are we to do if we find ourselves adrift in this seemingly endless waiting game?

First, let's remember the Bible is clear that for the Lord, a thousand years are like a day. He is not in a hurry. But we can take confidence in the fact that, despite our frustration, his timing is always perfect. Second, we can be intentional about praying the Lord will help us to not waste the situation. We can ask if there's something he wants us to learn in the waiting, with the hope of coming out the other side a better Christ follower because of the experience. Finally, we can simply learn to wait patiently for the Lord to show up.

Our God is a good God. He knows everything and has the power to take care of all our needs. We can trust him to always respond perfectly, just in time. What are you having trouble waiting for right now? Will you renew your mind again in the hope of his promises for you? Shalom!

TODAY'S READINGS

Psalm 90:1-6, 13-17 | Deuteronomy 34:1-12 | Matthew 22:34-46
1 Thessalonians 2:1-8

Monday | OCTOBER 26

> Speak and act as those who are going to be judged by the law that gives freedom, because judgment without mercy will be shown to anyone who has not been merciful. Mercy triumphs over judgment. | James 2:12-13

Mercy Triumphs

This passage scares the hell out of me. I think often about what it will be like for me on the day Christ returns and I have to give an account for all my poor choices. I think in that moment everything will be laid bare. There will no longer be any manipulation of the truth or making excuses or blaming others. It will just be Jesus and me face to face.

Now, I have confidence he will forgive me for my disobedience, but I'm not looking forward to the gory details. This is why I love this passage. James seems to be advocating we become people steeped in mercy. That's what I want for us. I would love for us to be famous for our mercy.

My experience is most everyone is already convinced of their own guilt. What they desperately need is the kind of mercy only flawed but hopeful folks like you and I can provide. So, let's go out today and be responsible for bringing mercy to every place we find ourselves. God will go ahead of you and prepare the way of peace. Mercy triumphs over judgment. With whom will you feel and ooze beautiful mercy today? Shalom!

TODAY'S READINGS

Psalm 119:41-48 | Numbers 33:38-39 | James 2:8-13

Tuesday | OCTOBER 27

As the body without the spirit is dead, so faith without deeds is dead. | James 2:26

Dead Faith

I love how James just lets us have it with both barrels. For the past few hundred years in the United States, Christianity has been obsessed with behavior modification. Our leaders have taught us the key to a successful Christian life lies in our ability to abstain from sin. I call it, "The Gospel of Don't."

The thought was if we could deny ourselves enough of the negative influence of our culture, we would be able to live lives pleasing to God. The problem inherent in this teaching is it ignores our divine calling to not merely abstain from negative behavior, but also to immerse ourselves in positive behavior.

This is why we're so passionate around here about "finding hurting people and helping them take their next steps toward Christ." We're convinced James served his master well when he called us to get to work. But what if we don't feel like helping others? Well, my AA sponsor is always quick to remind us that "we don't think our way into right acting, but we act our way into right thinking."

My encouragement for you today is simple. Ask God to help you find someone who is hurting and help them take their next step. Get going! Shalom!

TODAY'S READINGS
Psalm 119:41-48 | Exodus 34:29-35 | James 2:14-26

Wednesday | OCTOBER 28

All who have this hope in him purify themselves, just as he is pure. | 1 John 3:3

Almost There

John is speaking here about what we are about to become as the redeemed of Christ. Think about this, won't you?

When Christ returns, we will *be like him*. This is a staggering statement made by the old apostle. What will being like Jesus look like? Well, we will no longer sin or even be given to sin. We will always and in every situation, just like Jesus, be strong and gentle. We will never say anything unless it is true, encouraging or necessary. We will always build each other up by encouraging one another in faith, hope and love.

So, this got me thinking about our treatment of each other. It is possible for us to live like this today as we wait for Christ's glorious return? We absolutely have been given the power through Christ's resurrection to live glorious lives. The older I get, the more convinced I am that 90 percent of the battle is just showing up every day with the conscious attitude of living like we're right on the brink of becoming like Christ. Just taking that next step.

We are almost there. Jesus is coming soon. Let's treat ourselves and each other like he is already here. Then watch his blessings pour into our lives. How might you live your life today in the spirit of "Jesus is about to show up"? Shalom!

TODAY'S READINGS
Psalm 119:41-48 | Matthew 5:1-12 | 1 John 3:1-3 | Revelation 7:9-17

Thursday | OCTOBER 29

Have I not commanded you? Be strong and courageous. Do not be afraid; do not be discouraged, for the Lord your God will be with you wherever you go." | Joshua 1:9

Be Strong

I can only imagine what Joshua was feeling before going to war with the people who occupied the Promised Land. They were veteran warriors trained in battle, living in fortified cities. The people Joshua was leading were sons of slaves with no military training and probably very limited equipment.

Any military expert would have to agree there was no way on earth this ragtag group of bricklayers was ready to go to war. There was no visible reason "on earth" this military battle would turn out well. But the Lord reminded Joshua their hope was not in horses and military equipment, but was in the Lord, who promised to do the fighting for them. Joshua's job was to simply stay connected to the word of God and see to it the people showed up when it was time for the conflict.

The battles we face today are sometimes small, but a few of them seem insurmountable. If we dare to, we can embrace the same command as well as the same promise God gave Joshua. We need to be strong and courageous and reject discouragement because the same sovereign God who went ahead of his people in Jericho will go ahead of us today. His promise of his continuous presence has been passed down to each of us who claim the name of Christ. "Never will I leave you. Never will I forsake you." These are the words that have lifted the people of God and driven his Kingdom forward for thousands of years. It came true for all of them and it's true for you today. So take heart, dear Christians, the Lord is near. He will fight your battle. You just show up and immerse yourself in his word and watch how he blesses you today. What battle can you trust to the Lord today? Shalom!

TODAY'S READINGS
Psalm 107:1-7, 33-37 | Joshua 1:1-11 | Romans 2:17-29

Friday | OCTOBER 30

> "Woe to you, teachers of the law and Pharisees, you hypocrites! You shut the door of the kingdom of heaven in people's faces. You yourselves do not enter, nor will you let those enter who are trying to. | Matthew 23:13

Be Damned

Wow! Talk about speaking the truth to power!

These were the most revered and respected men in the nation of Israel and Jesus has just let them have it. He's not pulling any punches here. His concern and ultimate disgust appear to be twofold. Number one: They are men who have not actively pursued a relationship with God. Their lives have been consumed with the exterior, with no regard to the interior. They were refusing, as we say, to take their "next step" toward God. Two: Not only were they spiritually empty, but they were teaching and leading others to follow them down this same selfish path to destruction.

What does this have to do with us today? We need to passionately pursue our paths toward Christ. He and only he is our way to spiritual wholeness. And we should be wary of "blind guides" who hold positions of power in our culture and claim to follow the God of the Bible. Our country is awash today with elites who claim the authority to lead us and are quick to be our moral leaders. Let us humbly pursue "justice, mercy and faithfulness" through our passionate pursuit of the one who shed his own blood for our souls. To Jesus be the power and the glory.

Today, take a fast from social media or the news and "take up your cross and follow Christ." Consider who you are following and listening to. Shalom!

TODAY'S READINGS
Psalm 107:1-7, 33-37 | Joshua 2:15-24 | Matthew 23:13-28

Saturday | OCTOBER 31

"Now then, please swear to me by the Lord that you will show kindness to my family, because I have shown kindness to you. Give me a sure sign." | Joshua 2:12

God's Protection

Everything Rahab had heard reinforced the fact that this God of the Israelites does what he says he will do. It was her hope that if she could somehow come under his people's protection then she would escape the coming destruction of Jericho.

Rahab knew the only way to be protected from destruction was to risk everything about herself. To have faith in God, she had to lose faith in everything else! She based her faith not on who she was—a woman of Jericho, a prostitute, a woman living in a home built into the walls of the city near its gate. Instead, Rahab based her faith on who God was—the God who does what he says he will do, who keeps his promises, and who protects and saves his people. In doing so, Rahab willingly surrendered everything she had to his mercy!

This is why Rahab's faith was honored so much later on in the New Testament. When a person surrenders everything and places everything they know, love, and trust on the line and at the mercy of God … when a person willingly trusts God with their very life, not trying to control it in any way themselves… then God rewards their faith. This is the kind of faith that can move mountains.

The point of this story is not to make you think whatever you fear most about trusting God will become a reality in your life IF you abandon yourself to him! The point is that WHEN you abandon yourself to God the things he ends up doing in your life will be things you want him to do. What is your Rahab moment? Have you had one yet? Can you lay your wrong beliefs down and put your faith in who God is? Shalom!

TODAY'S READINGS
Psalm 107:1-7, 33-37 | Joshua 2:1-14 | 2 Peter 2:1-3

Sunday | NOVEMBER 1

The greatest among you will be your servant. | Matthew 23:11

Glorious Humility

Jesus really lays it on the line here for anyone who is serious about following him. The only path to the Kingdom of God is paved with humility. We must make a conscious decision every day to humbly serve everyone we meet.

Think for a moment about the context here. Jesus is in the middle of addressing the abuse being showered on the rank and file by the religious leaders. These were men with unprecedented power in the lives of God's people. They had developed a governing system that afforded them the power to facilitate the execution of God's only Son. They obviously wielded their power with an iron fist.

But Jesus contrasts that by saying real power—the kind of power that will ultimately change the world—is that which is borne by men and women on their knees, humbly serving their God and their neighbor.

So, as far as we're concerned, we come to this human experience from two simple places: We are to be students of the word of God and humble servants to all. We will go forward from this place in time bathed in the humility that sent the King of all kings and Lord of all lords to his humiliating death. In that one great act of humility, Jesus demonstrated his unmatched greatness. So, may he fill you today with his humility as you reach out to serve everyone you encounter. How will you become humble servant to all today? Shalom!

TODAY'S READINGS
Psalm 107:1-7, 33-37 | Joshua 3:7-17 | Matthew 23:1-12 | 1 Thessalonians 2:9-13

Monday | NOVEMBER 2

> And we also thank God continually because, when you received the word of God, which you heard from us, you accepted it not as a human word, but as it actually is, the word of God, which is indeed at work in you who believe | 1 Thessalonians 2:13

Message Received

Paul was thrilled because the church at Thessalonica had received his teaching as the very word of God. I'm not certain if Paul realized this letter he is writing would one day become part of the yet to be formed compilation we know as the New Testament. I sense he did not know he was literally writing holy Scripture.

However, I believe God in his infinite wisdom spoke through little more than a handful of men and divinely inspired them to create these wonderful books. Then he in his infinite power placed his hand of protection upon these words, preserving them to enable you to take your "next step" toward Jesus Christ today.

That's why I'm always quoting Scripture in our teaching time. It's the only thing I say each week that I absolutely know is correct. So, the lesson for us from this passage is to reaffirm in our hearts and minds today the glorious importance of God's written word. And, the fact that he has preserved it for the building up of our very lives. How has God's word been vital to your faith journey? What verses speak powerfully to you today? Shalom!

TODAY'S READINGS
Psalm 128 | Joshua 4:1-24 | 1 Thessalonians 2:13-20

Tuesday | NOVEMBER 3

You will eat the fruit of your labor; blessings and prosperity will be yours. | Psalm 128:2

Fresh Fruit

It seems the desired blessings for God's people change dramatically after Christ's coming. The Old Testament is ripe with blessings about financial prosperity, children, and a long life. But after the life, death, burial and resurrection of the Lord Jesus Christ, we see the writers of the New Testament embrace his different perspective on blessings.

We don't see Peter pray his parishioners would live long, happy, fruitful lives. Instead, he blesses them amid their horrendous suffering for the cause of Christ. Paul doesn't bless the early church with long life to see their grandchildren. In fact, he argues that for some it's best if they never marry at all or have children.

In his wonderful letter, James, as a revered leader of the church, not only neglects to pray for their financial success, but he scolds them for even giving preferential treatment to the wealthy. It appears the blessings pursued by the people of God on this side of the cross are always focused on the spiritual aspect of their lives.

Paul prays for the church at Ephesus—not for physical prosperity, but that the eyes of their hearts might be enlightened. This is something I'm wrestling with. I grew up as a good red-blooded American who embraced the ideal of the "American Dream." But that pursuit seems hollow or empty compared to the spiritual blessings advocated by Christ and pursued by his early followers. I encourage you to think about this with me for a season. Think, what is your prayer focus today? How do your desires for blessing line up with what is important to Christ? Shalom!

TODAY'S READINGS
Psalm 128 | Joshua 6:1-16, 20 | Acts 13:1-12

Wednesday | NOVEMBER 4

Jesus replied, "And why do you break the command of God for the sake of your tradition? | Matthew 15:3

Misdirected Traditions

Think about the "religious leaders" who constantly tried to discredit Jesus. They were the powerful elite of their day—educated and, for the most part, revered by ordinary citizens. Extremely dedicated to their traditions, they were, as we'd say today, "good church-going folks." This makes me ask, "Why was Jesus so frustrated with them?"

Two reasons jump out at us. First, Jesus was always the people's "Good Shepherd." His consistent passion was to save and protect the "lost sheep of Israel." And he believed the greatest threat to the people he cared for was these "sheep in wolves clothes," the Pharisees and teachers of the Law.

Second, he learned the reason these men had wandered so far from God's path was because they had allowed their "traditions" to take precedent over "Scripture." I believe this unfortunate misdirection was started from a good place—an attempt to lead all of Israel into lives of faithful service to God. However, the more rules they developed beyond Hebrew Scriptures, the farther they drifted from God's perfect path. This is why Jesus said, "Why do you break the commands of God for the sake of your tradition?"

What does this have to do with us today? It's our divine right and responsibility to look at all teachings through the lens of Holy Scripture alone. Unfortunately, the enemy still uses the zealous misdirection of many in church leadership to keep us off course. That's why I'm so passionate we keep immersing ourselves in God's holy word. And that we remain unswerving in our commitment to follow it alone and not the traditions of sincere but misguided leaders. Can you identify any areas where you've allowed rules or traditions to steer you off course from God's all-sufficient word? If yes, let grace bring you back into his freedom. Shalom!

TODAY'S READINGS
Psalm 128 | Joshua 10:12-14 | Matthew 15:1-9

Thursday | NOVEMBER 5

The first woe is past; two other woes are yet to come. | Revelation 9:12

Uh-Oh

That first "woe" would be terrible enough—I can't imagine how dreadful it will be for those who must endure it. Studying the book of Revelation has always been difficult for me, mostly because I don't know what I should take literally and what to take figuratively.

However, there are two obvious points I'm left with from this reading. The first is I'm so thankful God rescued me from this horrible experience. I can only imagine the turmoil and utter chaos that will engulf the world during this awful period John is sharing with us from his divine revelation.

The second point is I don't wish for anyone to suffer this horrible fate. I need to be about God's business today as I take my "next step" toward Jesus through prayer, meditation, worship, study, fellowship and service. Everything I do has eternal significance. May each of us choose wisely so we can become vessels God uses to draw people to our Lord Jesus Christ. Thinking about the terrible day we never have to experience, what can you do today to save someone else from that fate? Shalom!

TODAY'S READINGS
Psalm 78 | Joshua 5:4-9 | Revelation 8:6 –9:12

Friday | NOVEMBER 6

The rest of mankind who were not killed by these plagues still did not repent of the work of their hands; they did not stop worshiping demons, and idols of gold, silver, bronze, stone and wood idols that cannot see or hear or walk. | Revelation 9:20

The Unvarnished Truth

One of the men who had a major influence on my life as a preacher and teacher was an old saint of God named Al. He was a farmer who, while in his forties along with his wife, cashed in everything so they could spend their lives ministering to the impoverished people in our community. They purchased a home right in the middle of the crime infested neighborhoods most of us would never even drive through at night.

Al has always had this no-nonsense approach to ministry that will have a positive impact on people's lives for generations to come. While my approach at evangelism has always been less confrontational than Al's, I have the utmost respect for his wisdom. I remember explaining to him once many years ago that I was afraid to be so confrontational when explaining the gospel because I didn't want to risk scaring people off. His down-home country charm rang true as he calmly asked me, "In their present condition, the Bible is clear that hell is waiting for them. Are you afraid you might send them to hell number 2?" Al wanted me to embrace the divine truth that only two fates await all mankind—either a life of eternal glory with God or a life of eternal suffering apart from him. I'm still as I write this uncomfortable with its uncompromising truth. Do you see this eternal issue as black and white with no wiggle room? Shalom!

TODAY'S READINGS

Psalm 78:1-7 | Joshua 8:30-35 | Revelation 9:13-21

Saturday | NOVEMBER 7

> …but the one who stands firm to the end will be saved. And this gospel of the kingdom will be preached in the whole world as a testimony to all nations, and then the end will come. | Matthew 24:13

Finish Strong

According to Jesus in this passage, our instructions regarding end times are pretty straightforward.

Number one: "Do not be deceived." And two: "Stand firm to the end." Okay, we can do those two things. We will faithfully wait for Christ's return, not accepting any counterfeit messiah. We will take comfort in all his glory so we will not be confused.

We won't wonder if perhaps this could be him. We'll know with certainty when he comes crashing in on the scene. And second, we will stand firm till the end. We will finish strong. Some believe we will experience some very difficult times as the end draws near. We will not allow that to deter us from our goal of finishing strong. Because we believe, with the people of God for the last twenty centuries, whatever we must endure for the cause of Christ will be small potatoes compared to the glory awaiting us on the other side.

I believe that to a large degree it is our current calling in life to embrace these commands of Jesus to not be deceived and to finish strong. No one knows the time when he will return, but even today we can be about the business of embracing the life he's called us to. What does it look like for you to "finish strong"? How are you standing firm in the faith today? Shalom!

TODAY'S READINGS
Psalm 78: | Joshua 20:1-9 | Matthew 24:1-14

Sunday | NOVEMBER 8

> The bridegroom was a long time in coming, and they all became drowsy and fell asleep. | Matthew 25:5

Big Snooze

I actually do feel like the Lord, our bridegroom, has been a long time in coming. In our reading from Matthew, Paul addresses this issue at its very beginning.

The early church seemed totally convinced the Lord was coming right back. When folks began to die of natural causes before he returned, they began to wonder what was happening. Now, we have experienced 2,000 years of waiting and watching. And it's only natural we tend to fall asleep.

I believe Jesus would have us live our lives with one eye constantly focused on his return. This means we live out each day, 24 hours at a time, as if we've been given inside information that today's the day he'll return. As we begin to do this, we adjust our priorities. To maintain our vigilant watch like the wise virgins, we must commit ourselves to embracing the truths of the gospel of Jesus Christ. The way we keep our lamps burning is by living out each 24-hour period completely focused on renewing our minds, taking our "next step" toward him.

We watch for him by praying to him and reading about him and meditating on his words and loving his church, and finally by reaching out to a lost and dying world desperately needing his love. That's how we become ready every day for his return. And we pray each day, "Come quickly, Lord Jesus." Amen and amen. How do you keep yourself at the ready, in a state of expectancy for the Lord? How does that affect how you live today? Shalom!

TODAY'S READINGS
Psalm 78 | Joshua 24:1-3, 14-25 | Matthew 25:1-13 | 1 Thessalonians 4:13-18

Monday | NOVEMBER 9

> And David shepherded them with integrity of heart;
> with skillful hands he led them. | Psalm 78:72

Heart Training

What a beautiful declaration to make concerning one man's life!

I love to study the life of David and to preach about how he engaged with God on his journey of faith. David was perhaps the greatest leader the world has ever known. He rose out of obscurity from the sheep's pasture to become the leader of God's people. However, one of the really interesting facts about David is how the Lord allowed him to suffer unbelievable trials and tribulations before he was crowned king.

I believe, through this fire of adversity, the Lord was shaping David's life to become first the boy and then the man and finally the king God wanted him to be. It was only after a couple decades of suffering that David was made ready to be God's heart and hands for the nation of Israel. And then David, inspired by the Holy Spirit, led the nation of Israel to become a major world superpower. It was this simple shepherd boy God used to lead his people to glory.

If you find yourself struggling through your own trials and tribulations today, take heart! Perhaps God is using this experience to mold you into a person "after his own heart." God rarely will use us greatly until we have been hurt deeply. How might God be molding your heart today? Will you search for it and thank him for it? Shalom!

TODAY'S READINGS
Psalm 78 | Joshua 24:25-33 | 1 Corinthians 14:20-25

Tuesday | NOVEMBER 10

> Then all the people went away to eat and drink, to send portions of food and to celebrate with great joy, because they now understood the words that had been made known to them. | Nehemiah 8:12

Party Time

I always think about the sharing of our meal together after every weekly service at the church I pastor. We want it to be an extension of our worship together. Each Sunday, faithful men and women prepare a wonderful lunch so we can "celebrate with great joy" that we've heard the gospel preached, that we've repented of our sins, and that we've received the body and blood of Jesus Christ. Now, that is something to celebrate!

Each week we are reminded of God's love and faithfulness to us as well as Christ's sacrifice on our behalf and the Holy Spirit's commitment to help us take our "next step" toward Jesus Christ. We are truly a blessed people.

Therefore, we have a party each Sunday. The love of Christ compels us to gather together as one body, in his great love, to enjoy one another and to encourage each other to continue down the path of faith. I'm convinced what goes on in the Eatin' Room is every bit as important a part of our worship as anything else we do. How will you join in the celebration today? Shalom!

TODAY'S READINGS

Psalm 78 | Nehemiah 8:1-12 | 1 Thessalonians 3:6-13

Wednesday | NOVEMBER 11

Heaven and earth will pass away, but my words will never pass away. | Matthew 24:35

Fireproof

I was thinking about the recent disastrous fires in California. In one case, almost 9,000 buildings were destroyed. Countless families were forced to leave their homes in a panic. It made me ask myself, "If my home was engulfed in flames and I was forced to leave, what one article would I grab to take with me? What is the one thing so precious to me that it would survive the fire?"

In this passage, Jesus is clearly referring to a time of complete destruction. He's talking about an event that could destroy everything existing in this world, as well as the world to come. This is utter annihilation. Nothing will survive except the very words of Christ. It sure makes me consider what kind of priority I should place on knowing and loving and sharing the words of Jesus Christ.

How could anything be more precious, more valuable, more honored? I love going to a traditional, liturgical worship service with readings from the Psalms and the Old Testament and the New Testament. And then the final reading is from the Gospels. When they're preparing to read the words of Christ, the congregation is required to stand out of reverence for his words. A small token of respect, perhaps? But it's a constant reminder that the words of Christ will ultimately be the one precious commodity to survive in the end. Can you share some precious words of Christ with someone today? Shalom!

TODAY'S READINGS
Psalm 78 | Jeremiah 31:31-34 | Matthew 24:29-35

Thursday | NOVEMBER 12

Have mercy on us, Lord... | Psalm 123:3a

Just Enough

I love the verse about God's mercies are new every morning. Because each day only has enough mercy in it for one day. God allows every day's troubles. And God appoints every day's mercies. In the life of his children, his mercies are perfectly appointed.

I just read this verse in my devotions and it fits perfectly here, "Therefore do not be anxious about tomorrow, for tomorrow will be anxious for itself. Sufficient for the day is its own trouble" (Matthew 6:34). Every day has its own trouble and every day has its own mercies. Each is new every morning.

How often do we tend to want to take on tomorrow's load of troubles along with today's? It makes me think of the manna God delivered every morning to his children on their way to the Promised Land—fresh and just enough for that day. There was no storing up; that way they had to depend on God's mercy.

God is just so cool, isn't he? You don't receive today the strength to bear tomorrow's burdens. You are given mercies today for today's troubles. What a faithful God we serve. What is your burden today? Will you freely receive the mercy you need from our loving Savior? Shalom!

TODAY'S READINGS
Psalm 123 | Judges 2:6-15 | Revelation 16:1-7

Friday | NOVEMBER 13

> The Lord had allowed those nations to remain; he did not drive them out at once by giving them into the hands of Joshua. | Judges 2:23

Cultural Idols

It's interesting how this story of the ancient people of God parallels the story of God's people today. Just like them, we desperately want God's blessing. But also like them, we stubbornly want to cling to people and activities we know are detrimental to our journey of faith. We find ourselves unable to take our "next step" with Christ because there is a part of us clinging to the things of this world.

No, we do not worship gods made of gold or sticks and stones. And none of us are considering sacrificing our children to evil deities. But, unfortunately, we have allowed cultural influences to seep into our lives and occupy a place of authority. I know, sadly, I've found myself guilty of these negative cultural influences—mostly from the media, whether it's movies or news or television shows. In so many ways my life has mirrored those of God's people in the days of Judah in Israel.

I want to be a faithful follower of Christ while immersing myself in the "Great American Dream." And so, I've been guilty of the sins of my culture, like consumerism and idolizing celebrities who are opposed to the advancement of God's Kingdom. But all the while I prayed for and desired God's blessing, rarely recognizing our God is a jealous God who refuses to share us with the idols of our culture. Let's take a minute today, as we ask for God's blessing, to have him examine our hearts and shine a light on any cultural influence that he finds offensive. Shalom!

TODAY'S READINGS
Psalm 123 | Judges 2:16-23 | Revelation 16:8-21

Saturday | NOVEMBER 14

Then it goes and takes with it seven other spirits more wicked than itself, and they go in and live there. And the final condition of that person is worse than the first. That is how it will be with this wicked generation." | Matthew 12:45

Fill'er Up

In this passage, Jesus had begun his assault on the religious leaders of his day. They weren't used to someone calling them out for the evil in their hearts. He called them "whitewashed tombs," all clean and shiny on the outside but full of dead men's bones on the inside.

What he is accusing these men of, we need to be mindful of ourselves. I notice here, that after the demon was driven out, when it returned it found the man empty. In other words, he hadn't replaced his evil activity with something good. I am painfully aware of that scenario.

When I first quit drinking, my life was cleaned up, so to speak. But in many ways it was like an empty house. I never replaced the bad activity with something good. Oh sure, I was praying and studying and serving every day. But in those down times I was empty. So, the temptation to drink again was overwhelming—until I began woodworking. What once filled my house with horror, God helped me replace with something good.

To this day, whenever I feel a trigger to drink, I head to my woodshop and pray to God for relief. Then I busy myself with the work of my hands. We must learn to always replace bad behavior with good, to fill our houses with something that's healthy. Are you struggling to empty yourself of ungodly desires? What will you fill your house with today? Shalom!

TODAY'S READINGS

Psalm 123 | Judges 5:1-12 | Matthew 12:43-45

Sunday | NOVEMBER 15

> To one he gave five bags of gold, to another two bags, and to another one bag, each according to his ability. Then he went on his journey... | Matthew 25:15

Compound Interest

Jesus uses this teaching at the end of his ministry as he prepares folks for his departure and the certainty of his return. He refers to himself as the master and his audience is represented by the three servants.

Each of the servants is given a large sum of gold. One bag of gold would be equivalent to five years' wages. Each man was entrusted with more money than any of us will ever hold. Jesus is teaching all of them using something with incredible value: their very lives.

We would say the gold represents their time and talent and treasures. The two faithful servants invest what the master has entrusted to their care wisely. But the third had developed a very negative opinion of the master. I believe the people listening to Jesus would come to understand the third servant was the Pharisees and the teachers of the Law. In all their passion to hold onto their power over God's people, they refused to recognize Jesus as a kind and loving master. They did nothing with the treasure of the message of the Kingdom of God.

There are many applications for us to embrace in this teaching. One is to make sure we each know and understand the character of the master. Ultimately, what we believe about his love and goodness toward his servants will determine how we invest the time and talents and treasures he entrusted to our care. If you're convinced as I am that Jesus is the kindest, most loving and powerful, self-sacrificing man who has ever lived, and if you believe he is the Son of God sent to rescue us from our own selfish lives, then nothing will stop you from taking your next obedient step with him today. What are some ways you can invest your time or talent or treasure into God's Kingdom today? Shalom!

TODAY'S READINGS
Psalm 123 | Judges 4:1-7 | Matthew 25:14-30

Monday | NOVEMBER 16

So when you, a mere human being, pass judgment on them and yet do the same things, do you think you will escape God's judgment? | Romans 2:3

Stop It

The phrase "mere human being" jumped out at me as I read this passage. We say, "Just who do you think you are anyway?" Or as we used to say as kids, "Who died and made you boss?"

The sad, tragic truth is, in our flawed humanness we all have a constant desire to play God. It's God's job and his job alone to judge. Yet, left to our own desires, we all secretly and perhaps subconsciously want to play God, as we are prone to judge. I'm convinced the key to stop being critical of others is to simply learn to stop judging.

In other words, don't let your mind entertain the thought of evaluating someone's motives or even their actions. Just reject the thought whenever it comes into your mind. This will take a great deal of discipline because we're preprogrammed by our own flawed desires to pass judgment—because there's a payoff when we do it. The payoff is the time we spend criticizing others' actions temporarily distracts us from our own failings. It's the genius behind programs like *The Jerry Springer Show*.

As a recovering alcoholic, I've noticed this is quite common. When I see folks who are critical and openly judgmental of recovering addicts, it's not too hard to see they may be suffering from their own issues, whether it's overeating or some other type of dysfunction. This is why we consistently remind each other that we are ALL flawed but hopeful. Today, be aware of how you might be judging others and stop those thoughts before they gain a foothold. See what God might want to say about you, and be transformed. Shalom!

TODAY'S READINGS
Psalm 83:1-4, 9-10, 17-18 | Judges 4:8-24 | Romans 2:1-11

Tuesday | NOVEMBER 17

And we urge you, brothers and sisters, warn those who are idle and disruptive, encourage the disheartened, help the weak, be patient with everyone. | 1 Thessalonians 5:14

Always Patient

Some things never change.

What was true for the apostle Paul in his fledgling church is still true for our church 2,000 years later. Hardly a week goes by when I'm not confronted with someone who has fallen headlong into the sin of gossip and being judgmental. It is by far the most frustrating aspect of being a pastor.

I find it fascinating here that Paul is calling out those who are "idle and disruptive." Almost without exception, the people who get caught up in other people's business are those having extra time on their hands. Their days are not filled with working a full-time job or other productive activities. So, to their great disgrace and to the detriment of the cause of Christ, they busy themselves being disruptive. It breaks my heart.

However, I notice here that after Paul's command warning those who are hurting the cause of Christ, he doesn't advocate tossing them out of the church. In fact, after reminding them to show compassion to the hurting, he says to "be patient with everyone." This is my calling as we move forward. Think, what is your calling? How will you fill your mind and your time and your day today? Shalom!

TODAY'S READINGS
Psalm 83:1-4, 9-10, 17-18 | Exodus 2:1-10 | 1 Thessalonians 5:12-18

Wednesday | NOVEMBER 18

> Let them know that you, whose name is the Lord—that you alone are the Most High over all the earth. | Psalm 83:18

Name Knowing

Our Lord wants us to know his name, to know who he is! Why? So we can praise his name, allowing us to call on him.

As Christians it's easy to get caught up in serving more than one god. With one breath we claim to honor God, and with another we serve the gods of this world. We aren't alone in this. The nation of Israel did the same thing. We must ask ourselves—what drives us?

In a time when we can be or do just about anything we want, how do we make the right choices? How does God factor into our decision-making? The answer, as we search our hearts today, is that we call on the name of our Lord as this verse suggests—the one who is most high in our hearts, our minds and our lives.

Though the world may not acknowledge him, the day will come when all men will bow before him and proclaim him the one Lord, Most High over all the earth. We testify to this future glorious truth by every decision we make today in collaboration with him. How will you glory in his name today? Ask him to reveal more of his nature to you. Shalom!

TODAY'S READINGS
Psalm 83:1-4, 9-10, 17-18 | Esther 7:1-10 | Matthew 24:45-51

Thursday | NOVEMBER 19

Know that the Lord is God. It is he who made us, and we are his; we are his people, the sheep of his pasture. | Psalm 100:3

First Step

This is a great place to take our "first step" with God. For anyone considering becoming a follower of the God of Scripture, first we must determine if we believe the Lord made us. And since he did, he therefore has the sovereign right to do with us as he pleases.

Are we okay with that? If we are, then it only makes sense for us to spend the rest of our lives learning who he is and what he wants from us. Look—he is either in control and worthy of our pursuit or he is not.

I've been convinced for the last 33 years that he absolutely is worthy of pursuit. That one single truth drives me to work at knowing him more intimately day by day. I believe the way we accomplish knowing him better is through a combination of the daily study of his word, a commitment to pray without ceasing, spending time each day "thinking rightly" about him, and pouring out our heart in worship. It is a relationship, in many ways, like any other. The more we invest in it, the more intimate we become. As you meditate on his worthiness today, choose how you will draw closer to him in pursuit of his presence. Shalom!

TODAY'S READINGS
Psalm 100 | Genesis 48:15-22 | Revelation 14:1-11

Friday | NOVEMBER 20

> The grass withers and the flowers fall, but the word of our God endures forever... | Isaiah 40:8

Enduring Words

I believe the prophet Isaiah wrote these words long before the people of God returned from their Babylonian exile. At just the right time, they had these prophetic words to encourage them as they returned to their homeland. It was a place void of all its glory—a hollowed-out landfill of turmoil, awash in seemingly unending crisis.

However, Isaiah's encouragement for them was that they already possessed the solution to their tremendous problem. They had hidden in darkness the light that would lead them to peace. It wasn't going to be a great king or judge or prophet who would save them. They were all men and women like Isaiah who would flourish like flowers for a season but then eventually fade away and die.

No, the hidden treasure, the only true hope for the people of God was his enduring word. And guess what? The solution for God's people 2,500 years later remains hidden in plain sight in this wonderful book we call the Bible. Absolutely everything we need to know about our Lord and what we need to do to be his faithful followers has been preserved for us in these very words you have read today. Today as you meditate upon the enduring quality of God's word, what does that do for your faith? Give God praise for his bedrock of truth. Shalom!

TODAY'S READINGS

Psalm 100 | Isaiah 40:1-11 | Revelation 22:1-9

Saturday | NOVEMBER 21

> He replied to him, "Who is my mother, and who are my brothers?" Pointing to his disciples, he said, "Here are my mother and my brothers. For whoever does the will of my Father in heaven is my brother and sister and mother." | Matthew 12:48-50

Sibling Rivalry

This is one of those moments in Jesus' ministry when you can feel the intensity of his words. I cringe a little, thinking how it probably sounded very hurtful to his biological family. And, maybe it was.

However, I can imagine how it would have touched so many who felt left out. For the outcasts and people who were grieving or hurting, Jesus is promising their family would be determined by obedience, not blood, not politics, or power, or money.

What I love is how this offer still stands today. The promise is just as true for us now as it was for those who were hearing the words directly from Jesus himself. This doesn't mean just because we're hurting we are automatically a part of his family. Nor is it just for those who hang around hoping for a miracle. No. He is specific here. His divine siblings are those who join with him, in a flawed and hopeful way, to do the will of our Father in heaven. How does this difficult verse speak to you today? Are you convicted to be obedient? Shalom!

TODAY'S READINGS

Psalm 100 | Ezekiel 34:25-31 | Matthew 12:46-50

Sunday | NOVEMBER 22

> I pray that the eyes of your heart may be enlightened in order that you may know the hope to which he has called you, the riches of his glorious inheritance in his holy people, and his incomparably great power for us who believe. That power is the same as the mighty strength he exerted when he raised Christ from the dead and seated him at his right hand in the heavenly realms. | Ephesians 1:18-20

Power Play

It is obvious to me here Paul believes, as followers of Christ, we have the same power residing in us that God used to raise his Son from the dead. Wow! This is monumental!

It brings to my mind two important truths for us to wrestle with today. The first is, why do we keep praying for power Paul declares we already possess? How often do we pray, "Lord, just give me the strength…"? We pray this for ourselves and we pray it for others as well. But Paul prayed not for power; he prayed for the awareness of the power believers already have been given.

Second, if my interpretation here is accurate, we don't just have power—we have *unlimited* power. Paul compares it to the kind of power that not only raised Christ from the dead but the strength that gives him complete and utter dominance over all that exists.

This makes me feel like stretching my spiritual muscles a bit. So, for the past several years, I no longer pray folks will receive strength from God to do this or that. I simply ask the eyes of their heart may be enlightened so they might know they already have at their disposal the same power that raised Christ from the dead and enables him to reign in sovereignty over all of creation.

Pray the eyes of your heart will be enlightened so that you might know his power working in your situation, whatever it may be today. And thank him for what he has already done. Shalom!

TODAY'S READINGS
Psalm 100 | Ezekiel 34:11-16, 20-24 | Matthew 25:31-46 | Ephesians 1:15-23

Monday | NOVEMBER 23

> Praise the Lord, all you nations; extol him, all you peoples. For great is his love toward us, and the faithfulness of the Lord endures forever. | Psalm 117:1-2

Faithful Love

Too often, it seems, I get so caught up in the day to day struggles of ministry that I fail to just take the time to stop and think about God's faithful love for me. It exists perfectly and fully without me striving to receive it or conjure it up. It's waiting there, hovering over me like a love bomb waiting to drop. But did I slow down long enough to enjoy him?

So, to that end, let's just pause here today and crank up our favorite praise song or even just sit for a moment in the glory of God's goodness. Let his love settle upon you with the full weight of his majesty. May this experience inspire us today to tackle whatever is before us with supernatural confidence. You are a child of the King of kings and he loves you perfectly. Yay, God! Shalom!

TODAY'S READINGS

Psalm 117 | Jeremiah 30:1-17 | Revelation 21:5-27

Tuesday | NOVEMBER 24

The earth is the Lord's, and everything in it, the world, and all who live in it… | Psalm 24:1

Got It

Although I know in my mind that God is in control, the message oftentimes doesn't travel the 12 inches to my heart.

For my entire adult life, I've been given to depression and anxiety. Some of it may be attributed to a chemical imbalance. I don't want to disregard that, especially in others who suffer.

But I'm learning the more I attach myself and live in constant awareness that the Lord is in control, the less I suffer. For me, and this is just me, most of my anxiety springs from my lack of faith. If I really believed God's got this, then why am I so frightened?

Whenever I'm afraid and running around with my hair on fire, one of my most beloved spiritual counselors always says, "God's got this." At first this was very encouraging to me, but after a while I noticed she says the same thing every time I'm afraid. "God's got this."

Could she be right? Is that the answer to all my frightened confusion? Is it that simple? What I'm learning to do whenever I'm faced with an uncertain outcome is to say out loud, "That's God's problem." And while he will not always bring each situation to my own control-freak preference, I know that everything is the Lord's, including me. Are you anxious or worried or afraid about anything today? Will you simply hand it to him and trust God's got this today? Shalom!

TODAY'S READINGS
Psalm 24 | Isaiah 33:17-22 | Revelation 22:8-21

Wednesday | NOVEMBER 25

> Many have undertaken to draw up an account of the things that have been fulfilled among us, just as they were handed down to us by those who from the first were eyewitnesses and servants of the word. With this in mind, since I myself have carefully investigated everything from the beginning, I too decided to write an orderly account for you, most excellent Theophilus, so that you may know the certainty of the things you have been taught. | Luke 1:1-4

Eye Witness

Luke wasn't one of the apostles of Christ. He wasn't even a part of the three-year ministry.

But he subsequently gave his life to Christ and joined the apostle Paul on several missionary journeys and was an eyewitness to the birthing of the church.

He was also a brilliant man and an excellent historian. Today, even atheist scholars admire Luke's work as an ancient historian. Luke's divine task was to interview those who walked with Christ, and then use their information to compile an orderly rendering of the life of Christ.

I believe that Luke, under the direction of the Holy Spirit, was inspired to share with us the story of the good news of Jesus Christ. It's a wonderful accounting of the most glorious story ever told. And it is our great privilege to have it secured these 20 centuries for us. I never get over the wide-eyed wonderment of the fact that I'm hearing the very experiences of those who actually spent time with Jesus. God's word is indeed my greatest blessing in life. As you read these verses today, be aware of what God is quietly speaking to you through his word. Shalom!

TODAY'S READINGS

Psalm 24 | Isaiah 60:8-16 | Luke 1:1-4